TRENCH WARFARE 1914–1918

The Live and Let Live System

TRENCH WARFARE
1914–1918
The Live and Let Live
System

Tony Ashworth

First published 1980 by
THE MACMILLAN PRESS LTD
*London and Basingstoke
Companies and
representatives
throughout the world*

Printed in Hong Kong

British Library Cataloguing in Publication Data

Ashworth, Tony
    Trench warfare, 1914–1918
    1. European War, 1914–1918 – Campaigns –
Western
    I. Title
    940.4′144   D530

    ISBN 0-333-25766-9

To my daughters, Shura and Selby Louise

Contents

Contents

List of Plates

Every effort has been made to contact all the copyright holders of
the material used in the compilation of this book, but if any have
inadvertently been missed, the publisher would be pleased to make
any necessary arrangements.

Acknowledgements

Much of the material upon which this book is based was written by trench fighters, and these sources which include diaries, memoirs and autobiographical fiction are mostly listed at the end of the book. I have spent many pleasant, sociable hours talking with and writing to soldiers of the First World War. I owe them a debt, firstly for their time and reminiscences and secondly, for their example of adversity borne with fortitude and sometimes humour, and remembered without rancour. In particular, I should like to thank Captain C. Allen, M. C., Sergeant W. Mitchenor, and Private W. Watts. Colleagues have helped and contributed in various ways and, among these, I am especially grateful to Dr Michael Walker, whose constant interest, quick insight and comment served, in informal lunchtime workshops over the years, not only in shaping this book but also as necessary encouragement. I will always be indebted to my first teacher, Professor Norbert Elias, who has introduced so many students to the fascinating world of social enquiry. Additionally, I wish to thank the following: Professor Ilya Neustadt, Anthony Giddens and Jack Winkler for encouragement at an early stage; Professor Percy S. Cohen, Clive Ashworth, David Owens, Dr Helmut Heisler and Dr Paul Atkinson, who have had either a direct or indirect influence on the book. I also wish to thank Professor Martin Albrow of University College, Cardiff, for arranging invaluable study leave when the research was in a formative stage. Further, the often enthusiastic contributions of students made in tutorials during the duration of the research should not go unmarked. I am grateful to the library staff of University College, Cardiff, for their efforts in getting books through the inter-library loan service. Finally, Miss Diana Davies has my thanks for valuable editorial assistance, and Mrs Myrtle Robbins for typing the manuscript so efficiently.

Llantwit Major, South Glamorgan   TONY ASHWORTH
2 February 1979

xi

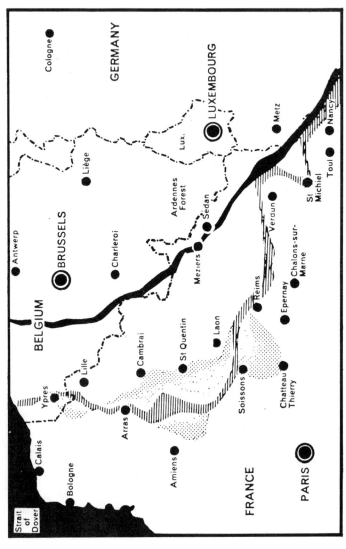

Map showing the whole of the Western Front, 1914–1918 (the dotted area represents the extreme advances of both sides; the horizontally lined area shows the Western Front for most of the war (1914–17); the darker line shows the Armistice line of 1918).

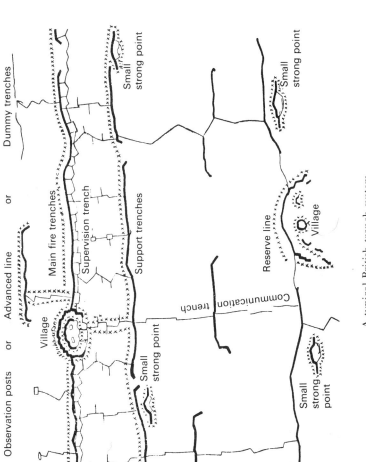

Observation posts   or   Advanced line   or   Dummy trenches

Village

Main fire trenches

Supervision trench

Support trenches

Small strong point

Small strong point

Village

Communication trench

Reserve line

Small strong point

Small strong point

Village

A typical British trench system.

I

The First World War on the western front began as a war of rapid movement, and this opening phase of less than four months contrasted vividly with the static trench warfare which ensued for nearly four years. Early in August 1914, the German armies swept through Belgium, checked but momentarily by a series of short, sharp battles with the Belgian, French and British armies. But by 24 August, the comprehensive retreat of the Allied armies from Mons to Paris had begun. Meanwhile, in Lorraine, Alsace and the Ardennes, the French armies had assaulted the Germans, but some initial success turned quickly to defeat, retreat, and then entrenchment. The German advance on Paris was halted in September by the four-day battle of the Marne, and there then followed the race for the sea, where, moving rapidly northwards to the Belgian coast, the French and Germans tried to outflank each other, but neither gained the advantage; for as one side brought up a new unit, the other had one to face it. At the outset of October, the B.E.F., entrenched near the Aisne, where it repulsed several German attacks, was transferred gradually to the north, entrenching along a line from Ypres to Bethune. At Ypres, the British army fought, in November, the last battle of the first phase of the First World War.

During this phase of open warfare, the soldiers of all armies had at times entrenched, but this was conceived as a temporary tactic consistent with the offensive ethos which prevailed in contemporary military thought. In 1914 the authoritative view was that future wars would be both mobile and short. Although trench war had occurred in the American Civil War, the Russo-Japanese conflict of 1904–1905 and elsewhere, military theoreticians judged these as atypical, caused by conditions unlikely to recur. Consequently, all armies on the western front were technically, and psychologically, geared for an open war of movement, to which the fighting between August and November 1914 appeared to correspond. But expectations and events no longer corresponded by mid-November, when at the end of the first battle of Ypres and the last of open war, the primary event evolving on the western front was static trench warfare, which became the characteristic form of war for the following four years. During this war, armies were deadlocked, and movement was more often measured in yards than miles, as, above ground, trench fighters hammered each other with bullet and bomb and, below ground, mined and blasted each other in unremitting trench battles . I have distinguished between an early and a later phase in trench warfare, and each phase is described in Chapter 3.

Such trench fighting has been the subject of much analysis and comment. Here, however, the subject is not the whole of trench warfare but a part of it, one particular aspect. From the start we must distinguish trench warfare firstly as intermittent, large-scale battles, where one side attacked the other, striving to kill the enemy, capture his trenches, and break through them into the open ground behind, and secondly as continuous but small-scale attacks where each side aggressed the other in a multitude of ways, while remaining mostly in their respective trenches. The former were the massive, dramatic episodes of the war: the battles of the Somme, of Passchendaele, Verdun and many more; but the latter was the ceaseless struggle in trenches, which occurred not only *within* the intervals between large battles but also *throughout* a given battle, such as the Somme, but elsewhere in the line. Our concern is with this less spectacular, routine or normal trench warfare, which, unlike large battles, was going on at all times of the war, on some part of the line and which from this point I shall refer to simply as trench warfare.

From the perspective of combatants, trench war was the larger part of the total war experience, since most soldiers for much of the time fought this form of war. Yet from the perspective of military and other historians, it seems that trench war is of less consequence and interest, and certainly, historical works attend less to trench war than to large battles. For instance, in the two volumes of the official war history for 1915, the number of chapters about large battles and trench war is thirty two and two respectively; in the two volumes for 1916, the number is thirty and four. This emphasis is usual in most histories but is entirely reversed in the present book, which treats directly and at length of trench warfare and more indirectly and incidentally of large battles.

The reader will find it useful to have a preliminary sketch of the physical environment of trench warfare and the organisation and movement of military units. As we have seen, the open war ended in November 1914, and static war then prevailed along a trench system roughly 475 miles in length. This long, narrow zone of violence stretched, in the form of a shallow S, from the North Sea to Switzerland, passing through different nations and types of terrain. From north to south, the western front started on the beaches of Belgium, and for the 40 miles (approximately) between Nieuport near the Belgian coast and Armentières in France, the trenches crossed the flat and sometimes flooded fields of Flanders. This ground created problems of trench drainage and construction and, most frequently, they were not dug into but built on top of the ground in the form of breastworks; on part of this line lay the Ypres Salient, where, from high ground, the German trenches overlooked the British on three sides. Along the next segment, that is, Armentières – Givenchy – Lens—about 20 miles, the British trenches first ran through flat French farming country and were again overlooked at places by the German trenches. But between Givenchy and Lens, the farms gave way to a drab region of mining villages, dotted with pitheads and slagheaps. In contrast, the next 70 miles between Lens and Lassigny consisted, aside from the marshy valley of the Somme, of dry and rolling chalk downland, ideal for building long trenches and deep dugouts. From Lassigny to Rheims—about 50 miles—the trenches passed over a closer more uneven country and, in places, ran along the ridges and crests of hills. Between Rheims and the Argonne forest, the western front once more crossed dry, open chalkland—the Champagne—where the French Army trained in peacetime. Then, cutting through the Argonne, a rugged area of broken hills, heights, thick forests and streams, the line encircled the fortress at Verdun, before dropping down to the Plain of the Woëvre. For the remaining 100 miles of its length, the western front continued southwards, crossing the Vosges mountains, where sometimes a series of strongpoints replaced a continuous trench line, and finally ending on the Swiss border.

Much of the ground along the western front was not fitted for large-scale battles. Nevertheless battles were fought on ground whether it was suitable or not. For instance, artillery fire made parts of Flanders into a great swamp, making infantry movement well nigh impossible. But the battle of Passchendaele was fought on (and partly under) exactly such a swamp. Similarly, some parts of the western front were more suited than others for trench warfare, but the latter was possible upon all parts of the line, whatever the geographical or climatic conditions.

What were the relative positions of the Allied armies along the western front? These positions changed somewhat during the war, but the overall picture in November 1914 was not vastly dissimilar from that of September 1918. During 1915 and 1916, however, the positions of the Allied armies were relatively static. On the northernmost point of the western front, the Belgium army held a sector approximately 15 miles long from Nieuport to a point just north of the Ypres Salient. The British and Commonwealth armies were entrenched along 85 miles from the Ypres Salient to the River Somme, and between the Somme and Switzerland lay the French army. Obviously, the French sector was far longer than the British but was less densely held with troops, especially below Verdun. In 1917, the arrival of the Americans altered the picture. At first units of the U.S. army went individually into the French and British sectors for training in trench war; but, during 1918, the U.S. army held a sector from the Argonne to a position 80 miles to the south.

The reader now has a rough idea of the geography of the western front as well as the relative positions and length of sectors held by the Allied armies. The Germans and some Austrians were, of course, just 'over the way'. Now let us turn our attention to the trenches.

The western front first emerged as the infantries of each deadlocked army huddled in countless hastily dug and unconnected rifle pits, then joined these together into two continuous but parallel and opposing trench lines. From this simple beginning, the British, French and Germans evolved somewhat different but equally complex trench systems, which combined the functions of offence, defence, communication and supply. Between, and separating, the trenches of each opposing army lay no-man's-land. This was a continuous strip of ground held by neither army but patrolled at night and fired across by day by both. The length of no-man's-land was that of the western front itself; but its average width varied from 100 to 400 yards, although it narrowed, in some places, to as little as 5 to 10 yards and widened, in others, to as much as 1000 yards. The trenches of each side were roughly parallel to and stretched back from the outer boundaries of no-man's-land.

Upon British sectors, the fully developed trench system comprised three parallel trench lines: the front, support and reserve. The trenches were built either below or above ground as breastworks, or were part trench and breastwork combined. The latter was most frequently found. Usually, the front line consisted of two trenches: the fire and the command trench. The fire trench was continuous, but not straight, and traversed at intervals by earth buttresses, which protected against enfilade fire and shell blast. Buttresses were about 9 to 13 feet thick, and, between each buttress, the length of trench or 'bay' was 18 to 30 feet. Trench bays were occupied by a small group of soldiers, sometimes under a junior N.C.O., who had weapons, loopholes in the parapet, periscopes and so forth in order to harass the enemy. Frequently, a group was not only a weapon unit but a social group; for instance, soldiers brewed tea, fried bacon and 'chatted' together (a chat was a louse, and to chat was to rid oneself of lice by searching the uniform and underwear). This was a social as well as an individual event, as trench fighters gathered in groups and chatted, that is, deloused and gossiped.

About 20 yards in front of the fire trench, a continuous belt of barbed wire, some 10 yards broad and 3 feet high, was staked in no-man's-land; occasionally, a second wire obstacle was built beyond the first, with its outer edge 40 or 50 yards from the trench. Soldiers had access to no-man's-land through tunnels in the parapet of the fire trench and lanes through the barbed wire defences. Sometimes a sap trench jutted into no-man's-land for 20 or 30 yards and served as an observation or advanced warning post.

About 20 yards behind the fire trench and parallel with it, the command trench was located. The latter was connected with the former at frequent intervals, thus giving easy lateral communication along the front line. The command trench contained both dug-outs, which gave protection against shell splinters, and latrines, which attracted them, since from the air a latrine looked like a gun position—a favourite artillery target. Finally, machine guns were sited in the front line often in concealed strongpoints.

The front, support and reserve lines were connected at frequent intervals by communication trenches, along which passed reliefs, rations, supplies of ammunition and telephone cables to battalion and battery H.Qs. Communication trenches were not traversed but dug in a winding way to prevent enfilade fire and blast effect. Slit trenches, 2 feet wide and 7 feet deep, were dug at right angles to, and either side of, communication trenches and gave protection during bombardments.

From the command trench, the communication trench stretched back into the support trench—some 70–100 yards. This was a traversed trench with deep dug-outs, but no parallel command line, which accommodated support troops for the front line garrison. The latter sometimes retired to the support trenches either during a heavy bombardment, or to regroup for a counter-attack after an enemy raid upon the front line. Usually, the support trench was continuous and was protected by wire obstacles.

Roughly 400 to 600 yards behind the support trench lay the reserve line, which consisted of a line of dug-outs and trenches containing a garrison which reinforced front and support trenches. All trench systems contained mutually supporting strongpoints, sited in the ground between the front, support and reserve lines. Generally, these were infantry redoubts with parapets around their perimeters, containing machine-guns and trench-mortar emplacements. Such strongpoints were manned by a garrison, which might vary from a section to half an infantry company—about 100 men. Finally, the artillery was sited behind the trench system of front, support and reserve lines and out of the range of enemy small arms fire.[1]

The trench system of the French was somewhat different from the British and developed by an earlier date. It comprised two lines: the front and support. Unlike the British front line along which men were more or less equally distributed, the French front line was segmented, and fully garrisoned and fortified trenches alternated with trenches garrisoned merely with sentries. The former defended the latter with enfilade fire. In no-man's-land, two belts of wire, 10 yards thick and 5 yards apart, ran parallel to the front trench, and like the British, these contained passages for the entry and exit of French patrols. The French support trench was fully garrisoned and contained deep dug-outs for protection against shelling. The power of the quick-firing French guns compensated for the lack of a reserve line.

From early in the war, the trench system of the German army corresponded to the defence in depth perfected by them later in 1917. For instance, in 1915 at Neuve-Chapelle, the system comprised a continuous, fully garrisoned front trench, defended by wire obstacles in no-man's-land, with troops in support trenches 2000–3000 yards behind, and more in reserve trenches some 2000 yards behind the supports. The defence was supplemented by a line of machine-guns, in concrete strongpoints, 800 yards apart, positioned roughly 1000 yards behind the front trench.

The depths of the British, French and German trench systems

varied, from a minimum of about 1000 yards with the British, to a maximum of 4000–5000 yards with the Germans. Thus the three trench systems were basically similar in that each offered roughly the same range of opportunities for aggressing the enemy during trench warfare. This is true of all save exceptional sectors, where a fundamentally different trench system affected the pattern of trench war, for instance, in the Vosges a chain of isolated outposts ran up, down and over mountains, replacing the usual continuous trench lines.

It was noted above that from the start to the end of trench war, the trench systems of the western front remained in the shape of a shallow S, from Belgium to Switzerland. But the western front was not entirely static and from time to time shifted somewhat. Frequently movement occurred after a battle, such as the Somme, where one side, having captured the other's trenches, converted these for its own use, while the ejected enemy built other trenches; this completed and the battle ended, trench war recommenced but upon different ground. Alternatively, one side might withdraw for strategic reasons from its trenches to others further back. For instance, in March 1917, the Germans broke off trench warfare and withdrew, for an average of 20 miles along a front of 65 miles, to the Hindenburg line. Generally, though, the western front was mostly immobile for the greater part of the war; for instance, trenches near Laventie, on the British sector between Armentières and Lens, did not move from 1914 until the final advance of the war in 1918.

As a preliminary, the reader should know something not only of the ecology of trench warfare, but also of the organisation and movement of military units within the trench zone. British units are described in what follows but, in essentials, these did not differ greatly from their German and French counterparts.

The battalion figured largely in the lives of most infantrymen, since it was large enough to minister for their basic needs, yet not so large as to seem impersonal; on the contrary, all officers, and most N.C.O.s and private soldiers of a battalion knew each other by sight at least. The battalion was an administrative and fighting unit, which not only organised its members in and for battle, but fed, paid and clothed them, arranged their leave and saw to their religious, recreational and medical needs. A battalion contained about 1000 men and 35 officers, organised into subgroups which comprised: 4 companies, 16 platoons and 64 sections. These subunits contained respectively about 240, 60 and 14 men; commissioned officers commanded companies and platoons, and non-commissioned officers commanded sections and sometimes platoons. Some private soldiers were battalion specialists: signallers, cooks, transport men, Lewis gunners and many more. These positions had a more than intrinsic attraction for trench fighters, bestowing an immunity from other onerous duties, such as drill, fatigue and working parties. Moreover, a specialist might enjoy a wide discretion, which made some unlikely jobs seem most attractive. For instance, an officer, wishing to reward a soldier for good conduct, was amused when the latter asked to be made company sanitary man.[2] But this man was no fool. Although he would care for the primitive loos of 200 men, he would also be excused parades and left alone by authority to look to his loos as he saw fit. Needless to say, old soldiers were often found in these jobs.

In the form of its commanding officer, the battalion sometimes protected the interests of trench fighters against demands of a non-combatant high command. An officer of the 48th Division commended his colonel for 'the uncompromising way in which he confronted brigade from whom he stood no nonsense'.[3] Similarly, in temporary command of the 2/Royal Welch Fusiliers, Robert Graves protected his battalion against high command, who planned to use it for a small attack, which all of the unit agreed was 'unnecessary, foolish and impossible'. Graves arrived at the brigade H.Q., and when the general 'inquired in a fatherly way whether I were not proud to be attending a commanding officers' conference at the age of twenty one, I answered irritably that I had not examined my feelings, but that I was an old enough soldier to realise the impossibility of the attack'. Graves was supported by other battalion C.O.s and the attack was called off. At the battalion, 'the officers were much relieved to hear of my stand at the conference'.[4]

Some battalions evolved into communities and became the core of the soldiers' formal military experience and their socio-emotional lives.[5] In such cases, strong friendship cliques with a high degree of solidarity emerged, at section and platoon level among private soldiers and N.C.O.s, and at company and sometimes battalion levels among commissioned officers. Community sentiment within regular battalions was associated with regimental honour and tradition, and within the 'pals' battalions of the New Army, it had something to do with recruitment from a single area, for instance a neighbourhood, or an occupation.[6] While a guest at an infantry officers' mess, a gunner was impressed by regimental solidarity commenting that 'it was much to be envied', and added that he regretted the artillery's lack of regimental tradition, which he felt, 'would bind us all together more'.[7]

Brigade was next above battalion in the chain of command. An infantry brigade consisted of 4 battalions, machine-gun and trench-mortar units all commanded by a non-combatant brigadier general and his staff of about 4 officers. Brigade H.Q. was the lowest rung of the high command ladder; 'brasshats' and 'red tabs' started here. Unlike battalions, brigades did not often develop a sense of solidarity or *esprit de corps*.

Beyond brigade lay division, which was the smallest unit possessing all—or nearly all—arms and auxiliary services. A division comprised about 20,000 men, organised into 3 infantry brigades—12 battalions, 4 artillery brigades, machine-gun and trench-mortar units, engineer units and supply, transport, medical and signal services. All this was commanded by a major-general and his staff of officers at division H.Q. The division was a self-contained and self-supporting unit which held a front line approximately 4000–6000 yards long. If strategy is defined as the art of moving and conducting fighting units and selection of their positions, and tactics as the art of handling and directing troops when in actual contact with the enemy, the division was the largest tactical unit of the war and its main function was to train and direct men in large-scale battles and trench warfare. Further, the division was the largest unit to maintain a permanent establishment (larger units such as corps and army did not) and might keep its original infantry and artillery units throughout the war. Perhaps this permanency had something to do with the development in some divisions of a high *esprit de corps*, and, according to one authority, 'divisional pride and esprit de corps were at the very least as high and important as regimental'.[8]

Following the outbreak of war, the number of divisions on the western front increased rapidly from 4 in August 1914, to 21 in July 1915, 58 in July 1916—the start of the Somme battles—62 in February 1917, and 64 in November 1918.[9] Some divisions served both on the western and on other fronts including Gallipoli, Salonika and Italy. Some divisions did not serve on the western front at all. The total number of British divisions which served on the western front for a period of 3 months and more was 57.[10]

Divisions were either regular, New Army or territorial. Regular divisions consisted of professional, permanent army units; a New

Army division was comprised of units created in wartime, for instance, the 'service' infantry battalions; a territorial division was composed of units manned by part-time volunteers in peacetime, committed to full-time service in war. Of the 57 divisions, which served for 3 months and more on the western front, 12 were regular, 27 New Army and 18 territorial. In some cases, however, these titles were misleading; some regular divisions contained New Army battalions and conversely, but territorial divisions remained entire throughout the war.

The division was thus the basic tactical unit of the B.E.F. Moreover, the division is a basic unit of analysis in this study, which intends to make assertions about the battle behaviour of trench fighters. With regard to these assertions, one problem was the possible objection that they had been derived from an unrepresentative or biased sample of sources. Therefore it was necessary to examine material from fighting units drawn systematically from throughout the B.E.F. The division was chosen as the basic sample unit because the total number of divisions was small enough to be manageable for research purposes, yet the division itself was a large enough unit for at least one of its members to have written about trench war. The reader should know that this book is based on material contributed by at least one trench fighter from each of 56 divisions, that is, 98 per cent of the total number of divisions;[11] further, there are on average more than 3 sources per division. The sampling has not been unsystematic and it has been as intensive as time and resources allowed; thus neither the sources nor the conclusions drawn therefrom can be dismissed as unrepresentative.

The sources themselves include diaries, letters, accounts of trench war written at the time, various forms of reminiscence as well as battalion and divisional histories, which were usually written or edited by ex-trench fighters, and always contained material written by them. The official war diaries were not used as sources since, as the reader will soon see, they could not record the types of behaviour and events which are the subject of study here.[12] I have interviewed and talked at length with some ex-trench fighters, and what they have had to say mostly confirms the events described in the written sources. However, I have not included oral material because while trench fighters can very well remember that certain events occurred, they cannot remember exactly where and when. This is a difficulty of researching the 'small' rather than 'large' events of the war; but in the written material the particulars of time and place are either given or can be researched.

Returning to our outline of the military hierarchy, battalion, brigade and division were mobile units, but the corps, next above division in the chain of command, was a static formation, which held more or less permanently a sector often 12 miles in length. For the most part, the function of corps was strategic and administrative, namely, to position and direct the fighting divisions along its front in battle and trench war; but corps had some permanent fighting units, chief among which was the heavy artillery. A corps H.Q. had an establishment of 24 officers and was commanded by a lieutenant-general. Like other units, the number of corps expanded greatly during the war, for instance, two corps existed in 1914 and sixteen in 1916.

An army was a static unit with strategic and administrative functions similar to corps, but on a larger scale and higher level. Further, an army was commanded by a full general. An army front could be 25 miles in length and contain several corps. The number of armies in the B.E.F. grew from one in 1915 to five in 1916.

Above army and at the apex of the hierarchy was G.H.Q., commanded until December 1915 by Field Marshal Sir John French, and subsequently by Field Marshal Sir Douglas Haig. Theoretically, then, the chain of command worked something like this: G.H.Q. issued policy directives, concerning large battles and trench warfare, which were channelled downwards through army, corps, division, brigade and battalion H.Q.s. In this process, G.H.Q. directives became less general as they were adapted by successive H.Q.s to local circumstances, until, finally, specific orders for particular attacks at specified times and places were issued direct to combatants.

In June 1916, shortly before the battles of the Somme, the B.E.F. filled an 85-mile sector of the western front from Boesinghe near Ypres in the north to Mericourt near the Somme in the south. The B.E.F. front was divided into 4 army sectors, subdivided in turn into 16 corps sectors, along which 39 fighting divisions were distributed.[13] This front was continually active not only with the struggle between the armies but also with the rotation of fighting units in and out of the trenches. During the battle of Verdun in 1916, the French established the principle of 'roulement' whereby the fighting divisons were 'rolled' in succession through army and corps sectors, where the battle was occurring, and then were transferred to trench war or training and rest. 'Roulement' spread to the British and German armies and was applied both to large-scale battles of attrition, as when all British divisions save one were 'rolled' through the Somme, and to routine trench warefare. Thus a division would usually move into and out of several army and corps sectors in the course of the war; for example, the 48th division circulated through three army and six corps sectors in the war.

But the picture is still more complex, for there was a parallel movement in and out of trenches among the units of a division, along a divisional sector. Frequently, a divisional sector was divided into two brigade subsectors, through which the three infantry brigades were rotated. Thus at any time two infantry brigades were in the line and one at rest. All artillery brigades, however, remained in the line until the division was relieved. Heavy artillery, which was either an army or corps formation, never came out of the line, since the latter were static units. An infantry brigade of four battalions usually had two in the trenches and two behind, billeted in farms, barns and villages. Likewise, the two battalions in the line had two companies in the front and support trenches, and two in the reserve trench; the two forward companies had two platoons in the fire and command trenches and two in the support trench. Every eight days, or thereabouts, the two battalions in the line changed places with the other two billeted behind.

Briefly then, divisions succeeded each other upon army and corps sectors, and brigades and battalions were rotated in and out of divisional sectors. Divisional artillery stayed put until the division was relieved, but heavy artillery was in the line at all times, although some miles behind the front line. Despite this constant circulation, trench war went on without cease.

No introduction to the war of the trenches is complete without mention of the high command/trench fighter relationship. 'We all hated the sight of staff officers', bluntly asserted one old soldier, who served four years on the western front, 'the only damned thing the majority seemed to be any good at was to check men who were out of action for not saluting them properly'.[14] Elsewhere the same old soldier remarked, 'during the whole of the war I never saw a general above the rank of brigadier general in a front line trench'.[15] Front fighters held generals in contempt and offered up many a 'prayer'[16] for the souls of the 'velvet arsed buggers'[17]—such prayers were meant, of course, to speed the souls of high command from the earthly to the other state. Moreover, the growth in the number of high command personnel as the B.E.F expanded did not go unnoticed by the line, 'A gibe among us was that the war would end when a staff job had been found for everyone and there was no one left to man the fire step'.[18] Without a doubt, many trench fighters shared sentiments similar to these; yet, even in the war, a minority view existed, for instance, the diary of a German artillery man reads 'People often talk drivel about staff officers not daring to come up to the front. For one thing as I see it, it's their duty not to expose themselves to danger, but on the other hand, we have quite a number of inspecting generals up at the front'.[19] After the war and in retrospect, some trench fighters changed their view of high command; for example, one officer, who during the war happily hid behind a trench dam and let loose a 'mass of slime' and 'stinking sewage'[20] upon an unsuspecting general and his staff walking up the trench, commented of high command in 1965, 'The simple rule blame the corps commander would pass when one was young and ignorant but won't do as an historical verdict'.[21]

However, I am not much concerned here to argue for or against the view that higher commanders were either fools or knaves, although some conclusions which will later emerge may bear upon this controversy. On the other hand, the high command/trench fighter theme is central to both this and many other works on trench war, but the theme's usual emphasis will here be reversed. Thus the aim is not to show how the decisions of a few generals affected thousands of soldiers, but, rather, how the decisions of thousands of soldiers affected a few generals. It is no secret that the resentment of trench fighters towards high command was expressed in derisory and colourful language, but it is less well known that such resentment was also translated into subtle, collective action, which thwarted the high command trench war strategy.

But first, exactly who were high command? British soldiers often spoke of the 'staff', 'brasshats' or 'red-tabs', but these terms denoted two distinct categories of officer: firstly, there were the generals or higher commanders, who commanded units higher than battalion, such as brigade, division, corps, army, and, ultimately, G.H.Q; secondly, there were officers who served on staffs of the former, and these are properly called staff officers. To some extent, the term high command was relative. Some brigade and divisional staff officers—perhaps generals also—did not think of themselves as belonging to high command, which, from their point of view, was comprised of

generals and staff officers of corps and above. But no such fine
distinctions were drawn by trench fighters, who saw non-
combatants who directed battles as one species, and those who
fought battles as quite another, and it is the front-line meaning of
the term high command that is used in this book.

At this point, the reader knows of the difference between large-scale
battles and routine trench war, and also something of the latter's
physical and social organisation. Now we turn our attention to
social behaviour among the antagonists of the trenches.

Whether of the battle or routine type, the image of trench war
held by most persons is probably of persistent, violent and bloody
conflict. This image is conveyed in mass media, for instance, the
B.B.C.'s Great War series, and is found in the work of military and
other historians. Thus the introduction of a recent study of trench
warfare stated:

> the intensification of combat was mutual and progressive, and
> seemingly obeyed mathematical rather than human laws. Hence
> the inhumanity of its conditions and the helplessness which the
> individual subjected to those laws so very often felt. 'Attrition'
> 'materialschacht', 'guerre d'usure ; in whatever language sought
> to describe the character of trench warfare, they expressed the
> same idea.[22]

In a similar vein, the editor of a war diary wrote, 'What was it that
men endured there, and what was the secret of their great capacity
for endurance?'.[23] The picture of combatants helpless before 'laws'
working independently of their wills, causing misery and des-
peration, which is then passively endured, represents some part of
the trench war experience; but if it is meant to describe either the
whole or 'average' war experience, the image is misleading, and,
perhaps, is less than just to trench fighters who were resourceful as
well as brave.

Much research into social situations has shown, where persons
are exposed to the working of 'laws' which are inconsistent with
either their wills or needs that they remain neither passive, 'helpless'
nor 'powerless' but actively strive to modify the working of such
alien 'laws'.[24] A concept of trench warfare, which blocks the insight
that soldiers might act upon conditions of trench existence to render
these more tolerable, is inadequate. For the fact is, soldiers strove

with success for control over their environment and thereby radically changed the nature of their war experience. To show how this was achieved, one must first distinguish between active sectors of the front line, which corresponded to the conventional picture of trench war, and other sectors which did not. The latter are the main subject of this study and will now be defined.

In their accounts of trench war, combatants distinguish between quiet or cushy sectors of the front line and active sectors where aggression prevailed. 'Cushy' was a term used to describe any comfortable state,[25] but especially those sectors where the reciprocal violence of enemies was small in volume and perfunctory in performance. On a cushy sector, life was relatively safe, tolerable, even comfortable, and greatly contrasted with life on an active sector, where continuity and zeal marked the fighting. According to one infantry officer, a 'profound difference' existed between sectors where 'a perfunctory showing of the daily discourtesies of war' predominated, and sectors 'whose quality took the form of a permanent manifestation of evil. The fire of bitter antagonism never died down to ashes in such places . . . the wind of every passing shell would fan the embers into a blaze of fury. Battle strode the air night and day without respite'.[26]

Trench fighters described this 'profound difference' both figuratively and factually, but rarely in detail. For instance, Winston Churchill, after serving an apprenticeship in trench war with a Guards battalion, commanded a battalion of the 9th division elsewhere in the line. In a letter to his wife, he briefly illustrates with hard facts the difference between the two sectors, 'it is a very quiet part of the line . . . the casualties run only to 5 or 6 a day on the front of the division which is no more than is lost in one battalion of the Guards'.[27] Assuming that both divisions had 4 of 12 battalions in the line, the difference between active and quiet, measured in flesh and blood, was 20–24 daily casualties in the Guards division, and 5–6 in the 9th. But it was quieter still on other parts of the line, for instance, a battalion of the 48th division had only one officer casualty from April 1915 to Spring 1916 while holding a series of quiet fronts.[28]

The statistical treatment given to trench war casualties often conceals the difference between active and quiet fronts, and it thereby distorts the reader's mental picture of trench fighting. For example, the official history describes the time from May to September 1915 as 'a period of trench warfare with a steady toll of

300 casualties a day'.[29] From this statistic—an arithmetic mean—
the reader cannot tell whether 300 casualties occurred on most days,
or whether the figure was much less on some days but much more on
others; nor can he tell if the 300 casualties were more or less equally
distributed among different units and sectors, or if casualties were
high upon some sectors and low upon others. As a consequence, the
reader could believe 300 was the most frequent figure and these
casualties were distributed in equal parts among sectors and units.

But such a belief is quite wrong; firstly, it entirely obscures the
difference between active and quiet sectors, and, secondly, it
represents as a normal case of trench war, a possible, but unlikely or
limiting case.

Nevertheless, historians continue to give casualty statistics in this
way. Thus Middlebrook asserts that during trench war in the first
half of 1916, a battalion could expect to lose about 30 men each
month through death and wounds.[30] But this should not be taken to
mean that each battalion lost about 30 men for each 30 days in the
line. Some battalions lost more and some less than 30. We saw above
that a Guards battalion might lose 150–180 men per 30 days, while
other battalions might lose far fewer during a similar time. However,
if these varying rates are added and averaged, a figure of about 30
casualties per battalion per month might well emerge. But such a
statistic leads easily to the view that trench war had a uniform
intensity and continuity which, in fact, it did not.

To illustrate this important point, let us look briefly at the
distribution of casualties in two battalions of the 35th division[31]
from February to May of 1916. The battalion with the least
casualties lost 38 men, whereas that with the most lost 96 men. But
each battalion did not lose about the same number in each of the 4
successive months, that is, 9 and 20 men respectively (though this
figure is correct as a mean average). On the contrary, the monthly
casualty rates show that the battalion with the least total casualties
lost as many as 18 men in one month and as few as 3 in another;
similarly, the battalion with most casualties lost 72 in one month
and 4 in another. Clearly, mean averages, which conceal the
variation of casualty rates upon quiet and active fronts, could be
calculated for all battalions of the 35th division. But such statistics
convey an unreal image of invariable conflict in trench war and
leave the reader unprepared for, and perhaps puzzled by, allusions
to the other face of trench war, such as the following:

For twenty one days we held 'E' sector, . . . so peaceful was the outlook we might have been cloistered in a monastery . . . it was not even considered worthwhile to change the positions of the companies after the appropriate interval. 'A' company on the right were approached to be relieved by 'D', but, not desiring the incidental trouble of interruption, they protested, with some judgement, that any alteration of the existing dispositions could not prove more salutary. They therefore begged to be left alone in the firing line. Their appeal was respected and 'D' company remained in reserve.[32]

Without doubt the choice to stay put was neither heroic nor foolhardy but deliberate; for, as another trench fighter pointed out, 'on a very quiet sector it might be better to be in the line than out, because there were fewer fatigues and inspections'.[33]

In 1930, an ex-infantry officer of the 63rd division criticised those 'disenchanted' authors of war books, who described trench war as unremitting violent struggle managed by generals who were either fools or knaves, on the grounds that they distorted the reality of trench war, which was, more accurately, a mingling of active and quiet sectors where 'boredom' and 'inactivity' made up 'nine tenths' of the life of the infantry soldier.[34]

All this vividly illustrates the 'profound difference' between active and quiet sectors, and further, it certainly gives rise to a number of questions. How could it happen that soldiers found life more 'salutary' in the front line than out of it? What sort of battlefield can be likened to a monastery? Exactly how did 'the fire of antagonism' die down, flicker or whatever? How is it possible that the armed trench fighters of each army, separated sometimes from each other by several feet only, were 'bored' and 'inactive' for much of the time? If no war existed in the trenches, then what did? The answers lie scattered and in fragments throughout the documents of trench fighters, seldom, if at all, systematically rendered as a dimension of trench experience, but frequently found in distinct and implied forms.

In accounts of trench warfare, some authors merely mark while others look more closely at the difference between quiet and active sectors, and, regarding this, it is useful to distinguish retrospective material from that contemporary with the war. In the latter, the authors' aim was to describe the new type of static war between the European powers, to a public anxious for details. Written from the trenches shortly before their publication, such accounts were informal dispatches, and gave the reader an eye-witness and representative sample of large and small events in trench war. These dispatches noted the difference between sectors, and not in= frequently described the underlying principle, as well as some particulars of the cushy front.[35]

In much retrospective material, however, the evocation of trench war is based rather upon a selection than a representative sample of events. This is true of many memoirs and much autobiographical fiction of the inter-war era which expressed a theme of disenchantment, or qualified disenchantment, with the war. By qualified disenchantment, I mean a perspective wherein the author is estranged from war as an instrument of human purpose, yet, at the same time, is profoundly moved by the comradeship of the trenches—an intense social bond generated ironically by the very war rejected by all. However, the expression of either theme meant the selection of limited aspects of an author's war experience, and, as a consequence, an unintentional yet systematic neglect of other forms of war experience is often characteristic of these two genres.

One exception is that acknowledged classic *Undertones of War* by Edmund Blunden, a seasoned and decorated infantry officer of the 39th division. While he wrote from a stance of qualified disenchantment, Blunden viewed the war experience comprehensively, and, as Cyril Falls has observed, his memoir is 'almost a perfect picture of the small events which made up the siege warfare of France and Flanders'.[36] In his preface, Blunden designates these 'small events' as the 'undertones', 'oracular events' and 'front line meaning' of the trench war.[37] The latter were mostly represented by the author in an indirect and figurative form; but lest an especial 'undertone' escaped the uninitiated, Bluden explictly referred the reader to, 'the observance of the "LIVE AND LET LIVE" principle, one of the soundest elements in the trench war'.[38] Further, the author commented that the rule was 'unfortunately . . . not invariably observed'.[39] In the following chapters, we will examine both the nature and operation of live and let live as well as the extent of trench fighters' compliance.

The phrase 'live and let live' was not coined by Blunden, but appeared during the war at least as early as summer 1915 in the dispatches of Ian Hay,[40] and thereafter in material written in the course of the inter-war and post-World War Two periods.[41] Further synonyms are found in sources written during as well as after the war. 'One felt that the recent occupants of the sector had erred in the direction of a laissez-faire policy',[42] wrote Siegfried Sassoon at the time of a battalion relief, while serving with the 74th division; similarly, in the 51st division, an infantry officer remarked on the 'principle of laissez-faire'.[43] Other phrases include: 'rest and let rest';[44] 'let sleeping dogs lie';[45] 'mutual obligation element';[46] 'tacit truces';[47] 'mutual understanding';[48] and less economically, 'characteristic trench warfare, sort of take the thick with the thin, compromise, and be mighty glad to be alive'.[49]

Live and let live was a truce where enemies stopped fighting by agreement for a period of time: the British let the Germans live provided the Germans let them live in return. Essentially, the term live and let live denoted a process of reciprocal exchange among antagonists, where each diminished the other's risk of death, discomfort and injury by a deliberate restriction of aggressive activity, but only on condition that the other requited the restraint. The 'profound difference' between the quiet sector and the active sector was, therefore, the exchange of peace, according to the rules of live and let live on the former, and the exchange of aggression according to the rules of kill or be killed[50]—the high command policy for normal trench war—upon the latter. The quietness of a sector did not signify either a social void or vacuum between enemies but the replacement of one form of exchange with the enemy by another, which trench fighters found more consistent with their needs.

Truces were usually tacit, but always unofficial and illicit. The agreement between antagonists was unspoken and expressed in certain actions—or non-actions—which were meaningful to front fighters but not always to others. Truces were illegal at all times for they were neither created nor legitimated by authority but explicitly forbidden. The unofficial policy of live and let live was the antithesis of the official kill or be killed.

The size of truces varied considerably. The smallest truce involved only two adversaries, chatting, perhaps, after a chance meeting in no-man's-land, like that described in his diary by an officer of the 24th division:

Visited the sentry posts at 7 a.m. and at the bottom of the largest crater I found Pte Bates . . . who was rather undersized and comical looking . . . fraternising with a German . . . The fol-

20 *Trench Warfare 1914–1918*

lowing was their conversation. Bates: 'What rank are you in your army?' 'I am a corporal', indicating stripes on his collar. 'What rank are you?'— 'Oh', replied Bates, 'I am Company Sergt.-Major'.[51]

On the other hand a truce could implicate hundreds of soldiers: infantrymen, gunners, trench-mortar crews and so forth, and extend along several thousand yards of the front line. Such large-scale truces often surprised new troops on their first trench tour, whose expectations of trench war contrasted with its reality. 'Probably the most outstanding impression gained was the prevailing quietude', remarked an officer of the 41st division. 'It was difficult to believe that there was a war on and that this was really the front line'.[52]

The duration of a truce varied from a few minutes, as with small groups of fraternising trench fighters, to several days, weeks or even months in rare cases where large numbers and areas were involved. Moreover, while the abstract principle of live and let live (exchange) was at all places and times the same in trench warfare, truces assumed a multitude of concrete forms. Clearly, a few soldiers overtly fraternising face to face in a shell crater was a very different situation from one where a large number were covertly involved in a truce and communicating with each other, not directly in a face-to-face situation, but indirectly and over long distances. The former was a definite, explicit agreement between antagonists, whereas the latter was an implicit agreement, comprised of the mutually held assumption of seasoned trench fighters of both sides, that the adversary was in the mood to exchange peace, given a chance. Nevertheless, despite their relatively indefinite form, the influence of large-scale tacit truces was real enough in the trench war, as we will see.

According to the present account, the western front was interspread with active and quiet or peacetime sectors.[53] But the reader must not take this to mean a sector was active or quiet according to its nature—for instance its terrain—and regardless of its tenants' temper. More often, a sector was active or not, according to the attitude of the units in situ and irrespective of other features. In brief one sector was quiet because soldiers were disposed to live and let live, and another was active because soldiers wanted to fight. Since units circulated freely among sectors, a peacetime sector might very well become a small-scale battlefield, and conversely.

Thus truces were mobile and not geographically fixed, and, at any time on the western front, some sectors were active, some quiet, while the pattern changed frequently as units of different dispositions passed among sectors.
     Yet exceptions existed. Trench fighters knew of some sectors which were active without cease, such as the notorious Ypres Salient—Wipers to the troops; and others which were usually cushy, for instance Ploegsteert—Plugstreet to the soldiers. Further, for the course of the war, little activity occurred in the French sector between Nancy and the Swiss border. For reasons we will examine later, mining sectors were mostly active whatever their location.
     The disposition of trench fighters was, then, the prime factor in the emergence of truces. But there are no simple answers to questions about which units in the B.E.F. tended to rest and let rest, and what proportion of the total these were. However, the reader will find it useful to think of units, that is, battalions and divisions, as varying in terms of aggressive spirit in a threefold way.
     Firstly, some units aggressed the enemy for most of the time during trench tours. These were élite fighting units in which 'there was no thought of abstaining from action for fear of reprisal . . . no "live and let live" idea', and which, 'declined to purchase a peaceful time at the expense of making life easy for the enemy'.[54] It is invidious to name some élite units and not others, but these included the 1st and 2nd Battalions The Royal Welch Fusiliers, the 1st Battalion The Royal West Kent Regiment, and the 1st Battalion The Gloucestershire Regiment. Secondly, some units were variable and were aggressive for perhaps half of the time but content to live and let live for the rest. Finally, some units were willing to 'let sleeping dogs lie' for most of the time. Robert Graves speaks of the 'pessimism' of units of the 1st division whose 'spirit in the trenches was largely defensive; the policy being not to stir the Germans into more than their usual hostility'.[55]
     But another factor complicates this question. As sectors fluctuated in activity, so units fluctuated in terms of fighting ability. Thus, in the course of the war, some units won and some lost élite status, but only a few remained permanently élite; further, many units were non-élite throughout the war. The general picture was one of flux: sectors alternating between quiet and active, and units becoming either more or less passive or aggressive.
     A corollary of this flux was that no single 'typical', 'average' or 'truly common' war experience existed, but rather a number of

diverse sometimes inconsistent experiences, each formed by the particular mix of sectors and units which characterised a soldier's war career.[56] Although all trench fighters were brave, and all war experience traumatic, it is also true that some experiences were more traumatic than others. Some of the most and least traumatic experiences corresponded to different and identifiable trench war situations. Consider the contrast between the situation where one élite unit opposed another élite unit in the line, for instance, on one sector the 2/Royal Welch Fusiliers faced an especially active enemy, but the 'deadly competition was entered into with zest',[57] and another situation where a non-élite unit comprised of 'very decent chaps but hopeless as soldiers; the only thing they ever became efficient in was swearing',[58] faced up to a succession of élite and deadly enemy units. In the former case, life was nasty and brutish, but compensated for by the comradeship of skilled trench fighters, and a regimental *esprit de corps*. But in the latter case, an élite unit ensured life was nasty, brutish and very short for their less skilled adversaries; further, where comradeship was weak in a non-élite unit, the individual endured the horrors and hazards of battle alone, without the emotional and technical support of others.

Consider also a third situation where a non-élite unit content to live and let live faced a succession of non-élite enemy units, each equally disposed to peace. This third situation generates another and quite different war experience from the preceding two, and one considerably less traumatic.

The reader might now comprehend, not only that the search for a single 'true' account of the war experience is misconceived, but also that the inconsistency between some interpretations of trench warfare is illusory; for each could be a valid and 'true' rendering of one distinct dimension of multi-dimensional phenomenon. Thus the contradiction between the image of trench war as an obscenity of death and degradation, found in the poems of Wilfred Owen,[59] and the image implied by a comment of an infantry officer: 'Could you ever have guessed how much I should enjoy the war',[60] is to some extent resolved with the knowledge that the opposition marks two different but possible trench war situations and careers.

There can never be a comprehensive history of the trench war, for it *was* an infinity of profound experience; perhaps that is why trench war continues to fascinate and to endure in the folk consciousness. In what follows below, I am saying that live and let live was endemic to trench warfare; that it is an insufficiently researched aspect of the trench war; and that one can know neither how men endured the war nor the nature of the war experience, without also knowing how trench fighters controlled some conditions of their existence.

2

At the outset of this study, we must distinguish between problems of the origins of truces, and problems of their persistence through time. Concerning origins, we want to know when and where tacit understandings first occurred, and also how they happened during battle, where each antagonist was ostensibly intent upon killing the other. Exactly when and where the first truce emerged can never be known; but the view that truces appeared for the first and last time during the Christmas of 1914 is incorrect. The Christmas truces were neither the first nor last instances of live and let live; for some truces occurred before the Christmas, and others for the duration of the war. A more correct view is that several forms of truce occurred throughout the trench war, and that truces briefly yet vividly emerged in the form of overt fraternisation on a widespread scale during the 1914 Christmas. The event can be likened to the sudden surfacing of the whole of an iceberg, visible to all including non-combatants, which for most of the war remained largely submerged, invisible to all save the participants. But how and when did truces first happen? Which activities were first involved?

Some evidence suggests that the first understandings were associated with meals, the times and conditions of which were common to each side. Both British and German rations were brought up to their respective trenches at about the same time each evening, and a British N.C.O. noticed this practice as well as its effect on truce formation as early as the first week of November 1914—which is around the beginning of trench war. The N.C.O. whose unit had been engaged in trench war for some days, observed that:

> The quartermaster used to bring the rations up . . . each night after dark; they were laid out and parties used to come from the front line to fetch them. I suppose the enemy were occupied in the same way; so things were quiet at that hour for a couple of nights, and the ration parties became careless because of it, and laughed and talked on their way back to their companies.[1]

Probably the N.C.O.'s supposition that British and German ration parties were not only doing the same thing, but were aware of it, was correct. Concerning the growth of the process where each antagonist made assumptions about the other's behaviour, and then acted on these assumptions, it seems quite possible that men who are forced to take account of each other's behaviour in battle in order to stay alive, will not stop when the pace of battle decelerates for whatever reason. The process of mutual empathy among antagonists was facilitated by their proximity in trench war and, further, was reinforced as the assumptions made by each of the other's likely actions were confirmed by subsequent events. Moreover, by getting to know the 'neighbour' in the trench opposite, each adversary realised that the other endured the same stress, reacted in the same way, and thus was not so very different from himself.

Again in respect of mealtimes, the early growth of this process is illustrated by a Private Hawkings of the 5th division who was looking over the parapet of his trench on the morning of 1 December 1914:

> I could observe the earthworks of a trench on the other side of the road. Soon after dawn a man looked out of this trench . . . and slid into ours. It was a sergeant . . . who had come to see how we were getting on. He warned us against peering lightheartedly over the parapet and opined that our earnest curiosity had not been greeted with a shower of bullets was probably due to the large breadth of no-man's-land, poor morning visibility and Fritz enjoying his breakfast.[2]

No doubt Fritz was busy with his breakfast. No doubt, too, that such knowledge influenced not only Private Hawkings but other trench fighters up and down the line. Certainly, breakfast truces later in the war became a common mode of live and let live, and Liddell Hart, the trench fighter and military historian, described them thus, 'Unforgettable too, is the homely smell of breakfast bacon that gained its conquest over the war reek of chloride of lime, and in so doing not only brought a tacit truce to the battle front, but helped in preserving sanity'.[3]

Similarly, ration party truces quickly became a custom of the quiet front, for instance, in April 1915, they were so well established on part of the 27th division's front that a private remarked, 'At night we went on ration parties across the open, which we came to regard

as safe';[4] and, in the summer of 1915, Ian Hay of the 9th division was
writing that:

> It would be child's play to shell the road behind the enemy's
> trenches, crowded as it must be with ration wagons and water
> carts, into a bloodstained wilderness . . . but on the whole there
> is silence. After all, if you prevent your enemy from drawing his
> rations, his remedy is simple: he will prevent you from drawing
> yours.[5]

But on an active front, of course, each side considered the other's
rations as a prime target.

Thus, early in the war and in spite of it, both sides were learning
that each had similar priorities and needs, and it seems that this
realisation first crystallised around basic needs such as food and
warmth. For instance, in December 1914 but before Christmas, the
same Private Hawkings was sentry in an advanced post near a
similar post manned by Germans. The weather was bitter.
Hawkings was told to keep a sharp look out, but he assumed that 'If
the members of the Fritz post were as cold, wet and sleepy as I, they
wouldn't be inclined to interfere with me'.[6] The Germans, it seems,
reasoned likewise, for the night passed in peace as neither side
provoked the other.

At some point in this empathic process where each antagonist
learned that the other shared his needs and priorities, overt
fraternisation, rather than covert trucing, was always a possible
outcome as, for example, where fraternisation might be necessary to
satisfy a shared need. Concerning the common need for warmth, a
German officer before the Christmas of 1914 commented upon 'The
fraternisation that has been going on between our trenches and
those of the enemy, when friend and foe alike go to fetch straw from
the same rick to protect them from the cold and rain and to have
some sort of bedding to lie on—and never a shot is fired'.[7]
Accordingly, the energy of each side was sometimes directed against
their common enemy—winter—but such energy was not in all cases
channelled back into warfare when conditions improved. One does
not know whether this process had evolved among few or many
units before the Christmas truces. Certainly, there is evidence that it
had occurred in some battalions, but, equally, there is evidence that
it had not occurred in others.[8] Some battalions did not participate
in the Christmas fraternisation, and whether there is a connection

between the growth of empathy and the restriction of aggression before Christmas, and truce participation on Christmas Day, is an interesting question, but one which cannot be answered fully here. Nevertheless, such a connection seems to make sense, and can be illustrated in the case of the 2/Scots Guards. Towards the end of November 1914, some Scots Guards raided the German trenches at night, and according to one officer:

> The morning after the attack, there was almost a tacit understanding as to no firing, and about 6.15 a.m. I saw eight or nine German shoulders and heads appear, and then three of them crawled out a few feet in front of their parapet and began dragging in some of our fellows who were either dead or unconscious . . . I passed down the order that none of my men were to fire and this seems to have been done all down the line. I helped one of our men in myself, and was not fired on, at all.[9]

The unintended consequence of such *ad hoc* truces was that antagonists were rendered more conscious of their similarities and less aware of their differences, and in so far as the mutual perception by enemies of their differences promotes war, the perception of similarities weakens it.

Thus it is probably no coincidence that, several days after the above truce, the same officer described in a letter plans for Christmas festivities which included gestures of goodwill for the Germans:

> We return to the trenches tomorrow, and shall be in them on Christmas Day. Germans or no Germans . . . we are going to have a 'ell of a bust, including plum puddings for the whole battalion. I have got a select little party together, who, led by my stentorian voice, are going to take up a position in our trenches where we are closest to the enemy, about 80 yards, and from 10 p.m. onwards we are going to give the enemy every conceivable form of song in harmony, from carols to Tipperary . . . My fellows are most amused with the idea, and will make a rare noise when we get at it. Our object will be to drown the now too familiar strains of 'Deutschland über Alles' and the 'Wacht am Rhein' we hear from their trenches every evening.[10]

Not surprisingly, a Christmas truce occurred between the Scots

Guards and the Germans.[11] Moreover live and let live had existed in some form on the battalion's front before Christmas, and hence the fraternisation of Christmas was neither a wholly spontaneous, nor an isolated event, but the substitution of an overt for a covert form of peace. More generally, the whole of the Christmas truces might not have been a spontaneous event as is often supposed but a visible and vivid manifestation of the already existing undertone of trench war.

Now attention shifts from the origin of truces to the more complex problem of their persistence. The two problems are different: the fact that a truce emerged at breakfast, or when rations were brought up, or when rain flooded the trenches, does not explain why the *ad hoc* agreement persisted after breakfast, or when rations had been brought up, or when the sun appeared. Neither does the origin of truces in non-combat activities explain their diffusion throughout, and persistence within, combat activities. Now, communication among parties to a truce was necessary for a truce's origin as well as its persistence, and if we understand how trench fighters communicated with each other, we will also learn a lot about the persistence of truces throughout the war. Such communication posed unique problems with live and let live, since it had to happen not only *within* each army, that is, among compatriots, but also *between* each army, that is, among antagonists. In principle, the former does not seem difficult, but the latter is more puzzling, for instance, how was peace negotiated in the midst of battle? Moreover truces in war were fragile things, for if either side suspected the other of duplicity, a pre-emptive strike was at all times possible as well as prudent. Some truces were destroyed, no doubt, by pre-emptive aggression, but others persisted for months. How did each adversary not only reveal to the other the wish to restrict aggression, but also stop the spread of suspicion for as long as the truce lasted?

But first we will discuss the less complex question of communication among compatriots. Obviously, the unofficial rules of peace were not officially published and passed among trench fighters for their information; yet all veterans knew of the rules whether they concurred with them or not. How was this knowledge conveyed within each army? There are two situations here: one involved experienced trench fighters, and the other inexperienced troops fresh from the home front. In the first, a circulation of veterans into and out of the line was occurring at all times as battalions were rotated in and out of divisional sectors, while divisions moved in and out of corps and army sectors. Given this continuous movement of men, how could a truce remain stable on a sector for several months? The second case concerns the circulation of new troops. Freshly trained soldiers were frequently fed into the war either singly or in drafts to make a unit up to strength or as whole units, such as battalions and divisions, as in the build-up of the B.E.F. during 1915–16. As part of their training, soldiers acquired the official image of trench war, namely, of perpetual conflict where 'there was no cessation of gun, trench mortar and rifle fire, nor neglect of mining, raids and small actions for local purposes'.[12] But where trench fighters first experienced war upon a quiet front the inconsistency of image and reality caused much surprised comment. The reaction of a member of the 61st division was typical: 'there was . . . an uncanny stillness in the air, broken occasionally by some spasmodic firing. It was very difficult to imagine that this place had any connection with a world war—it seemed so quiet'.[13] Likewise a medical officer of the 23rd division commented:

> It was my first visit to the trenches . . . There was still none of that roar of cannon and rattle of machine guns which we in our innocence had imagined went on more or less continually in trench warfare.[14]

The 'innocence' of some newcomers amused the old soldiers; for instance, one young soldier arrived in the front line calling out excitedly, 'Hi mate, where's the battle? I want to do my bit'.[15] But clearly such enthusiasm might disturb the peace. In both the above situations the general problem should be clear enough: the persistence of truces was consistent neither with their constant renegotiation by seasoned antagonists entering into and exiting from the line, nor with their constant rediscovery by successive units of unseasoned men. How, then, did truces stay stable through time?

Let us take the last case first: exactly how and when were the rules of the game passed on to new troops? In the B.E.F. fresh divisions usually went for an official tour of instruction into trenches held by veterans, and where the line was quiet the newcomers were often instructed in the art of peace as well as war. Such a situation was described by a private of the greenhorn 47th division who with others of his section had been instructed and now were about to take over the trenches from their tutors and, for the first time, hold them alone. The private spoke with the outgoing soldiers:

> The man Mike gave some useful hints on trench work. 'It's the Saxons that's across the road' he said, pointing to the enemy lines which were very silent. I had not heard a bullet whistle over since I entered the trench. On the left was an interesting rifle and machine gun fire all the time. 'They're quiet fellows, the Saxons, they don't want to fight any more than we do, so there's a kind of understanding between us. Don't fire at us and we'll not fire at you'.[16]

Likewise a unit of the 29th division took over trenches in France for the first time and was told by an N.C.O. of the garrison relieved that 'Mr. Bosche ain't a bad feller. You leave 'im alone: 'e'll leave you alone'.[17]

In much the same way when a single newcomer joined a seasoned unit, he might be told by an old hand both of his official duties and of the unofficial rules guiding their performance. R. C. Sherriff, who served with the 24th division, described such an incident where one officer takes his new colleague around the trenches. Together they crawl along a sap into no-man's-land. A German trench is nearby:

> 'Yes' said Trotter . . . 'that's the Bosche front line. Bosche looking over this way now, maybe, just as we are—do you play cricket?' he added . . . 'A bit' said Raleigh, 'could you chuck a cricket ball that distance?' 'I think so' 'Then you could do the same with a Mills Bomb . . . But you won't though' said Trotter . . . 'Come on, let sleeping dogs lie. If we was to throw a bomb you can bet your boots the old Bosche would chuck one back, and Mr Digby and Mr 'Arris (the soldiers occupying the sap) . . . are both married men. Wouldn't be cricket would it?'[18]

One can agree with Trotter: not that it isn't cricket; but neither is it war. Yet Trotter's brief homily on the undertone of war is neat.

We see then that the conventional image of trench war held by freshly trained units and individuals was modified, as the new soldiers experienced both the reality of a quiet sector and were initiated into the undertones of the war by their colleagues, and thus the stability of truces was assured. Neither was this stability effected by the circulation of experienced men moving in and out of the line for the official relief procedure allowed outgoing trench fighters to communicate the existence of tacit truces to incoming troops. Concerning trench relief, an official manual laid down:

> The first essential is a careful preliminary reconnaissance. Whenever a unit is about to take over a new line of trenches, parties from it will visit the trenches previously, by day if possible. In the case of a battalion, the party should consist of the C.O., adjutant and machine gun officer, and at least one officer and one N.C.O. from each company.[19]

Thus some incoming troops had direct knowledge of the line to be relieved and doubtless told others both of their own impressions, and also of the tenants' description. An officer of the 37th division described the take over of a new sector from the French:

> I made a preliminary tour of the whole line with Taudieres, a young French officer . . . of the French regiment we were relieving . . . it was the French practice to 'let sleeping dogs lie' when in a quiet sector . . . and of making this clear by retorting vigorously only when challenged. In one sector which we took over from them they explained to me that they had practically a code which the enemy well understood: they fired two shots for each one that came over, but never fired first.[20]

A private soldier of the 56th division described the same situation, 'the necessary arrangements were made for taking over our new section of front. These included a visit by several officers to the firing line, and, as usual on these occasions, we waited eagerly for their return in order to question . . . their mounted orderlies on the quietness or otherwise of our sector'.[21]

The above refers to troops moving from one sector to another; but most reliefs concerned different units moving in and out of trenches in the same sector, and in such cases a reconnaissance was not always necessary. Such reliefs were described by the adjutant of the 49th division:

> One relief is very much like another . . . The trench seems endless, but, at last the front line is reached. Other men covered with mud and wearing equipment are waiting there. The relief goes smoothly. Sentries are changed, duties are handed over, the

latest intelligence about 'Fritz' or 'Jerry' is imparted. 'Quiet tour. Not a casualty in our company. He doesn't fire if you lie doggo'.[22]

In this way a truce could persist for months, despite the continual circulation of soldiers in and out of the line, as the troops departing told those incoming of the existence of a truce, and thus constant renegotiation with the enemy was unnecessary.

The second problem is the more complex one of communication among antagonists, and here I shall distinguish direct and indirect truces, this distinction referring to different means of communication between antagonists. Direct communication involved the use of either verbal or written symbols, such as the spoken word with overt fraternisation. Indirect communication involved symbols unique to, and evolved in, the world of the trench fighter and it assumed one of two general forms: inertia or ritualisation. It is important to grasp that fraternisation, inertia and ritualisation were at one and the same time means of communication and forms of live and let live. The analysis starts with direct truces.

In so far as opposing trenches were within speaking or shouting distance of each other, commonsense suggests that truces were negotiated verbally and reaffirmed by the same means for so long as they persisted. The most famous of such truces were those of Christmas 1914 when nine British divisions held a front line of approximately thirty miles throughout which verbally arranged truces of varying lengths of time occurred.[23] The manner of the starting and ending of a typical Christmas truce was described by an officer of the 6th division. He met his German counterpart in no-man's-land where both agreed that neither wished to shoot on Christmas Day, although each had strict orders to allow no truces. A 24-hour truce was informally concluded and courteously ended at the agreed hour:

> At 8.30 I fired three shots in the air and put up a flag with 'Merry Christmas' on it, and I climbed on the parapet. He put up a sheet with 'Thank you' on it and the German Captain appeared on the parapet. We both bowed and saluted and got down into our respective trenches, and he fired two shots in the air, and the war was on again.[24]

The reaction of high command to these truces was immediate and negative, but on the whole appears to have taken the form of admonishment and warning; for instance, one battalion recorded that the truces, 'drew down the wrath of general headquarters',[25] who further demanded the names of the officers responsible but eventually dropped the matter. But the truces caused an army routine order to be issued asserting that soldiers 'were in France to fight and not fraternise with the enemy'.[26] For the Christmas of 1915 special measures were taken by high command to prevent a recurrence and these seem to have been successful, since only some units of the Scots Guards are recorded as having fraternised with the enemy. The reaction of high command was unequivocal. Two officers of the Scots Guards were court martialled; one was acquitted, and the other convicted and reprimanded.[27] According to one officer, all leave in the battalion was stopped.[28]

Despite the proscriptions of high command, verbally arranged truces were possibly widespread and probably the most common form of live and let live during the first few months of trench warfare. At about this time, an eyewitness wrote of British trench fighters that:

> They began to take something more than a professional interest in their neighbours opposite. The curiosity was reciprocated. Items of news . . . were exchanged when the trenches were near enough to permit of vocal intercourse. Curious conventions grew up, and at certain hours of the day . . . there was a kind of informal armistice. In one section the hour of 8 to 9 a.m. was regarded as consecrated to 'private business', and certain places indicated by a flag were regarded as out of bounds by the snipers on both sides.[29]

The custom which conferred immunity to an enemy on the loo is less curious, perhaps, than another where one side gave impromptu entertainments to the other. For example, we find in a battalion history that:

> On . . . the 4th April, the Germans made an organised effort to obtain a truce, which . . . lasted about two hours. While it was still dark, the Germans could be heard talking excitedly in their trenches which were not many yards away from our own. Later they began to sing and to shout remarks to the 1/2nd Londons and to the Leinsters . . . who returned the compliment with interest . . . it was amusing to see the heads of Germans popping

up and down like marionettes, behind their trenches, to the accompaniment of loud laughter. A German, standing on his fire step, juggled with three bottles; and when his 'turn' was ended, another German—a very small man—walked out as far as his own wire, struck an attitude, and hurriedly scampered back. A third then stood up and boldly challenged our men to play a game of 'soccer' against them in no-man's-land, but was immediately howled down when he confessed that they could not provide a football.[30]

Overt truces involving direct communication were not confined to the early part of trench war; for instance, in 1918—the last year of the war—along the front of the 38th division, 'where the lines approached, there was an exchange of messages, cigarettes and visits. By May the whole division was fraternising until a peremptory order from the G.O.C. stopped the practice'.[31] Whereas the latter truce involved large numbers of men along a divisional front, other direct truces occurred throughout the war on a much smaller scale, for example, a soldier of the 33rd division wrote, 'some of our sapheads were only fifteen yards from the German saphead. Each side could have easily thrown their bombs into one another's saps, but this was very rarely done and they generally lived in peace with one another; sometimes they held conversations'.[32] While some trench fighters generally lived in peace, others as Junger pointed out were, 'forever puzzling out the best possible ways of slinging over bombs with hand made catapults'.[33] The choice of aggression was always possible. Overt truces were arranged either in face-to-face situations by word of mouth as in the above illustrations, or, if the distance between trenches precluded face-to-face contact, trench fighters shouted across no-man's-land. Thus on parts of the 8th division's front during October 1915, the Germans frequently shouted over 'promising not to fire if we would not';[34] on moving to a quiet sector,a battalion of the 51st division heard the Germans shout, 'We Saxons, you Anglo Saxons, don't shoot', and apparently all went well, for a few days later the Saxons, 'shouted . . . that Prussians were relieving them, and asked us to give them hell'.[35] Written messages were sent to the enemy either upon a notice board raised above the trenches, or, more ingeniously but less effectively perhaps, inside defused missiles. For instance, opposite the 12th division, the Germans intimated a wish for the quiet life on a notice board which read, 'Don't fire East Surreys, you shoot too well';[36] on the front of the 18th division, bad weather prompted some light-hearted banter, 'a Teutonic voice was heard to call out "another dugout fallen in Tommie?" And . . . our neighbours across the way hoisted a board with the following inscription (in English) painted on it: "On and after the 13th inst. you can have these b---- trenches" '.[37] Using another means of communication, some sociable Saxons put a written message into a defused rifle-grenade, and dispatched the harmless missile into the trenches of a unit of the 12th division. The message read, 'To the opposition. We have sent by rifle grenades some newspapers. When you get it, stick up a white flag and we don't shoot. Wait a minute and newspapers come by non exploding grenades. Is peace in sight? Please answer.'[38] A unit of the 46th division recorded that:

the infantry opposite . . . were Saxons, and inclined to be friendly with the English. On one occasion the following message, tied to a stone, was thrown into our trench: 'We are going to send a 40 lb bomb. We have got to do this, but dont want to. I will come this evening, and we will whistle first to warn you'. All of this happened. A few days later they apparently mistrusted the German official news, for they sent a further message saying, 'Send us an English newspaper that we may hear the verity'.[39]

Similarly, Robert Graves, serving then with the 2nd division, remarked that his battalion—the 2/Royal Welch Fusiliers—received a message in a defused grenade from the 'German Korporals' to the 'English Korporals' inviting the latter to a 'good German dinner'.[40] In the 1st division, the Germans made 'coy advances' on the front of the 1/Gloucestershire Regiment and 'fired over a friendly message in a trench mortar bomb'.[41] But it was most unlikely that either this regiment or the 2/Royal Welch responded in kind, since both were élite units with reputations for aggressive trench fighting.

Some truces occurred for a specific and limited purpose; for instance, heavy rainfall made mutual aggression very difficult; for the trenches were flooded and mud made rapid movement impossible, and in these conditions an *ad hoc* truce not infrequently emerged. An officer of the Guards division recorded that, 'the rain brought the trenches tumbling in, and the mud was so bad that they simply could not be used. The Germans and ourselves were walking about on the top in full view of each other, neither side wanting to shoot';[42] an officer of the 50th division described a similar bad weather truce:

> fortunately Fritz was in much the same plight and did not bother us. He was only about 200 yards away, and at almost any hour of the day we could see two or three of them standing about on the top. We did not snipe at them, and they left us alone . . . Almost every day both British and Boche lose their way and get into the enemy lines.[43]

It might be thought that bad weather gave trench fighters no choice but to stop the killing for a while. But that was neither the case nor the view of high command. For example, on the 8th division's front, some trenches were two feet deep in water, and others entirely flooded; yet under these seemingly impossible conditions, the 1/ Worcester Regiment made the first raid of the trench war. In the same division another battalion with flooded trenches instantly fired upon Germans who quitted their flooded trenches in order to bail them out.[44] The choice of aggression was possible even under extreme conditions.

Once started *ad hoc* weather truces were sometimes prolonged and progressed to further exchanges between antagonists. For instance, in the 24th division, a weather truce lasting for several days developed into good morning greetings, friendly conversations and night truces between working parties; during one of the latter a British officer, walking by mistake into the German working party, got stuck in the mud and was pulled out by his orderly.[45] The logical outcome of such direct truces was, perhaps, the type of situation witnessed by Winston Churchill when visiting the French front line:

> The lines are in places only a few yards apart . . . the sentries looked at each other over the top of the parapet: and while we were in the trench the Germans passed the word to the French to take cover as their officer was going to order stone shelling. This duly arrived.[46]

Another British officer accompanied Churchill and described similar events:

> On the front we were on the Boche signals if the art. [artillery] is going to fire and shows the no. of rounds by holding fingers up.

They inform the French of the arrival of an officer by pointing to their shoulders & yesterday shouted 'pauvres Francais, explosion'. Measures were accordingly taken, & whilst we were there sure enough they exploded a comouflet.[47]

No doubt the French in their turn similarly obliged the Germans. Incidentally, it has been asked why Churchill wrote no war memoirs. He served with the Grenadier Guards for several weeks and as a battalion commander in the 9th division for several months. The 9th division held a front where live and let live was not infrequent, so that unless he described the latter, Churchill did not have a great deal to tell. Moreover most persons are familiar with a usual form of war memoir and would have expected the same from someone of Churchill's reputation. The state of the line was described by Ian Hay[48] whom Churchill met and described as, 'the author of those brilliant articles *The First Hundred Thousand*'.[49]

But to return to our theme: the British high command, perhaps aware of the outcome of uncurbed truces, were implacably opposed to all truces, whether these were brief events of no military consequence, or had some precedent and moral justification in the rules of war. The temper of high command can be gauged from the following events: after a minor attack, a battalion of the 16th division was invited by the Germans to collect its wounded in no-man's-land. Before the British and German commanders could stop it, a truce had been established and spread quickly along the front of the units concerned. The British battalion commander knew that despite its humane purpose the incident was 'highly irregular'. Further, and unfortunately for him, the truce occurred a short time after another for the same purpose had been conceded by the British to the Germans. The latter had caused the divisional headquarters to underline the order against fraternisation by a memo which stated:

> The Divisional Commander wishes it to be clearly understood by all ranks that any understanding with the enemy of . . . any . . . description is strictly forbidden . . . No communication is to be held with him . . . and any attempt on his part to fraternise is to be instantly repressed . . . In the event of any infringement . . . disciplinary action is to be taken.[50]

High command convened a court of inquiry into the above truce and issued even more stringent orders. The truce involved several hundred men along a battalion front; yet small-scale truces involving a few men along a few yards elicited from high command an equally severe response, as the brief event below recorded by an officer of the 39th division showed:

> a German officer and perhaps twenty of his men . . . with friendly cries of 'Good morning, Tommy, have you any biscuits' . . . got out of their trench and invited our men to do the same . . . our men were told not to fire upon them, both by C. and the other company's officer on watch; . . . there was some exchange of shouted remarks and after a time both sides returned to the secrecy of their parapets.[51]

When high command heard of this the two officers responsible were arrested, and shortly afterwards were marched off in open arrest to take part with their battalion in the battles of the Somme.

Although verbally arranged truces occurred intermittently for the duration of the war and were permanent in this sense, they were neither pervasive nor continuous. In the first case, overt truces could not exist without physical nearness and therefore could not diffuse into weapon groups which fought each other over long distances. For example, the opposing artillery and trench-mortar groups, unlike the opposing infantries, did not interact in face-to-face situations, and therefore could not arrange truces directly. Secondly, with rare exceptions, direct truces occurred neither in continuous succession, nor regularly at infrequent or frequent intervals; on the contrary, such truces were mostly irregular and ephemeral, since being highly visible they were easily repressed by high command, and therefore were never a serious and widespread problem.

However, live and let live evolved indirect and covert forms as well as direct, overt forms, and the former were an adaptation to the legal sanctions of high command, which threatened the existence of overt forms of live and let live. Accordingly, antagonists conveyed the wish to restrict aggression not only directly and personally, but also indirectly, impersonally and over long distances. Such communication involved a language of trench warfare, that is, a set of non-verbal symbols understood by trench fighters, but not outsiders, whereby antagonists who neither saw, spoke nor wrote to each other, nevertheless managed to convey reciprocally the wish to exchange peace. The process of indirect communication among antagonists assumed two main forms: inertia and ritualisation. (Ritualisation is examined in Chapter 5.) These, like overt fraternisation, were simultaneously forms of live and let live. Like direct truces, indirect truces occurred throughout the war; but unlike the former, the latter took a more subtle, less visible form and, as a consequence, were less vulnerable to the control of high command. As indirect communication was possible over long distances, such truces were pervasive involving artillery, trench-mortar and machine-gun weapon groups as well as the infantry. Moreover, as they could not easily be put down by high command, indirect truces continued without hindrance for many months on some sectors and were thus, from the point of view of high command, a serious and endemic problem of trench war. It seems that when referring to the undertone of trench war, Blunden had in mind these covert understandings which unlike overt truces were pervasive as well as continuous and subtle yet effective.

It was not the case that only one of the three forms of live and let live could exist on a sector at a given time, that is, a truce based upon either verbal contract, or inertia or ritualisation; on the contrary, all three forms could and sometimes did co-exist. For example, it could happen that infantry groups—hand-bombers—fraternised at sap-heads, while machine-gunners remained inert, and the opposing artilleries ritualised aggression. The sectors where all three forms of live and let live existed, and where all weapon groups exchanged peace were described in the literature as 'very quiet' or 'absolutely peaceful'[52] or 'like a convalescent home'.[53] Such sectors were not frequent and were, perhaps, as rare as active sectors where no agreements existed, and all weapon groups exchanged aggression. On the other hand, many sectors were a mixture of war and peace, that is, of exchanges of peace as well as exchanges of aggression and these were more frequent than either very quiet or very active sectors.

All three forms of exchange existed for the whole of the war; at the same time, it will be argued below that, in the early phase of trench war, live and let live typically took the forms of overt truces and inertia, whereas, in the later phase inertia and ritualisation were more characteristic (the two phases of trench war are defined in Chapter 3). But this is a matter of relative frequency only; for some fraternisation occurred in 1918, and some ritualisation occurred as early as 1914.

Having distinguished direct and indirect truces, and illustrated the former, we can now examine inertia both as a means of communication and as a form of live and let live. Not infrequently in trench warfare, a suspension of hostilities happened for no conscious decision or specific agreement, but merely because each side seemed disinclined to aggress the other. Antagonists sometimes shared a vague, general and passive attitude of mind. Although both sides would instantly retaliate against the other's aggression, generally neither would initiate aggression nor otherwise provoke the other, and, accordingly, both sides remained passive and inert. Such inertia should not be mistaken for the absence of either the ability or opportunity to aggress the enemy. Lack of capability was quite another thing. For instance, the British artillery was short of shells on the 4th and 46th divisional fronts in the spring of 1915, and, in consequence, the gunners were incapable of anything but inertia. Yet this shortage, which the press called 'the Shells Scandal'[54] does not entirely explain the quiet which at that time prevailed on the front of the 46th division, and which an infantry officer of that unit described thus, 'Life in S.P. 4 was gloriously lazy. The weather was perfect, the enemy was most peaceful, and there was little to do but lie on one's back and smoke, or write long imaginative letters home . . .'.[55] Unlike the gunners, the infantry had ammunition but chose not to use it. Thus the quiet of the front derived not only from the British gunners' shortage of shells, but also from the British infantry's inclination for inertia, which the German infantry shared—for it takes two to make peace. It is this latter voluntary type of inertia which concerns us here.

Inertia can be thought of as a negative situation void of meaning and communication, but, certainly, this was not true of inertia in trench warfare. In most sectors and at most times each side had the choice of either aggressing or not aggressing the enemy. In the situation where each antagonist had this choice, the non-aggression of one was neither negative nor meaningless to the other; on the contrary, it was as positive and meaningful as the alternative act of aggression. Mutual aggression was in a real and obvious sense mutual communication; for when trench fighters fired against each other, neither doubted that the other's intent was to kill or injure. Similarly, the choice of non-aggression instead of aggression was equally an act of communication, and this must be absolutely grasped by the reader, otherwise trench warfare will not be understood.

This crucial point must be spelt out: when the British (or German) trench fighter remained passive, the German (or British) thereby understood that either a special reason existed for the British (or German) non-aggression or the British had chosen not to aggress. The former possibility aside, the British choice of non-aggression where the contrary was possible meant to the German that the British desired peace. At the same time, the British passivity was not unconditional, and the Germans knew that if they responded to inertia with aggression, the British would retaliate in kind. On the other hand, the Germans knew also that to reciprocate the British inertia would establish a set of mutually contingent exchanges where neither side exercised its choice to aggress the other. As a means of communication, inertia was ambiguous, for it was sometimes difficult to decide whether inertia was a peace overture or not; notwithstanding this ambiguity, seasoned trench fighters generally understood the meaning of each other's passivity, and each remained inert in the expectation—and only in the expectation—that the gesture would be understood as well as reciprocated. Where this expectation was not realised, the exchange of aggression commenced, but where it was confirmed, the exchange of peace was either established or reinforced, or both. Moreover, the ambiguity of inertia as a means of communication diminished as peace exchanges continued and increased, and as each antagonist felt more confident of the other's response. Indeed inertia might be manipulated by an élite unit which would refrain from action to induce in the enemy a false sense of security that could be exploited by sudden aggression. Generally, however, inertia in trench war symbolised a willingness to give up the choice of aggression; it also served as a means of communication and was a form of live and let live. The meaning of inertia as exchange and communication among antagonists in trench war was put in a nutshell by the poet Charles Sorley, an infantry officer of the 12th division,'—without at all "fraternising"—we refrain from interfering with Brother Bosche seventy yards away, as long as he is kind to us';[56] and elsewhere Sorley wrote that trench fighters, 'have found out that to provide discomfort for the other is but a round about way of providing it for themselves'.[57]

We have seen that high command took instant legal action against fraternisation, but how did high command react to inertia? What was the attitude of the generals to covert truces, and what action if any, was taken? Sorley perceived the problem facing high command, 'the staff know that a sense of humour won't allow of this sitting face to face in a cornfield for long, without both parties coming out and fraternising, as happened so constantly a few months ago',[58] and, further, he reckoned that inertia would continue till trench fighters, 'have their heads banged together by the red capped powers behind them, whom neither attempts to understand'.[59] While they might not understand the generals, trench fighters could not ignore them; but exactly how did high command bang heads together? The answer will occupy us for much of this book.

Although tacit truces were less visible than fraternisation, high command was well enough aware of their existence; for the lack of fighting activity showed up on situation reports which the generals regularly received from front line units. Moreover members of high command sometimes visited the front where they witnessed events which might not be mentioned in an official report. For instance, a staff officer of the 51st division noted of a certain time in the war that: 'the diaries of senior officers contain frequent references in which they found the enemy working in daylight in full view, unmolested through want of initiative on the part of local commanders'.[60] But even where trench fighters walked around openly, inertia, unlike fraternisation, was neither a violation of specific orders nor a court martial offence. Nevertheless inertia was opposed by high command from the start of trench war because it was contrary both to the spirit of the offensive, which pervaded the military theory of the time and to an official British directive of 1915 which made active trench war mandatory.

In respect of the former, while no belligerent had a definitive doctrine of attack and defence in trench war, all existing manuals firmly asserted the necessity of the offensive spirit. The British *Field Service Regulations 1914* stated, 'Success in war depends more on moral than on physical qualities. Skill cannot compensate for want of courage, energy and determination . . . The development of the necessary moral qualities is therefore the first of the objects to be attained'.[61] Similarly, the German regulations instructed that, 'resolute action is . . . of the first importance in war. Every individual, from the highest commander to the youngest soldier, must always remember that supine inaction and neglect of opportunities will entail severer censure than an error in conception of the choice of means'.[62] One might object that these were principles for a war of movement and thus either redundant or of little relevance to a static war within trenches. But this was not so. Firstly, the spirit of the offensive was conceived as a principle applicable to all wars and all situations. Secondly, trench war was in some respects similar to siege war, and manuals contained a tactic of the latter which stressed the need for offensiveness when an army was on the defensive. For example, the British *F.S.R.* ran:

> the general principle which governs the defence of fortresses is that the offensive is the soul of defence . . . The most effectual means of defence is counter attack. It imposes caution on the part of the besieger, and imparts an inspiriting influence to the defender's troops, besides rendering them more fit for field operations in the event of the siege being raised.[63]

Clearly inertia was incompatible with the offensive spirit conceived to animate both attack and defence. On 5 February 1915, Sir John French reiterated these principles to army commanders in a G.H.Q. memorandum which laid down official guidelines for the conduct of trench war. The British commander-in-chief stressed the importance of constant activity and of offensive methods in general against the enemy even though the B.E.F. was on the defensive; he asserted that aggression must be encouraged since it would improve the morale of British troops and exhaust the enemy both morally and materially, and, further, that aggression was the most effective form of defence.[64]

It might be misleading to say that Sir John's memo established what was later called the British *policy* of active trench war, as neither the tactic nor technology of trench war had by that time been evolved,[65] but the memo did establish the *principle* of active trench war. However, the February memo had a limited effect for reasons we will later examine, and the advance of inertia continued; by September 1915, Sir John French was alluding to some veterans as 'sticky' on account of their 'trench habit'—indeed the lack of the 'trench habit' was a reason why he chose inexperienced rather than experienced troops as reserves for the battle of Loos.

In March 1916, a British training manual based largely on 1915 events identified inertia as both endemic and problematic, asserting in a section named 'The Offensive Spirit in Trench Warfare' that 'There is an insidious tendency to lapse into a passive and lethargic attitude against which officers of all ranks have to be on their guard, and the fostering of the offensive spirit . . . calls for incessant

attention'.[66] The attitude of the French and German high commands towards inertia was the same as the British. The official
French manual for infantry officers (1917) affirms that 'The war of
the trenches is neither a relaxation nor a guard duty; it is a phase of
the battle. It is necessary that the adversary feel in front of him a
vigilant hatred and know that we wish no rest before his defeat. It is
necessary that each hostile company go back from the trenches with
the loss of at least twenty men'.[67] The German high command's
concern for the fighting spirit goes back to April 1915 at least, when
it was noted that 'the infantry had become enfeebled by trench
warfare, and had lost its daring'.[68] In 1917, Ludendorff appointed
officers to divisional and army H.Q.s to lecture 'with a view to
maintaining the fighting spirit of the army';[69] but Rudolf Binding,
an officer of divisional cavalry who was selected for one of the latter
posts, had been lecturing already to young officers on the spirit of
field service regulations and had stressed the error of 'supine
inaction'.[70]

All this shows the several high commands' knowledge of, and
concern for the problem, and inertia was clearly neither part of
official policy nor something to which high command turned a
blind eye. The next question is clear: what could high command do
about inertia? And the short answer is—not a great deal in the early
part of the war. During 1915 the British high command could do
little against inertia except issue to combat units general directives
to harass the enemy. General directives are less effective than
specific orders as a means of control; for the greater discretion of the
former allows a subordinate to choose either evasion or compliance,
whereas the latter give a subordinate no choice but to comply—or
risk legal sanctions.[71] In 1915, however, high command was unable
to issue specific orders for aggression, since such orders meant
spelling out, with more detail than was then possible, the methods of
attack in trench warfare. Precise orders presupposed a specialised
tactic and technology of trench warfare, and at this time the latter
existed only in rudimentary and unstandardised form. For instance,
from 1916 raids were frequently ordered by high command. But in
1915 this was not possible, for the raid was not distinguished from
other minor operations, nor were raiding tactics and weaponry
developed. Further, few battalions had had actual experience of
raiding at this time. Thus high command had limited control over
combat units in 1915 and could do little about inertia but issue
general directives which affirmed the need for constant aggression,

but which could neither set in motion a specific tactic of trench warfare nor otherwise spell out exactly how to aggress the enemy.

By no means all British units remained passive, however. Some were forced to counter the aggression of élite German units, while others made it a point of honour to harass the enemy or responded to the spirit of high command orders. But for whatever reason, to be active was to innovate, improvise and specialise, and 1915 was marked by the gradual growth of specialised tactic and technology of trench warfare, that is, a body of technical rules, expert skills and weapons for attack and defence in trench war. While its progression was somewhat uneven and *ad hoc* within and between opposing armies, this technology was basically the same on both sides; for should one side gain advantage by innovation, the other had to imitate or otherwise counter so as to survive. For example, German trench-mortars were more advanced than either British or French at the start of the war, but Allied trench-mortars improved and the German advantage was reduced by the end of 1915; similarly, the British pioneered the raid, a major form of attack in trench war, but the Germans countered by developing their own raiding expertise. In respect of the infantry, élite battalions assumed the innovating role and exploited the opportunities offered by trench warfare for combat at close quarters through simultaneously adapting old weapons and evolving new.

Typical of these élite units was the 2/Royal Welch Fusiliers which, according to its battalion history, began to innovate as early as December 1914: 'The germ of specialism began to sprout vigorously at this time as new means of offence and defence were brought out'.[72] The energy with which the élite battalions went about the task of developing the new technology is illustrated in the history of the 1/Royal West Kents, which asserts of 1915 (and generally) that, 'When in the front line the time was spent in small aggressive actions calculated to make life uncertain for the enemy . . . Either we or the enemy were constantly retaliating . . . We always made ourselves as obnoxious to the Hun as orders and circumstances would allow'.[73] Both the 2/Royal Welch and 1/Royal West Kents were regular battalions, but some new army battalions were also very active in 1915; for instance, in the 37th division, the 10/Royal Fusiliers took over from the French a quiet front which was quickly turned into a hornet's nest.[74] Elite units such as these helped to build up a trench war technology throughout 1915, and in the next chapter we will look at some elements of this technology.

At this point it will be useful to summarise and underline some parts of our argument in this chapter. A distinction has been drawn between problems of the origin and the persistence of live and let live. In respect of origins, truces emerged before the Christmas of 1914 and first occurred in non-combat activities concerned with the fulfilment of basic needs. Probably these early truces were *ad hoc* and short-lived arrangements but once established they tended to persist and to evolve in accord with a circular process of cause and effect: live and let live entailed indirect or direct communication among enemies, and such communication implied mutual empathy, while empathy encouraged the evolution of live and let live in two ways—firstly, by reinforcing existing truces, and, secondly, by spreading truces into combat activities.

Accordingly, it seems that both sides soon started to make assumptions about each other's behaviour in respect of areas unrelated to war. For example, each side speculated that if we allow the enemy to breakfast in peace, they will allow us the same in return, since like us they are hungry. Mutual empathy was implied in such reasoning and this increased as assumptions were affirmed by events. Moreover the meaning of intertia both as a means of communication and as a mode of live and let live grew less ambiguous as empathy advanced. As a result empathy extended simply and logically to the thought that if we leave the enemy absolutely in peace they will also leave us in peace. When this expectancy was realised, the diffusion of truces from non-combat to combat activities had occurred. The peace within the war now persisted. All this concerns indirect communication, but the latter also communicated directly, for instance, by word of mouth. No doubt this was made easier as some Germans spoke English, having worked in the U.K., often in the catering trade; there was a joke about this: one day in the line a British Tommy shouted 'Waiter', and fifty Fritzes stuck their heads up above the trenches and said 'Coming Sir'.

High command was hostile both to overt and covert truces. Fraternisation was visible, and the authorities quickly and effectively moved against persons involved; in consequence, such truces were not endemic, although they occurred at intervals throughout the war. On the other hand, inertia was a subtle and tacit thing.

High command could neither identify nor prove that certain persons at certain places and times had colluded with the enemy. The generals defined inertia as a problem of morale rather than law, but their directives were ineffectual as a counter to inertia which became widespread during the early part of the war. In conclusion, a picture should be emerging by now of soldiers who were not so dominated by events that they were entirely powerless. If they chose, trench fighters could exercise some control over the matter of life and death.

3

At the start of this chapter I want to distinguish between two successive phases which occurred within the respective courses of routine trench warfare and large battles (the latter considered sequentially not separately). The first and second stages of development of large battles were concurrent with the first and second stages in the trench warfare: the first stages in both forms of war occurred at about the same time in 1915, and the second occurred from 1916 to 1918.

The first phase of trench warfare was described in the previous chapter. We saw that trench fighters learned to communicate indirectly with the enemy without risk of legal sanctions, and further that outgoing troops simultaneously handed over both truce and trench to incoming troops, thereby permitting a truce to persist indefinitely. This suggests that self-maintaining truces might have replaced trench warfare, except on sectors occupied by élite units. But the matter was not so simple; for factors inimical to inertia either existed or were nascent in the first phase and in the second phase these forced live and let live to adapt again in order to survive. These factors included the growth of a specialised tactic and technology of trench warfare as well as a centralised administration of violence, and the outcome tended to weaken inertia and promote ritualisation—another variant on the theme of live and let live.

However, this is to anticipate the narrative somewhat, and the plan of the present chapter is as follows: first we shall pick out two phases in the course of large battles and outline their chronology. We shall find that the development of each form of war followed a similar pattern; for instance, more bureaucracy existed in the second phase than the first in respect of large battles and trench war, adding a new dimension to the war experience, alluded to by Edmund Blunden thus: 'steel helmets now became the rule, their ugly useful discomfort supplanting our friendly soft caps . . . the dethronement of the soft cap clearly symbolised the change that was coming over the war, the induration from a personal crusade into a vast machine of violence'.[1] Next we shall return to trench war, and begin to examine those factors of the first phase which countered inertia, and whose effects in the second phase were associated with the 'vast machine of violence'.

In respect of large battles, the first phase commenced at the end of open war in 1914 and continued until the battle of Verdun in February 1916. The second was the period from Verdun until the re-emergence of a more mobile war in 1918. Deadlock between antagonists marked both phases. However, the first phase was one of experiment, with large-scale but short-lived battles, sometimes costly in casualties; whereas the second phase was one of attrition with large-scale, long-lived battles which were always costly in lives. The reader must remember that when a large battle was occurring on one front, trench war continued as usual on all others, and when no battle was in progress trench war occurred as usual on all fronts.

On the western front in 1915 the German strategy was defensive—the one German attack was the second battle of Ypres where poison gas was first used in the war, whereas the Allied strategy, and especially that of the French, was aggressive. Many generals thought that coordinated mass attacks on several fronts would punch a hole in the German trench system through which reserves could pour, fan out, and then decisively defeat a disorganised and demoralised enemy. The tactical problems of the strategy of breakthrough included the relative roles of the artillery and infantry in the initial breach of the German line, and, in particular, the duration of the artillery barrage which was to soften up the enemy defence before the infantry went over the top. A preparatory barrage could be either long or short—four days or four minutes. A short barrage surprised the enemy, but might also be ineffective, and then undamaged machine guns decimated assault troops. On the other hand, a long barrage might enable an attack to break into a weakened defence, but also gave notice of attack to the enemy, who then brought up fresh reserves to counter-attack the tired and depleted assault force, before the latter's relief by reserves.

Other problems included whether to assault on a wide or narrow front, for instance, twenty miles or two, as well as the 'fog of war', that is, inadequate communications between trench fighters and generals during battle. To attempt a breakthrough on a narrow front might be disastrous, for from either side of a narrow breach the artillery defence could dominate the assaulting infantry; yet an attack on a wide front might leave the assault troops thin on the ground. Concerning communications, if the infantry pierced the enemy line but could not signal their success to the generals, who were necessarily some miles back, then vital decisions, such as committing reserves, might be made either too late or not at all. The 1915 battles revealed a further problem, namely, the need for many more heavy guns to destroy strong, deeply sited enemy defences and dug-outs.

Until March 1915, the French made uncoordinated attacks in the Champagne and near Arras, but these achieved little, and there ensued a lull in the French effort until the late spring. Meanwhile, in March at Neuve-Chapelle, the British attacked with four divisions upon a narrow two-mile front, following a short (35-minute) artillery barrage. Certainly the enemy was surprised, and his defences were both weakly held and incomplete. Consequently, the centre of the British attack captured the village of Neuve-Chapelle, while on either side the flanks gained their objectives within five hours. Owing to communication difficulties, however, high command knew little of these successes for several hours, and thus neither was the reserve committed nor the first advance exploited. During this delay, the Germans brought up reserves and prevented further breakthrough. Subseqently, the line stabilised and deadlock returned. The battle of Neuve-Chapplle, which lasted for two days, taught the British that defences could be breached, and the Germans that defences must be strengthened to stop similar breakthroughs. This lesson cost each side about 11,000 casualties.

In May 1915 the French and British made joint attacks in the Artois and Aubers Ridge areas respectively. In Artois the French assaulted Vimy Ridge, and Foch, the overall battle commander, chose a long bombardment to destroy the defence, instead of a short barrage and the chance of surprise. Accordingly, French guns blasted the Germans for five days. The *poilus* attacked and, in the centre, pierced two and a half miles into the pulverised defence, reaching the crest of Vimy Ridge; but on either side of the centre, the infantry made no ground. The success of the centre was not exploited by the quick commitment of reserves, partly because of poor communications; but in any event the Germans, forewarned of attack by the long barrage, had reserves to hand which counter-attacked and restored the situation. The second battle of Artois continued until 15 May by which time the French and Germans had lost, respectively, about 100,000 and 75,000 casualties.

Meanwhile, fifteen miles north of Aubers Ridge, units of Douglas Haig's 1st Army went in upon a nine-mile front after a short bombardment of forty minutes. The Germans, as at Neuve-Chapelle, were probably surprised but, unlike Neuve-Chapelle, their defences at Aubers Ridge were strong and complete, comprising deep dug-outs, thick barbed wire and concrete machine-gun emplacements. The short barrage was ineffective and failed even to cut the wire, upon which some battalions were caught and swiftly slaughtered by the German machine-gunners. For instance, the 1/Northants and the 2/Royal Sussex lost 551 and 560 men respectively. Elsewhere the infantry made only two small and temporary lodgements in the German line. At Aubers Ridge the Germans had no need of reserves, and Haig stopped the assault after twelve hours. The British suffered 11,000 casualties, but the Germans far less.

Immediately, the British made fresh plans to support the French, still fighting at Vimy Ridge, with an assault at Festubert. To avoid another disaster like Aubers Ridge, Haig planned a four-day artillery barrage in order thoroughly to soften up the German defence. On 15 May the infantry attacked at night and the élite 7th division fought its way 500 yards into the enemy trench system, but the Germans, alerted by the long barrage, had hurried reserves to the threatened front and again blocked a breakthrough. Nevertheless, attack and counter-attack went on till 27 May, when the British had won a length of German line, but had lost 16,000 men; German losses were less. Ten divisions of the B.E.F., that is, about 50 per cent of the total number, took part in the battles of Aubers Ridge and Festubert.

A lull now emerged upon the western front. No large battle occurred in the summer of 1915. But Joffre, the French commander-in-chief, was planning a large Allied attack for the autumn, and once again the attack was to be mounted upon the Artois and Champagne fronts. Both the spring and autumn offensives had the same object: to break through the German line and end the deadlock. By the autumn of 1915, the Germans had weakened their manpower on the western front, having moved reserves to the eastern front where a decisive success was sought; on the other hand they had strengthened their trench system with a second fortified line some two to four miles behind the first.

On 25 September the Allies attacked at three places: the French in both the Champagne and Artois, upon twenty- and twelve-mile fronts respectively; the British in Artois—at Loos—on a six-mile front.

In the Champagne, the French after a three-day barrage penetrated the German line to a depth of 3000 yards; but even before the bombardment the Germans had anticipated the attack and had withdrawn troops and artillery to the second line which was the pivot of their defence. Consequently, the *poilus* attacked a skeleton garrison and suffered heavily in the German counter-barrage. Although the French breached the German second line at one place, in general the assault did not succeed, and the battle became a static slogging match, which went on at intervals until 6 October. The French losses were 143,000 men, and the German 113,000.

In the Artois, some French troops made little progress, whereas others, according to one authority, did not attack in earnest since some fighting commanders, less sure of breakthrough than the generals, annulled orders, 'by gentle evasion in places'.[2] Nevertheless, the third battle of Artois, which finished on 4 October, cost the French 48,000 casualties.

The British part in the Artois offensive was the battle of Loos. Haig's 1st Army attacked after four days artillery fire. Some divisions made little or no headway; but others carried the German front line, and one New Army division—the 9th (Scottish)—reached the second line, while another—the 15th (Scottish)—bored two miles into the German trench system. But success was not exploited, as reserve divisions were not immediately available. Fresh reserve divisions had been released by the Commander-in-chief, Sir John French, to the battle commander, Douglas Haig, some hours after the battle commenced on 25 September, but too late for use until the next day. Meanwhile the German reserves had deployed and counter-attacked, and their machine-gunners massacred the British reserves when these attacked on 26 September. Breakthrough was thus prevented, but the battle continued until 4 November, when the British casualties totalled 48,000 and the German somewhat less. Eighteen infantry divisions—about 50 per cent of the total in the B.E.F.—took part in the battle of Loos.

Given the 'fog of war', whether the British reserves could have acted without delay, even if available on 25 September, is an open question. However, Sir John French's handling of the reserves at Loos resulted, in December 1915, in his replacement as commander-in-chief by Douglas Haig.

The autumn battles in the Artois and the Champagne were the last of the first phase and, like the earlier battles, they were strategically barren for the Allies. Indeed, by the end of 1915, leaders no longer thought of a short war but of a long arduous process of attrition,[3] and, further, it was felt that a greater unity of effort among the Allies was needed for victory. Accordingly, delegates from Britain, France, Russia and Italy met in December 1915 for an inter-Allied military conference. It was decided that in 1916 the Allies would attack simultaneously, and in strength, upon the western, eastern (Russian) and Italian fronts, so that the Germans could not move their reserves between fronts. Further, the conference resolved that before the decisive blow was struck the German reserves must be worn down by vigorous action. Thus attrition was an integral part of the allied strategy for 1916.

The characteristic ethos of the second phase, manifest both in large battles and trench war, was set by the policy of attrition. Attrition involved a more systematic and comprehensive mobilisation of men for war than occurred in the first phase; for instance, phase-two battles generally implicated a higher proportion of the total divisions in the B.E.F. than phase-one battles. Moreover, the mobilisation of the second phase implied a greater degree of centralised administration than existed in the first. For example, the administrative role of higher levels of the B.E.F. high command—especially that of corps formations—increased as that of division and brigade tended to decrease; thus corps H.Q.s planned the British attack on the Somme right down to the movement of individual battalions.

The extended power of the military mandarins of the second phase created a change in the climate of the war of which trench fighters were quite conscious. Of the 1915–16 winter, a Royal Welch Fusilier observed, 'A mechanistic theory of the conduct of war was being developed which bade fair to make cyphers of the individual and the unit. The foundation of a bureaucratic means of handling operations was well and truly laid during this winter'.[4] For Ernst Junger—a German storm trooper—the steel helmet symbolised the new era of bureaucratically organised violence, 'The spirit and tempo of the fighting altered, and after the battle of the Somme the war had its own peculiar impress that distinguished it from all other wars. After this battle the German soldier wore the steel helmet, and in his features were chiselled the lines of an energy stretched to the utmost pitch'.[5]

Thus both German and British trench fighters likened the war of the second phase to a massive impersonal mechanism which racked men beyond endurance and generated a new form of war experience. But what of the chronology of large events during phase two?

On the western front the British and French planned a combined attack for 1916 upon a sixty-mile front from Lassigny to Arras, and Joffre proposed that the British should wear down the enemy until the start of the battle. The Germans however, pre-empted both the Allied assault and strategy by striking at Verdun—a battle which set the pattern for many others of phase two. Nothing less than the attrition of the entire French army at Verdun was the aim of Falkenhayn, the German commander. He argued that a break-through in mass was not necessary for victory. An alternative was an attack where, for both moral and military reasons, the French army would never retreat but would defend to the last man. Verdun was such a place. The French would not allow this fortress town to fall, since Verdun was not only of strategic value but also symbolic of Gallic resistance to ancient invasions by Germanic tribal hordes.

Falkenhayn's strategy of attrition assumed a new tactical form, namely, a sequence of assaults which progressed by stages, each with a limited aim. Accordingly, an assault would not aim at breakthrough but merely to carry a small part of the French line, which had been earlier smashed by a short intense barrage, rendering defenders unable to inflict heavy loss on assault troops. The latter were then to consolidate their gain. Next the German artillery would develop a hurricane barrage through which the inevitable but doomed French counter-attack would pass and be decimated. This process was to be repeated time and time again. Each time the French losses would exceed the German, and therefore the French must be worn down at a relatively greater rate than the Germans, and would eventually collapse.

In the event, Falkenhayn's plan of attrition foundered on the rock-like resistance of the French *poilus*, and the power of the French artillery. A million shells were fired by the Germans on the first day of Verdun and, as the battle developed, such holocausts destroyed communication between the fighting men and higher commanders of each side. Verdun was not a general's battle. Isolated, and acting alone, small groups of men fought blindly, ferociously, on ground which became in equal parts earth, blood and bone, as bodies were shattered by one shell and scattered by the next. The agony of

French and German trench fighters was ceaseless as the seasons of 1916 merged into an endless time of violence. During the spring, summer and autumn 80 per cent of all French infantry (259 battalions from a total of 330) were systematically rotated in and out of battle by high command. Verdun was not only the longest battle of the First World War, but of any war.

Falkenhayn's thinking was in part right: the French would indeed have defended Verdun to the last, but otherwise it was wrong; for French losses were not greatly more than the German— 360,000 and 330,000 respectively, and therefore both armies were worn down in similar proportions. Falkenhayn lost his job, and Hindenburg became the new German commander-in-chief.

The battle of Verdun went on from February to December 1916. On 1 July the British and French attacked on the Somme. Of the Allies, the British played the major part and assaulted with sixteen divisions along an eighteen-mile front. Most of these divisions met with misfortune or disaster: each of four divisions lost over 5000 men, and just a few succeeded in either breaking into the German line, or avoiding heavy losses—only four divisions lost less than 3000 men. If Haig had hopes of a breakthrough, he was disappointed: for the sole spectacular effects of the first day's fighting were the courage of and casualties (60,000) among the British soldiers. During the summer, autumn and winter of 1916, the British high command systematically rotated fifty-five divisions (about 98 per cent of all B.E.F. infantry divisions) through the continuing carnage. Similarly, about fifty German divisions (around 45 per cent of all German divisions on the western front) were moved in and out of battle. Some divisions returned twice or more to the conflict, and during this time of unremitting violence, hitherto little-known place names, such as Delville Wood, High Wood, Mametz, came to symbolise the same horror, hell and honour to the British and Commonwealth troops that Verdun symbolised to the French. The battles of the Somme persisted for five months. The British lost 400,000 trench fighters, the French 190,000 and the Germans about 600,000.

Both the Verdun and the Somme were 1916 battles, but further large-scale attrition was planned for 1917 by Joffre, the French Commander-in-chief. However, Nivelle, an exponent of break-through, replaced Joffre and immediately designed a powerful French/British attack for early 1917 to rupture the German front. The British duly attacked at Arras, just a few days before the French struck at Chemin des Dames and west of Rheims on 16 and 17 April respectively. No breakthrough occurred and attrition set in. On 29 April, however, large numbers of French soldiers spontaneously substituted peace for war, thus manifesting an explicit and uncompromising form of live and let live, an event which the world came to know as the French army mutinies of 1917. Meanwhile the British resumed attrition further north, where the third battle of Ypres, or as it was more widely and notoriously known, Passchendaele, lasted from 31 July to 16 November 1917, and British and Germans fought each other to a state of utter exhaustion and immobility in a welter of mud and blood. The British casualties reached nearly 250,000 and the German probably as many as 400,000. Douglas Haig now ordered a defensive attitude, although trench war went on as usual, while the British awaited the expected German offensives of 1918. The latter were made possible by the transfer of German troops from the eastern to the western front, following Russia's collapse after the Revolution. On 9 April 1918, the first German onslaught fell against the British, and on 11 April Haig issued his famous 'Backs to the Wall' order. The British held on, but were attacked elsewhere, before Ludendorff halted the offensive on 30 April. British and French casualties totalled 331,797 and German 348,000. Then followed in May, June and July, three offensives against the French, which exhausted the German army; in August, the French, British and American armies counter-attacked in what was the last major offensive of the war.

Very briefly, such was the background of large events running parallel with the smaller events which are the subject here. The story of both large and small dimensions of the First World War is, to some extent, one of increasing bureaucratisation: the conflict grew progressively more vast and specialised, as well as more and more centrally controlled and regulated by formal rules; whereas areas of personal and local discretion diminished.

The theme for the rest of this chapter is the growth of the specialised tactic and technology of trench war, that is, the build up of the means of aggression, and this will be traced from its rudimentary beginnings in the first phase to its sophisticated state in the second; further, the limited capability for aggression in the first phase will be contrasted with the vastly augmented capability of the second. The technology of aggression is dealt with in two parts: firstly, weapons and tactics used for aggression over medium and long distances, that is, between about 300 yards and several miles, and these included the rifle, machine-gun, trench-mortar and artillery; secondly, those used for aggression over short distances of less than 300 yards, such as the hand-grenade, fighting patrol and raid.

Sometimes it is said the hand-grenade was the characteristic weapon of trench warfare, and this was true with respect to aggression at close quarters; but neither the rifle nor marksmanship was ever redundant, for sniping over long distances was always a mode of mutual harassment. At the start of the war, each British battalion had at least four specialist snipers—one for each company—and sniping emerged as early as October 1914. In the 2/ Royal Welch Fusiliers, sniping organisation was flexible; for in addition to the company specialist, any soldier was allowed to snipe if he felt inclined.[6] This flexibility encouraged informal specialisation, and some soldiers improved their marksmanship and adapted it to the new conditions, for instance, an N.C.O. of the 2/Royal Welch had over a hundred notches on his rifle.[7] Sniping was important in the war, for the layout of the trenches gave snipers good chances to inflict material and moral loss upon the enemy, and, further, as Ian Hay observed, 'the sniper is a very necessary person. He serves to remind us we are at war . . . wherever a head, or anything resembling a head, shows itself, he fires. Were it not for his enthusiasm, both sides would be sitting . . . upon their respective parapets regarding each other with frank curiosity, and that would never do'.[8] Thus sniping was a means both of causing loss to the enemy and of controlling overt forms of live and let live.

Given its twofold function, it is no surprise that sniping organisation had been expanded, standardised and brought under a more centralised control by the second phase. During 1915 specialist sniping schools were set up at various levels of the high command hierarchy, and officers and N.C.O.s learned the techniques and organisation of sniping for trench war. Major Hesketh-Pritchard, a pioneer of these schools, reckoned that a corps school which he directed had by November 1915 trained at least one officer from all battalions which either were within, or had passed through his corps sector.[9] The growth of sniping schools was somewhat unsystematic, but each of the five armies in the B.E.F. had one by 1917. In 1915, however, some front line units welcomed neither the increase in sniping activity, nor the new battalion organisation taught at the schools, and conformed with the latter only when ordered by high

command. According to Hesketh-Pritchard, this front line reluctance derived from the prospect of enemy retaliation.

In most cases, the control of sniping[10] had passed at the start of
the second phase, from company to battalion headquarters, where
groups of about twenty-five specialist snipers and observers were
formed under the authority of battalion sniping and intelligence
officers. These snipers were distributed along battalion fronts in
concealed posts. Generally, they were paired, each member
alternating sniping with the observation of enemy lines both for
sniping targets and others (the latter were passed on to artillery and
trench-mortar groups) as well as intelligence information.

The potential fire power of the expanded and specialised sniping
organisation standardised in the B.E.F. by the second phase was
considerably greater than that of the first phase. For example, the
front line battalion, with ten pairs of snipers alternating among five
sniping posts along a front of 1000 yards, had a density of one sniper
and one observer per 200 yards, and each sniper was a specialist
marksman with a telescopically sighted rifle firing with lethal effect
into enemy lines for a depth of 2000 yards.[11] But the total sniping
power of a unit included company, as well as more specialised
battalion snipers. According to one manual,[12] company snipers and
observers numbered between 32 and 40 (say 36 for the following
calculation below), therefore a battalion with two companies had
a total of 46 snipers and observers along a 1000-yard front (36 from
two companies in the line plus ten from battalion who stayed in the
line while companies rotated), and this gave an approximate
density of one sniper or observer for each 21 yards. This ratio,
however, did not include the fire power of non-specialist riflemen.

Unless one side dominated the sniping war in a sector, the
number of snipers on each side was roughly equal, and therefore a
minimum of ten British specialists might be firing at ten German
snipers—as well as all other visible Germans—or any number up to
46 snipers and observers—specialists and others—might be firing
against their German counterparts.[13] All other weapon groups
aside, the potential violence of snipers with special skills, techniques
and weapons after the reorganisation was considerable, and, on an
active front, the slightest exposure was fatal, 'None save the very
rash would dare to thrust his head over the top, for the snipers on
both sides were appallingly quick and accurate',[14] wrote an
Australian infantryman; similarly, a battalion historian observed,
'To show one's head over the parapet was to commit death. It

should be borne in mind that artillery and rifle fire never ceased by day or night—it was only a matter of degree'.[15]

In diverse ways the rifle was adapted to the conditions of trench war; for instance, as early as December 1914 a unit of the 4th Division recorded, 'Both sides had "rifle batteries" laid on an object and fixed, a soldier being detailed to fire a round at stated intervals'.[16] Fixed or clamped rifles were aligned and sighted on parts of the enemy's line, such as a latrine entrance or a gap in the parapet or junction between trenches, and rifles were fired at unexpected times, especially at night. While this practice was something of an innovation in 1914, by 1916 it was commonplace and an official duty of battalion or company snipers.[17] With the shortage of artillery shells in 1915 some élite battalions improvised means to attack what in usual times were artillery targets, such as roads along which trench garrisons were supplied. The historian of the 1/Gloucesters recorded, 'At night the rumble of transport on the *pavé* roads behind the enemy lines was incessant and again attempts to persuade the guns to fire were unsuccessful, so long-range rifle fire had to be tried'.[18]

The rifle was used not only for long-range aggression but also, in an adapted form, to fire grenades over shorter distances of 200–300 yards. The principle of a rifle-grenade was simple: a rod with a hand-grenade attached to one end was placed in a rifle barrel; the rifle was then loaded with a blank cartridge and fired. Both British and Germans used rifle-grenades from the beginning of trench war, and in November 1914 the B.E.F. received about 630 weekly[19]—a number which multiplied rapidly within a few months. In the B.E.F., battalion rifle-grenade specialists were organised, either as a battalion unit, or at company level, where each company had its own rifle-grenade section of five to ten specialists under a N.C.O.[20] Assuming a company front of 500 yards, weapon density was at least one rifle-grenadier per 100 yards. The average width of no-man's-land was 250–300 yards, and thus some part of each side's trenches was within range of the other's rifle-grenades. This weapon gave little warning of its approach and was lethal if it burst on or within a few yards of a person; on the other hand even modest earthworks gave a good protection.

For mutual harassment over medium to long distances, machine-guns as well as rifles and rifle-grenades were used, and at the start of the war the B.E.F. had both Vickers and Maxim machine-guns, but the former shortly became standard. The Vickers had a crew of six, fired 500 rounds per minute, for long intervals, for a maximum range of about 2500 yards. The gun, however, was relatively immobile, since it weighed fifty-eight pounds and was fired from a fixed tripod. Machine-guns were much used in trench war, and in February 1915 the establishment of two Vickers per battalion was increased to four, and at about the same time the German army's establishment was likewise increased. Moreover, in December 1914 the British founded a machine-gun school which ran a monthly course for specialists, who numbered 250 in May 1915. The need for specialists, however, was so great that in June 1915 the school more than doubled in size and gave two monthly courses each attended by 500 men.[21] In October 1915 a machine-gun corps was created, and this involved a reorganisation where control over the Vickers was centralised from battalion to brigade. Each of the four battalions in a brigade gave up their four Vickers which were then formed into a brigade machine-gun company of sixteen guns and crews commanded by an officer under orders from brigade. Now machine-gunners were not only members of a specialist weapon group but also operated more autonomously than before, and awareness of this new status was a matter of pride for a gunner of the 12th division:

> It was exciting to feel that we were no longer in a small unit, subject to the whims and dictates of every infantry officer and N.C.O. From then on, as members of a special corps, we came under the orders of our own superiors . . . this meant that an unpaid lance-corporal in charge of a gun in action, who became detached from his own superiors, would be the sole judge as to the best position for his gun, and when and where it should be fired.[22]

The reorganisation of Vickers guns started in some divisions in the last quarter of 1915, but most divisions were not reorganised until the first half of 1916, that is during the second phase, because neither guns nor crews were brigaded until they could be replaced by Lewis guns and crews, and these were scarce in 1915.[23] The following figures for weapon density refer to a division before reorganisation. Where a division held a sector of 6000 yards with all three brigades, and where each brigade had two battalions in the line and two in reserve, weapon density was one heavy machine-gun per 250 yards of divisional front.[24] But sometimes battalion Vickers, which normally moved out with their unit, stayed behind to strengthen the line, and weapon density was higher in such cases. After the reorganisation, however, the Vickers were brigade not battalion weapons and stayed in the line with their brigade, while the latter's battalions were rotated; therefore weapon density was higher in the second phase of trench war than the first, although the number of Vickers guns in a division was the same. In the second phase all divisions had three brigade machine-gun companies each of sixteen guns—a total of forty-eight—giving a weapon density along a 6000-yard sector of one Vickers per 125 yards, that is, twice the minimum figure of 1915. Moreover, machine-gun density was augmented not only by reorganisation but also by supplementation, as each battalion received eight light Lewis guns in place of the four heavy Vickers.[25] But before we examine the density of the second phase, a brief description of the Lewis gun is necessary.

The Lewis was a mobile, light gun filling a definite need in trench war. The Vickers had a crew of six, weighed fifty-eight pounds and was fired from a fixed tripod in a specially built emplacement; whereas the Lewis had a crew of two, weighed twenty-eight pounds and was fired from the shoulder anywhere in the trenches. Further, the Lewis' rate of fire—600 to 700 rounds per minute—compared with that of the Vickers, although it had to be fired in short bursts. A Lewis-gun school was started in June 1915, by which time some units had the weapon. The first official establishment was eight guns per battalion, which was soon doubled to sixteen,[26] and this number had been issued to all battalions by the first day of the Somme—1 July 1916. A further and final increase was sanctioned in 1918, and by July all battalions had 36 guns.[27]

It is difficult to judge weapon density on a divisional sector between October 1915 and 1 July 1916, for some battalions waited longer than others for the sixteen-gun allotment, as demand exceeded supply. Nevertheless at the end of 1915 some divisions had the eight-gun allotment, giving a total of 96; but these were controlled by battalions of which half were in the line at any given time, and thus 48 guns were usually *in situ* on a divisional front, a density of one light machine-gun per 125 yards. By July 1916 all battalions had sixteen guns, giving a total of 192 of which 96 were in the line—a density of one gun for about 62 yards. This density was constant for most of the second phase until changed by the 1918 allotment of 36 guns per battalion to a density of one gun per 27 yards.[28] An illuminating yet conservative idea of the truly massive potential violence of machine-guns during most of the second phase is given when all Vickers and Lewis are added together and the density calculated: the total is 144, and the density one heavy or light machine-gun for each 41 yards of divisional front.

In the first phase of trench war, machine-gun tactics were developed from experience, and in the second they were published in official manuals for distribution throughout the B.E.F.; in both stages tactics were taught at high command schools existing at G.H.Q. and corps level. The Vickers were severally situated in front and support trenches as well as in concealed positions between, from where they fired indirectly—often at night—on targets in the enemy's trench system and back areas, which were some 2000 yards behind the front line. These targets included the enemy's lines of communication to the trenches, crossroads, road junctions, and small towns. Direct harassing fire included counter-machine-gun work; general fire into enemy trenches, especially along parapet tops to lop off unwary heads; night fire at the enemy working on trenches, and, of course, the destruction of such other targets as appeared. Sometimes machine-guns, both Vickers and Lewis, aggressed the enemy in concert with other weapon groups; for instance, a common plan was where a trench-mortar blew a breach in the enemy's parapet and wire, which was then exploited by machine-gun fire into the gap during daytime as well as night, which stopped the enemy making good the damage. Weapon group cooperation was also involved in the raid. When British raided Germans, the Vickers cooperated by firing into the enemy's trenches, to prevent the arrival of reinforcements; when Germans raided British, the Vickers fired into no-man's-land to prevent the former getting to and from British trenches. In general, the Lewis was more versatile than the Vickers, except that it was used less for indirect fire. The weapon's mobility allowed its use as an automatic rifle both within and without the trenches; for instance, the Lewis was moved within front and support trenches to search for targets in enemy trenches inaccessible to the less mobile Vickers; further, it was used outside the trenches in no-man's-land by night-fighting patrols, 'Our patrols are always accompanied by one or two Lewis guns on the principle impressed on all ranks, "Always engage the enemy when he is close at hand" '.[29] Clearly the Lewis enabled patrols to aggress the enemy where otherwise it was not possible.

Like the rifle, rifle-grenade and machine-gun, the trench-mortar[30] was used for aggression across long and medium distances; but unlike other weapons, mortars fired an explosive bomb effective not only against the enemy's person but also against his deep dug-outs and other earthworks. In October 1914 neither British nor French armies had a mortar establishment, whereas the Germans went to war with 160 light, medium and heavy mortars. The British were forced to counter the German advantage and in the first phase evolved effective mortars, skills and tactics. The British Royal Engineer and Ordinance workshops quickly extemporised various means of hurling bombs into enemy trenches, which included catapaults powered with string or elastic, as well as the more usual explosive gun. Nearly as many models of mortar as there were local workshops existed, but all early guns were similar in lack of accuracy and reliability, and, further, some were distinctly dangerous to operate—the French gave the British some mortars used in the Crimean war.[31] For much of 1915, the organisation of mortars was as haphazard and *ad hoc* as the guns themselves, and in the B.E.F. crews were severally drawn from field and heavy gunners, infanteers, pioneers and engineers; moreover this diversity existed in respect not only of mortars and crews but also of modes of control. In August 1915, mortars were placed under divisional control[32] which before rested in either division, brigade or battalion, according to local circumstance; for instance, the élite 1/Royal West Kents 'won' a weapon and formed a mortar team from their own ranks under an N.C.O. when mortars were scarce in March 1915.[33]

The *ad hoc* nature of mortar type, manning and organisation existed to a degree for all of 1915, and to give a general idea of mortars at this time is not easy. Nevertheless, the official history shows that the number quickly increased in 1915. The U.K. produced 75 mortars and over 8000 shells during the first quarter of 1915 and 524 mortars and over 180,000 shells in the fourth quarter[34]—some of the latter, however, were used for training. Further, the B.E.F. comprised 37 infantry divisions and possessed 244 mortars in September 1915,[35] and assuming guns were distributed equally among divisions, and a divisional front was 6000 yards, one arrives at a density of slightly more than one trench-mortar per 1000 yards.[36] But the ratio of weapons to front before September is difficult to guess.

During the second phase a great increase in mortars from 244 in September 1915 to 3022 in 1918[37] occurred, and the production of shells in the first quarter of 1916 was five times that of the last quarter of 1915.[38] The increase in numbers went hand in hand with the standardisation both of mortars and their organisation, and thus weapon density is more easily measured in the second phase. In terms of size, three types of trench-mortar were standardised: light, medium and heavy. The most successful light mortar was the Stokes, which had replaced all others by May 1916. The Stokes was an efficient, mobile weapon and was easily assembled for action and dismantled after; further, it had a rapid fire rate of up to thirty shells per minute, of which several might be airborne at one time. Somewhat earlier than the British, the French had developed and standardised a light mortar which fired a 35 lb shell over a maximum range of 500 yards. At about the same time, that is May 1916, a medium mortar was made uniform in the B.E.F. and known variously as the toffee apple, football or Christmas pudding, because of its large round shell to which a long rod was attached. These guns fired 60 lb footballs for a distance of 500 yards, from pits eight or nine feet deep within 150 yards of the front trench.[39] The B.E.F.'s heavy mortar, regularised in the latter half of 1916, fired rather erratically and for 1000 yards, a bomb 150 lbs in weight and four feet in length, which was promptly called the flying pig. Heavy mortars were fired in positions 25 feet from the surface[40] and caused craters 25 feet in depth. No dug-out was proof against a pig. The German counterpart fired a larger shell—200 lbs—but for a lesser distance—600 yards.

In the B.E.F. mortar organisation was finally rationalised in March 1916. Medium—and later heavy—mortars became part of divisional artillery and were manned by specialist gunners, whereas light mortars formed a brigade battery and were operated by specialist infanteers. By July 1916 each division had three batteries of light and three of medium mortars, to which was later added a battery of pigs. In most cases a mortar battery comprised four guns and a crew of about four officers and fifty N.C.O.s and men. Trench-mortar groups, whether infantry or artillery, led an independent and semi-nomadic life in trenches free from the scrutiny of parent units; thus an infantry officer who transferred to a Stokes battery wrote 'after the life of an infantry platoon officer, everything was extremely free and easy and the subalterns were given a greater degree of responsibility';[41] likewise, an artillery officer who went to divisional mortars commented 'I was fortunate enough to be transferred to a trench mortar battery . . . here I found myself in as jolly a crowd as I ever met in the war, and amongst whom I spent my happiest times'.[42]

But there was another view of trench-mortars and their crews.

For instance, Lord Moran asserted, 'when a battalion was ordered to send men into the Trench Mortar Company . . . it often seized the chance to get rid of its rubbish. These misfits of war were pushed from one unit to another';[43] Graves also mentions a case where an inefficient officer was sent to the light mortars.[44] It seems this practice occurred not only in the infantry but also in the artillery, for in respect of recruitment to medium mortars, a gunner observed that, 'Battery commanders soon got into the way of picking out those they could easily spare whenever they were asked to find men for the work'.[45] Whether this practice was general, I do not know; but an indifferent infantry or artillery officer might make a good mortar man. Generally, it is true the infantry disliked mortars, as one infanteer delicately put it, 'Though sometimes supplied, the cooperation of this arm was never asked for';[46] but this dislike derived not from the characters of men who manned mortars but from the characteristics of mortars as weapon groups. Mortar crews were not, as Lord Moran asserted, a mob of 'misfits'; on the contrary they sometimes developed solidarity, a distinctive life-style and interests, which occasionally coincided with infantry interests but more frequently did not. The relations of infantry and trench-mortars will be examined later.

In respect of weapon density and the ratio of potential violence to space, the picture in the second stage is more clear than in the first. In July 1916 the B.E.F. comprised 55 divisions each with six mortar batteries of four guns,[47] which gives an overall total of 1320 mortars and a divisional total of 24 mortars; where a divisional front was 6000 yards, density was about one mortar per 250 yards.[48] Subsequently, each division received a heavy mortar battery[49]— pigs—which contained two or more guns, increasing density to one light, medium or heavy mortar per 230 yards. Thus mortar density increased fourfold between September 1915 and the summer of 1916, that is, from one to four mortars per 1000 yards. Moreover mortars of the second phase were more efficient, their crews more specialised and organisation rationalised. In short, during the early part of 1916, a comprehensive trench-mortar technology emerged—a technology capable of producing immense aggression in trench war.

How was this aggression used? High command expected mortars to harass the enemy by creating and seizing opportunities to inflict loss. Targets were received from brigade and division,[50] otherwise mortar crews foraged among infantry company and battalion

H.Q.s or spotted their own. There was much to fire at; fighting and working groups of enemy; fighting trenches and earthworks; the enemy's defensive wire; enemy saps in no-man's-land; communication trenches especially when crowded with men, for instance, during the relief of one unit by another; enemy snipers, machine-guns and trench-mortars. At times light and medium mortars combined for a strafe, and the pigs joined in occasionally (a strafe was a short, intense and powerful assault, but the term had a wider currency, for instance, some trench fighters were arguing whether ample or slender females were better made for love, and one put his case for the lavish, briefly yet with feeling, 'Give me a woman I can strafe'); further and finally, mortars were expected to coordinate their activities with the infantry, particularly for raiding.

Up to now some elements of the technology of aggression for long and medium distances have been examined, and differences between the first and second phases of the war in respect of this technology are now shown in the following tabulation of data concerning the density and distribution of weapons and men (see Table A). While figures are approximate, the tables clearly contrast the aggression capability of the B.E.F. in 1915 and after. The table is not comprehensive, for some weapon groups are not included. Concerning the calculation of weapon density, suppositions were made which, while realistic, took little account of local variation and practice. One assumption was that a divisional front was 6000 yards long; but in fact some fronts were longer, and some shorter. For example, in December 1916, three divisions held the ten-mile front of VI corps, giving each a line of about 5860 yards; on the other hand, one division held the four-mile—7040 yards—front of XVII corps; and three divisions each with a front of about 3520 yards held the six-mile front of I corps.[51] Bearing these variations in mind, 6000 yards seems neither unreasonable nor misleading. Concerning the distribution of weapons and personnel, it was assumed each division had three infantry brigades in the line, whereas sometimes two brigades were in trenches and one in reserve; secondly, each brigade had two of four battalions in the line and two in reserve, which was not uncommon although variations existed; finally, each battalion had two of four companies in trenches and two in reserve. Given these assumptions, it follows that six battalions held a divisional front of 6000 yards, and each battalion front was 1000 yards long.

TABLE A   The distribution of specialist weapons and personnel along battalion and divisional fronts for the first and second phases of trench war

| | Battalion front: 1000 yards. Two Infantry Companies in the Line | | | | Divisional front: 6000 yards | | | |
| | First phase | | Second phase | | First phase | | Second phase | |
	No. of weapons	No. of personnel	No. of weapons	No. of personnel	No. of weapons	No. of personnel	No. of weapons	No. of personnel
Rifles: sniper	2	2	23	46	12	12	138	276[1]
Machine-guns: Vickers	4	24	4	24	24	144	48	288
Machine-guns: Lewis	—	—	8[2]	16	—	—	96	192
Trench-mortars: light and medium	1	12	4	48	7	84	24[3]	288
Total	7	38	39	134	43	240	306	1044

Weapon density: number of weapons per given length of front line[4]

	First phase	Second phase
Rifles: sniper	1 weapon per 500 yards	1 weapon per 42 yards
Machine-guns: Vickers	1 weapon per 250 yards	1 weapon per 125 yards
Machine-guns: Lewis	—	1 weapon per 62 yards
Trench-mortars: light and medium	1 weapon per 1000 yards	1 weapon per 250 yards
Total and average	1 weapon per 580 yards	1 weapon per 120 yards

NOTES: [1] Snipers and observers were paired, and this figure refers to the combined total, that is 138 snipers and 138 observers from battalion and company.

[2] This figure is based on the 16 per battalion allotment achieved by July 1916.

[3] This figure does not include heavy mortars of which each division received one battery in either 1916 or 1917.

[4] One must remember weapons were not lined up evenly at fixed intervals along a line as the table might suggest; on the contrary, weapons might be bunched for tactical reasons, and, further the front line might be 2–3000 yards in depth, and some weapons were nearer, some further, from the enemy line. In this sense, the figures for weapon density are notional.

Table A indicates the augmented size and complexity of the technology of trench war during the second phase. Along a battalion front there had been, firstly, a more than fivefold increase in the number of specialist weapons, that is, from 7 to 39; and, secondly, well over a threefold increase in specialist operators—from 38 to 134. Along a divisional front, there had been a sevenfold growth in the number of specialist weapons—from 43 to 306, and a fourfold increase in specialist personnel, from 240 to 1044; further, the density of specialist weapons increased from one weapon per 580 yards in the first phase to one weapon per 120 yards in the second. Obviously, the potential volume of, and opportunities for aggression, were vastly more in the second than in the first stage of trench war.

Moreover Table A does not show the growth in the technology and tactics of close-combat aggression, such as hand-grenades, patrolling and raiding; but before this is examined, a brief look at the heavy and field artilleries will be taken. While the number of divisions in the B.E.F. was greater in the first than second stage, the number of field guns per division did not change much throughout the war. In 1914 each division had 76 guns, but after a re-organisation in April 1916, this number dropped to 64[52]—a density of one gun per 90 yards (approximately). On the other hand, the number of heavy guns increased greatly from 105 in June 1915[53] to 761 in July 1916[54] and to 1157 in early 1917[55] and, finally, to 2200 in October 1918.[56] Field guns were part of division, but heavy guns belonged to either corps or army units, and their twentyfold increase was a striking feature of the trench war.

The next problem concerns the mutual harassment of antagonists at distances of 300 yards and less, and we shall examine three elements of close-combat tactics and technology: hand-grenades, patrols and raids. A hand-grenade is a small bomb thrown for 40 yards or less and is one of two types according to its exploding device: percussion bombs explode upon impact, and time bombs explode at an interval fixed by a time fuse. In 1914 the B.E.F. used both types, but in 1916 the Mills bomb, with a time fuse, became standard. The Germans used a time-fuse bomb throughout the war. At first both British and French armies had few bombs—in November 1914 the B.E.F. received 70 bombs a week from the U.K.,[57] and this supply was augmented by corps workshops, but demand and supply rose rapidly, and by July 1916 the B.E.F. was receiving 800,000 Mills bombs weekly from the U.K.[58]

The organisation of grenade-weapon groups took one of three forms: brigade, battalion or company. In some divisions, brigade drew about 30 men from each of its four battalions and formed a brigade bombing company of 120 specialists[59] under bombing officers whose H.Q. was brigade itself. Usually, the group was split into four subgroups of 30 men, with one group always in the line. This organisation gave a density of one bomber for each 66 yards of the 2000-yard brigade front. More often, however, hand-bombers were a specialist group within the battalion, controlled by a specialist officer; sometimes they were rifle-grenade specialists also.[60] A battalion grenade group was probably 20 to 30 men, and assuming 30 bombers worked two alternating shifts of 15 men along a battalion front of 1000 yards, density was about one bomber per 66 yards or similar to brigade organisation. Battalion bombers evolved a solidarity and collective identity, as a new bombing recruit was aware, 'I became a member of the toughest crowd in the battalion . . . (which) . . . formed a community within the battalion and, supported by our own bombing N.C.O.s, stubbornly defied all attempts to make us work or drill'.[61] Lastly, in some battalions bombers were organised at company level, where each of the company's four platoons had a section of about five bombers. Company organisation gave a density higher than either brigade or battalion, namely, one bomber for each 25 yards of the company's 500-yard front.

In respect of tactics and training, the earliest bombers were trained by the Royal Engineers,[62] but high command schools were soon instituted[63] and instructional manuals issued.[64] Bombing skills were useful in trench war not only generally but in at least three particular ways: firstly, where the narrow distance between opposing trenches allowed bombers of each side to bomb each other's trenches—if trench war was active and trenches close, intensely violent bombing fights, which shattered bodies into bloody and singed gobbets, continued night and day, and of one notoriously active front, a soldier commented, 'According to report, the crater and trench fighters of the brigade were slinging at Jerry an average of 30,000 bombs a day, for three days. The enemy retaliation was equally terrible, and we suffered 3000 casualties in the fourteen-day spell in that area';[65] secondly, bombing skills were crucial where fighting patrols met nightly in no-man's-land, and grenades were the favoured weapon; finally, the bomber was most necessary in a raid.

Much close combat in trench war came about as antagonists were either raiding each other or patrolling no-man's-land. Concerning the first phase, we can look at raids and patrols together, for in 1915 raiding was neither distinct nor evolved from patrolling. Patrols were of two types: reconnaissance and fighting. In practice, however, the distinction blurred; for reconnaissance patrols might fight to get information or return with it, and fighting patrols, which by chance got information, then avoided fighting to bring it back. On the other hand, a raid necessarily involved fighting, since it was a small but murderous attack against enemy trenches, which were occupied briefly by raiders, who inflicted in minutes the maximum of death and destruction upon the enemy, and then got out before he counter-attacked. Some prisoners were taken for intelligence, but, essentially, a raid was 'smack and back'[66] as one trench fighter put it.

Throughout 1915 élite battalions were active in developing tactics for the patrol and raid, and the 1st and 2/Royal Welch were prominent among these. At the start of trench war, a policy of aggressive patrolling of no-man's-land was established by the officer commanding the 2/Royal Welch,[67] and this was conceived more as a means to maintain the fighting spirit and honour of the battalion than as a response to high command orders or part of a programme of specialisation. At the same time in the same brigade, a similar practice was instituted by the 2/Cameronians, 'when nights are suitable', an officer's diary runs, 'the company sends a small patrol into no-man's-land . . . The main object . . . is to prevent morale deteriorating'.[68] The limited effect on battalions of high command directives during the first phase is well illustrated by comparing the number of patrols of the 2/Royal Welch and 2/Cameronians with that of the 5/Scottish Rifles—a territorial unit of the same brigade—in the spring of 1915. The history of the 5/Scottish Rifles records no patrol activity before May 1915, by which time the 2/Royal Welch were experts. Lord Reith, who served with the 5/Scottish Rifles then, recorded that a company commander stopped his officers from patrolling on several occasions.[69] High command directives did not move the 5/Scottish Rifles, while the 2/Royal Welch moved of their own accord.

According to Graves, who joined the 2/Royal Welch in July

1915, it was still a point of honour to dominate no-man's-land from dawn to dusk,[70] but other units thought patrolling 'a mad escapade'.[71] In some élite units the patrol had a further function. Early in 1915, the 2/Royal Welch first received temporary instead of regular officers as replacements for casualties, but such officers, although officially posted to the battalion, had to validate their courage by means of a patrol, otherwise the 2/Royal Welch 'unofficially' posted them to a lesser unit.[72]

In the history of the 2/Royal Welch one can trace the unplanned development of specialist skills and tactics concerning close combat aggressions in no-man's-land. In the first days of trench war the battalion learned 'the techniques of night defence',[73] of which patrolling was one; at the same time it experimented with defensive and offensive patrols, which destroyed snipers and harassed working parties as well as an embryonic raid, during which a nearby unit gave covering fire to the raiders, who set out at dusk and destroyed two barns in no-man's-land which concealed snipers.[74] According to one authority, the 2/Royal Welch did not order men to patrol but called for volunteers,[75] and before the end of 1914, there were signs that specialisation was occurring in an unplanned yet systematic way; for the same persons volunteered for successive patrols thus developing the skills and techniques of close combat in no-man's-land with constant practice. The unit history recorded informal specialisation as soon as December 1914 when it commended the constant night patrols of a private soldier.[76] By March 1915, it was generally known throughout the battalion that two officers through numerous night patrols had acquired special skills in aggressing enemy patrols and gaining useful information by hiding unseen near enemy trenches.[77] The aggression of this battalion was such that one night a patrol, all bombs thrown at the enemy, returned to the trenches not to rest on its laurels but for more bombs to continue the fight.[78] Another officer, specialising in patrols, evolved from experience a patrol formation which prevented its members either from being surprised by or blundering into the enemy.[79] In March 1915, high command, probably impressed by its aggression, called on the 2/Royal Welch to make a Chinese attack,[80] which was a small assault made at the same time as a large one elsewhere to confuse the enemy—a year after high command would have ordered a raid, but in March 1915 neither term nor tactic existed. The general selected the two officer patrol specialists with twenty others for the raid, which was made with artillery cooperation at a few hours notice. Although the raiders were skilled and reached and bombed the enemy's line, the operation was but a partial success; for the need to plan as well as rehearse a raid, revealed by such experimental affrays, was not appreciated in the first phase of trench war.

The techniques of trench war, evolved discretionally in 1915 by élite units, were codified and bureaucratically imposed throughout the B.E.F. in the second phase, and, consequently, aggression was then managed more by an impersonal than personal control system. Sir Douglas Haig, the British commander-in-chief for the second phase, was a prime mover in this process, which is the theme of the next chapter. In close-combat aggression, the domination of no-man's-land at night was no longer a spontaneous, locally controlled practice whereby élite units maintained regimental honour, but an integral part of the trench war technology, of which the skills and rationale were taught at high command schools[81] and published in official texts. High command spelt out the various functions of the patrol which included the maintenance of morale and the fighting spirit;[82] the domination of no-man's-land, so that patrols could obtain, without hindrance from enemy patrols, the facts necessary for high command plans for large battles as well as small raids— such intelligence included facts about the enemy's defences and the ground over which the troops would assault,[83] moreover, where patrols controlled no-man's-land the enemy was denied intelligence; the identification of enemy troops by patrols which was, 'a very important duty'[84] at all times, but especially when a battle raged elsewhere; attrition[85] was a further function of the patrol which in this was similar to the raid. The success of the raid, which was the most skilled form of small assault in trench war, depended in part upon control of no-man's-land by patrols in the period preceding the raid; it is to the latter tactic we now turn.

According to the official history, the first raid was carried out in February 1915 by the 1/Worcestershire Regiment (8th division);[86] but other battalions had made small local attacks against the enemy well before this date.[87] Such attacks were simple, impromptu affairs, involving little or no concerted action with other arms, little specialisation within the raiding party, and a minimum of planning and preparation. In most cases it seems a small group of volunteers quickly crossed no-man's-land, bombed and fired into the enemy's trenches and then hurried back with prisoners and information of the enemy's defences and dispositions. Such affairs were more like fighting patrols than raids, and the official history does not say why the 1/Worcester's attack was called a raid rather than a fighting patrol, for all these crude, early affrays bore little resemblance to the sophisticated and complex raid of the second phase.

As a developed tactic, the raid emerged in November 1915 when a Canadian unit[88] made an attack, the instructions for which were regarded as an exemplary model throughout the B.E.F.[89] The comparison of these instructions with early rudimentary attacks shows that by the end of 1915, the raid was clearly distinguished from other forms of minor assault, such as the fighting patrol. The instructions were both an official account[90] of the Canadian raid and a summary of principles which were to guide the preparation and planning of future raids; further, they were based in no small degree on experiences of élite units in close-combat aggression during 1915. It is interesting to note that in February 1915, when the 2/Royal Welch had developed close-combat skills, Captain Stockwell, one of their officers who had encouraged the development of these skills, was detailed to instruct the newly arrived Canadian troops.[91]

The raid was a complex tactic involving diverse skills as well as the coordination of weapon groups from several arms, and it comprised two successive parts: the preparation and performance. The former divides into an earlier and a later period. In the early period, fighting patrols established ascendancy in no-man's-land and gained intelligence of German defences and ground over which raiders would assault; the official account of the Canadian raid recorded that along the brigade front patrols, 'had been very active for a considerable period'.[92] During the later preparatory period, concrete objectives were selected, and attack plans formulated; volunteers were picked and withdrawn from front line duty to 'a good warm billet'[93] behind the lines, where by night and day they practised the attack over a specially built model of German trenches. According to the official report, the raiders did this with 'the same relish as if training for a football match'.[94]

It became customary to release raiders from duties and fatigues during this period. According to one authority, raiders were given better rations, felt themselves to be 'picked men', and lived together like a 'football team'. Successful raiders were decorated and sometimes given leave, for instance, one raiding party went for a 'seaside excursion' to Dunkirk.[95] All this suggests that something of a holiday atmosphere surrounded a raid; but about this there were two opinions: 'one sees a raid as a foul, mean, bloody, murderous orgy which no human being who retains a grain of moral sense can take part in without the atrophy of every human instinct',[96] wrote one infantry officer. However, it does seem in the preparatory period of some raids at least, raiders developed not only technical skill but solidarity which, in turn, increased the former.

However, the Canadian plan was a complex division of labour involving infantry, artillery and trench-mortar weapon groups. The infantry raiding group comprised assault, cover and support, and reserve elements, and each element was internally differentiated in terms of complementary, specialised skills. The assault group penetrated the German defences; the cover and support group gave covering fire to the assault of the German line and withdrawal from it and also contested German counter-attacks; the reserve group stayed in their trenches to prevent German counter-attack upon the Canadian line.

The assault group was divided into two self-contained subgroups, each attacking separately but simultaneously to confuse the Germans. Each subgroup was composed of 70 men and was divided into still more subgroups, each with a special function: a wire-cutting assault group (5 men); two bombing and blocking assault groups (14 men); two bridge-cover groups (6 men);[97] a trench-rifle group (10 men); a listening-post support group (13 men); a trench-reserve group (22 men).

The wire-cutting assault group were specialist scouts with a twofold task: firstly, to check that the trench-mortars and the artillery had blown gaps of sufficient size and number in the enemy's wire to give raiders access to enemy trenches, and, secondly, to lead raiders across no-man's-land. In the event, scouts found the gaps inadequate, whereupon they cut larger holes in the German wire—a task which took two and a half hours, and during which scouts were served hot cocoa. Then, at intervals of several minutes, the various sections of both assault groups left their trenches. For unforeseen reasons, one assault group failed to enter the German trenches and withdrew; but with the other all went according to plan. Surprising and stabbing the German sentry, the two bombing and blocking groups, which included two wire and two shovel men, entered the trench. One group turned left, the other right, and, 40 yards on either side of the entry point, the wire and shovel men quickly built trench strongpoints to block the German counter-attack. While engaged thus, shovel men were covered by the trench-rifle group, which contained a telephonist and linesman who established contact with Canadian lines.

Simultaneously, other sections of both right and left groups went about their tasks. The bombers—two throwers and two carriers—and bayonet men bombed German dug-outs between the entry points and the two strongpoints and killed some Germans and captured others, who, together with their equipment, were escorted across no-man's-land by the scouts and some of the trench-rifle group. In this way, the assault group killed or wounded about thirty Germans and took twelve prisoners within nineteen minutes. The order to retire was given. The raiders reassembled and withdrew entirely according to plan, and once they returned to the Canadian line, the artillery, which during the raid had bombarded the German rear trenches, shortened its range on to the German front trench to catch the counter-attacking troops.

4

At the onset of the second phase of trench war a vast structure of opportunities for aggression had been developed and positioned. The means of hostility were supplemented by further constraints towards it, such as high command rewards for aggression or punishments for non-aggression. Moreover, if one holds that man has violent needs, whether innate or learned, and these needs are an extra, underlying motive for warlike behaviour, then one would predict that generally men would with energy exploit the structure of opportunities for violence brought into being by the First World War in the manner indicated in Harold Macmillan's vivid sketch of trench warfare:

> One can look for miles and see no human being. But in those miles of country lurk . . . it seems thousands, even hundreds of thousands of men, planning against each other perpetually some new device of death. Never showing themselves, they launch at each other bullet, bomb, aerial torpedo and shell.[1]

Macmillan, however, served with the élite 4/Grenadier Guards, and other units had other methods; yet it is difficult to see how a fragile peace could persist in phase two with its vast potential for violence.

In passing, and with respect to the concept of innate aggression, it is fashionable to argue that man and animals are alike in certain ways, and, since animals have inborn aggression, man has also, and therefore this primordial instinct underlies human warfare. But the fallacy is clear enough, for if two things are alike in some respects, it does not mean they cannot differ in others. For instance, in medical science, it is useful to extrapolate the physiological behaviour of man from that of animals; but it can be most misleading to extrapolate man's social behaviour from that of animals, because man has culture, which determines his social behaviour (including war) and animals do not. To interpret the behaviour of men at war in terms of inborn aggression, genetic pre-programming, the R-complex or whatever, is to commit the same fallacy as to interpret the aggression of animals in terms of cultural rules, which is absurd. To reason by analogy thus, might be the first resort of the ethologist, but must remain the last refuge of the behavioural scientist. It is strange that ethologists, who warn against attributing human motives to animals, are the first to attribute animal motives to man. This view of human behaviour, namely that it is closely related to innate, *sui generis* faculties, is as old as Platonic philosophy, but is still widespread in the twentieth century. For instance, when George V went to the B.E.F. in France during the war, Douglas Haig observed that the king

> was inclined to think that all our troops are by nature brave and is ignorant of all the efforts which commanders must make to keep up 'morale' of their men in war, and of all the training which is necessary . . . to enable a company . . . to go forward as an organised unit in the face of almost certain death . . . we have to take special precautions during a battle to post police, to prevent more unwounded men than are necessary from accompanying a wounded man back from the firing line.[2]

Perhaps battle commanders have wished inborn bravery and aggression to exist, or that if they did exist, they had more force; but, as Haig pointed out, the experience and actions of commanders show that these behaviours were socially determined. The ascription of human warfare to an undefined, non-observable entity, assumed to exist in man, is conjecture and is a different form of explanation from that used by the social scientist who tries to relate acts of aggression to other identifiable social facts.

To return, however, to the analysis of social facts related to aggression, the theme of the previous chapter was the specialisation of means of aggression, while that of the present chapter concerns management of means of aggression. The thesis is that the personal, local control of violence in 1915 gave way in 1916 to an impersonal, centralised control, and, further, the latter more than the former constrained trench fighters to violence. More simply, trench warfare was bureaucratised and the incidence of violence increased.

This complex development involved, especially in the second phase, impersonal authority in human and non-human forms. By a human form of impersonal authority is meant hierarchical administration with transmission of orders from higher to lower levels, where levels are free from personal involvement, such as where high command and front line lacked personal ties.[3] This contrasts with hierarchical administration where personal ties bind followers to a leader, as existed in some battalions. Non-human impersonal authority means management through a mechanism which by its nature, in the absence or presence of generals, constrained men to aggression. Such devices included tactics and technology of trench war, whose growth has been described, and statistical records of aggression. I wish neither to employ nor to dwell upon more abstract concepts—'the drab garments of sociology' as called by some—than are relevant and necessary. But the disparity between a system where violence was impersonally controlled, in either human or non-human form, and one where it was personally controlled, was fundamental in trench war, for each system created contrasting war situations and experiences. For a short time at least it is necessary to carry the obscure and dull drapes of social science while amplifying these distinctions.

Concerning human forms of impersonal authority, the administration and production of violence was more personal and local in 1915 than afterwards, that is, fighting units like battalions decided the when, where and how of aggression, and then produced that aggression. In the second phase, however, the administrative and productive functions were divorced, and the former centralised in high command, which decided the when and where of aggression and then ordered combat units to action.

Both personal and impersonal systems of control were hierarchically organised, but they differed in other ways, such as the combat status of personal systems—battalions and so forth, and the non-combat status of centralised high command; in the fact that personal systems comprised not only formal ties of function and rank, but also informal ties of antagonism and friendship, shared experiences, interests and values, the paternalistic concern of officers for men and their reciprocal trust in some battalions; and, in élite battalions, the common commitment to regimental honour.[4] Such informal ties generated solidarity[5] which influenced the battalion's fighting record. Generally, solidarity worked either for or against the official policy of active trench war: where informal solidarity supported aggression, battalions conceived, planned and executed attacks with spontaneity and vigour; but where solidarity worked against aggression, this was variously restricted, and live and let live emerged. The important point is that in each case the battalion was executive both in management and in production of violence; decisions to attack or not were taken by trench fighters who were personally involved with others of the unit directly affected by such life and death orders. In contrast, neither solidarity nor informal ties existed between high command and fighting units, except perhaps in élite divisions where, for instance, the historian of the 29th division could assert that he 'never discovered that there exists any other point of view than that of the higher command. Broadly speaking, commanders and commanded have seen eye to eye'.[6] Consequently, when in the second phase, high command absorbed the administration of violence from the front line, decisions concerning attack were influenced less by informal personal ties among combatants, and more by the formal needs and strategies of non-combatants, which were often neither meaningful nor intelligible to trench fighters.

Non-human impersonal systems refer to situations where super-ordinate strata, for instance, high command, instal mechanisms which of themselves, more than the hierarchy, exert constraints upon subordinates such as trench fighters. Among such mechanisms were the tactics and technology of trench war—by this term I mean technical rules, methods, skills and weapons as well as their coordination within a division of labour designed for attack and defence. In ways to be examined, this technology together with statistical records of aggression had an effect on the rhythm of aggression which was independent of high command surveillance. However, this is not to say that no impersonal control existed in 1915, or that all aggression was then locally and personally controlled. We have seen that high-level directives, establishing an active front policy early in 1915, had little effect because their general nature gave much discretion to trench fighters, whose idea of the proper volume of violence sometimes differed from high command's; moreover, though stemming from regimental pride more than official directives, the activity of élite units was not entirely unrelated to impersonal control in 1915, since high command commendation, which rewarded aggression, increased regimental honour, and this was sufficient motive for action. Thus it is with the interplay of human and non-human impersonal control systems, and their combined, and separate, effects on the incidence of aggression, that this chapter is concerned.

The technology of trench war has been described, and its action as an impersonal system of control will now be analysed. While this technology was complex and diverse, it was also unitary in that all parts constrained combatants to aggression. These parts— weapons, skills and tactics—were several in scope and mode of working: some parts constrained all weapon groups at all times in all situations, whereas others were specific to certain groups at certain times and situations. Perhaps the most universal constraint was the official rationale for active trench warfare, which unambiguously laid down that the rhythm of aggression was to be determined by high command alone and certainly not by informal negotiation with the enemy. This theory made clear all sectors were active sectors in trench war, and the unofficial distinction of active and quiet sectors had no official sanction. In the 1915 narratives written for the home front, trench fighters described the difference between sectors and often explained and justified live and let live with private trench war theories—for readers might be puzzled about the peace within the war. One territorial soldier, for instance, put it this way:

> the real reason for the quietness of some sections of the line was that neither side had any intention of advancing in that particular district; it was simply a case of stone-walling while the other man made the runs—of holding the line while attempts at advancing were made elsewhere. Consequently neither side had much to gain by violence. If the British shelled the Germans, the Germans replied, and the damage was equal: if the Germans bombed an advanced piece of trench and killed five Englishmen, an answering fusillade killed five Germans.[7]

(the author leaves the corollary implied, namely, when the British did not shell the Germans, the Germans reciprocated, and the mutual benefit was an unofficial truce). But high command would disagree that no side gained from violence, and each lost equally; for there were good and indifferent trench fighters, and the former inflicted more losses than they sustained, which was the aim of attrition.

The official theory not only precluded unofficial interpretations but also explained the role of routine trench war in the wider conflict. The British war office manual *Notes for Infantry Officers on Trench Warfare*, first published in March 1916, distinguished two types of sector: firstly, where one's own trenches, the enemy's, or both, were sited where a major attack might at any time develop for military reasons, and if an attack occurred such a sector became a battlefield like Verdun, the Somme and Ypres; secondly, where neither the enemy's line nor one's own had strategic features making likely a large-scale attack.[8] Live and let live emerged more often on the latter than the former sectors, but the manual directed that the enemy must be harassed on both. The chief problem for infantry commanders was not whether to fight or remain inert but to ensure the maximum 'amount of work is done daily towards the subjection and annoyance of the enemy and the improvement of the trenches, consistent with the necessity for everyone to get a proper amount of rest and sleep'.[9] Aggression was mandatory on all sectors whether these had strategic value or not. At the same time, the manual sanctioned variations between sectors in amounts of time used for aggression against time for construction;[10] for much work was needed to make ready one's own line for launching major attacks when the enemy's line had strategic value, and, further, the same time was needed to maintain trenches as adequate defensive systems where one's own line had strategic import. Alternatively, where no prime objectives existed on either side, trenches as systems of offence and defence were of less importance, and therefore a relatively high proportion of time could be spent on aggression.

The official active front theory was but a small part of trench war technology, which mostly comprised weapons, skills and tactics. This technology produced aggression *sui generis* as a non-human impersonal control. It was non-human in the sense that aggression was generated independently of human factors, such as high command surveillance of zeal, or otherwise, of trench fighters. In a degree, the complex technology of the second phase moved men merely by its existence where the simpler technology of 1915 did not—of course, this is not to deny the former produced more aggression when used with energy than without. Probably General Bullard of the United States army was referring to intrinsic constraints of technology when he wrote in his diary 'I shall also organise in full and have a machine in the division, a machine that will work independently of the quality of the man who turns the crank'.[11] Bullard's metaphor of the machine is illuminating, for it points to the parallel between industrial and war technology. The industrial assembly line is a non-human impersonal control whereby superiors constrain subordinates' behaviour without supervision or constant orders. In motor car production, assembly line technology designed and installed by management exercises without further managerial supervision a constant constraint upon workers, showing which jobs, should be done, which materials and tools used, in which order and at which pace.[12] Trench war technology was partly designed by élite units but standardised and installed throughout the B.E.F. in 1916 by high command—Douglas Haig played a key role here.[13] Once installed, this technology diminished trench fighters' discretion by indicating that aggression was obligatory at all times and places; which mode of aggression was appropriate to which circumstance and time; which weapons and tactics should be used, and at which rhythm or pace; and which weapon groups should be coordinated. Thus, in the production of both cars and violence, a technology can continuously control the actions of subordinates, achieving the aims of superiors, even in their absence. In the case of trench war, this kind of constraint made aggression more likely and inertia less likely behaviour.

The specialised technology increased mutual harassment of trench fighters in other ways. Other things equal, it is logical that the incidence of violence during war[14] increases as war technology becomes more complex; for aggression is then possible where before it was not, while the greater the number of opportunities, the greater the number of aggressive acts, whether combatants are mostly bellicose or mostly passive. In addition, warlike persons are attracted to specialised weapons and tactics, since these offer more opportunities for violence—a machine-gunner commits more violence than a rifleman, and a member of a raiding party more than a sentry. Further, specialised weaponry not only recruits but also creates aggressive persons. In general, specialist weapons such as machine-guns are bigger threats to greater numbers of the enemy than non-specialist weapons like rifles, and therefore attract much more counter-fire. 'Machine-gun fire always provokes retaliation',[15] remarked a gunner, and such fire was countered not only in kind but with other weapons; accordingly, instigators had either to suffer the consequences, or to break off firing, or to force the enemy to break off by constantly escalating counter-fire—the principle of the latter was voiced by an officer of an élite unit, 'We are top dogs, and if there is any strafing, the last word must always be ours'.[16] But 'the last word' meant vicious fire exchange increasing rapidly in volume and force, thus exposing machine-gunners to more intense violence than ordinary soldiers. This degree of violence, however, was intrinsic to the combat role not merely of machine-gunners but also of specialist weapon groups generally.

The notion that specialisation made men violent is supported by a study of combat behaviour of the Second World War which found that specialist weapon groups were more aggressive in battle than other infantrymen.[17] In trench warfare, the relatively turbulent world of the specialists was acknowledged by others, for instance a trench-mortar crew was sometimes called 'a Suicide Club'.[18] Moreover, it seems the violent ethos, which surrounded the specialists in battle, influenced them out of battle towards wild reckless behaviour, which seemed bravado or bizarre to outsiders; thus one of a battalion bombing group remarked on its reputation as 'the toughest crowd in the battalion', which was not unrelated to their means of avoiding work and drill when pressed by authority. 'As a last resort, we had a pleasant trick of dropping bombs with feigned clumsiness which, with more of the uninitiated, achieved infallibly the result we wished.'[19] Feigned clumsiness or not, this was dangerous with the primitive bombs of 1915 when the author wrote. The same soldier, in training for a raid which he was later to lead, rebuked a raider for bravado when he 'perched himself on top of a tree to shout insults over to the German lines in the distance'.[20] This was not live and let live banter, for the raiders came from the élite 29th division. Similar wild behaviour was noted in a study[21] analysing how soldiers face up to war, that is, how they make the transition from a civilian world of everyday experience to an unprecedented world of massive violence, and the author argues that 'action out of place'—behaviour identified here as bravado— shows an incomplete transition from peace to war. Probably this is so in some cases. At the same time, one might argue that some bravado shows a successful passage between these vastly different realities, or, in other words, an adaptation to the combat role. The passage from peace to war is traumatic; for example, trench fighters had to brace themselves for combat each time they passed from rest to trenches; nevertheless the journey had to be made repeatedly; but if some of the violence of combat was carried from battle to rest as bravado, the inconsistency of the worlds of violence and non-violence—the source of shock—was diminished and became one of degree and not of kind.

To sum up, then, it may be that in a general sense war both attracts and creates violent persons, but the process is more marked with weapon specialists than others. I have found that violent attitudes against the enemy are relatively rare in personal documents of trench fighters and these attitudes seemed even less frequent among soldiers with whom I have spoken—one only, a shell-shock victim, admitted to hating Germans in the war. On the other hand, such sentiments certainly did exist among infantrymen and specialists but probably more often among the latter than the former. 'Speaking for my companions and myself, I can categorically state that we were in no mood for any joviality with Jerry . . . we hated his guts', bluntly asserted a machine-gunner of the 12th division. 'We were bent on his destruction at each and every opportunity for all the miseries and privations which were our lot. Our greatest wish was to be granted an enemy target worthy of our Vickers gun.'[22] Such an animus against the enemy is consistent with the relative violence of the specialist situation, ethos and war experience. Some believe that battle brutalises all soldiers, but if so, it dehumanises some more than others and in patterned ways.

Specialisation and aggression were linked in another way, which concerned the means whereby trench fighters involved in truces deterred hostile compatriots from aggressing the enemy, and thereby converting exchanges of peace into exchanges of fire. The control of warlike deviants[23] was simpler in the first than in the second phase, for fewer specialist weapon groups existed in 1915 than in 1916. The ratio of specialists to non-specialists shifted in 1916 in favour of the former, and therefore the number of trench fighters tending to disrupt peace, that is, specialists, relative to those tending to preserve peace—non-specialists—increased, or, what is the same thing, the ratio of peace-preservers to peace-breakers decreased. Additionally, in 1915, battalion personnel operated specialist weapons such as Vickers guns and trench-mortars, and if the battalion were solidly behind live and let live, the hostility of specialists and non-specialists was checked equally; whereas, in phase two, these specialist groups passed from battalion to brigade control and, consequently, were less influenced by battalions.[24]

So far the separate effects of impersonal constraints towards violence have been considered, and now we turn to the combined effects and mutual reinforcement of specialised technology and high command directives on the incidence of aggression in the second phase of trench war. High command orders constrained trench fighters differently in 1916 than 1915, whether these orders were oral or written. In 1915, directives lacked force, being issued into something of a void where weapons and skills were neither standard nor developed and morale had to compensate for established skills and techniques, if aggression was to increase. In 1916, however, directives put in motion a complex technology where modes of aggression were specified by technical rules set out in manuals and taught at high command schools. Further, this technology was not merely found, as in 1915, in some élite battalions but was uniform throughout the B.E.F. The combination of technology and oral or written orders was an effective control over trench fighters, for manuals not only prescribed efficient means of attack but laid down exemplary models of aggression, that is, yardsticks against which high command could evaluate the fighting activities of all units, élite and otherwise. From high command's point of view, technical rules decreed levels and means of aggression with which all units either complied or found good reason for non-compliance. High command could now ask battalions specific questions about particular fighting activities, such as what arrangements had the battalion made for patrolling its front. 'At night, higher ranks appeared in our midst' wrote Blunden in 1916, 'chief of all, . . . the Brigadier General . . . followed by an almost equally menacing Staff Captain. What was my name? I had not been round the company's wire? Why not? I was to go. Authority was at this time persistent that all officers should take their nightly constitutional in No Man's Land';[25] generals could ask whether a battalion's sniping organisation complied with the official pattern or not, and if not why not; and whether a battalion had plans for harassing the enemy in cooperation with either or both artillery and trench mortars as per official manual, which affirmed: 'In order to obtain full benefit from aggressive artillery action, close cooperation between infantry and artillery is essential. Every means must be used to induce the enemy to man his parapets or come out and expose himself and then catch him with artillery fire. Various schemes will suggest themselves, and can be worked out between infantry and artillery commanders.'[26]

Moreover, high command could ask specialists the same questions. For instance, in August 1916 a mortar officer of the 32nd division wrote in his diary, 'General Tyler, C.R.A.[27] of the Division, came around the line. He asked me to fire as much as possible'.[28] Now the reader must grasp that the force of this request in 1916 was quite unlike that in 1915, when very different conditions prevailed, and, in the words of the 5th division C.R.A., 'Our . . . armament of trench mortars was confined to one or two amateur weapons of the drain pipe order, firing canisters or old jam tins filled with explosive and shrapnel bullets, stones or boot nails'.[29] Clearly, sound reasons existed in 1915 why a request for frequent fire had little effect, for mortars were crude, and more dangerous to operators than enemy. Whereas the same order given in 1916 to trained crews of lethal mortars experienced in tactics and commanded by specialist officers, who might also have authority to coordinate light, medium and heavy mortars to strafe the enemy, boosted aggression to a considerable degree, unless crews could justify inertia to high command on grounds of special circumstances.

To conclude, then, the combination of high command directives and trench war technology in phase two acted as an effective impersonal system of control, which made aggression an even more difficult response for trench fighters to avoid; for orders primed and accelerated the motion of technology, which, in addition, had a movement of its own.

In the interplay between technology, orders and violence there was another vital variable, namely, the thrusters. These constituted a new stratum of military administrators among higher commanders and their staffs who had a particular power and influence in the second phase. It seems the term 'thruster' appeared among trench fighters quite early in the war; for instance, in June 1915, Lord Reith wrote in his diary, 'In the next trench spell we were visited by the G.O.C. 27th division to which . . . (we) . . . had been transferred. The new man had a reputation as a thruster so we thought we should be encouraged if not ordered to be more active than formerly'.[30] Thrusters were frequently young men and always vigorous exponents of active trench war and, as regimental officers of élite units in 1915, many had pioneered the methods of trench warfare which they energetically administered upon elevation to high command in 1916.

The rise of the thrusters was connected with the rapid expansion of the B.E.F. in 1915, which caused a shortage of both high command and staff officers, partly made good with retired officers; but the war made more mental and physical demands on 'dugouts'—as these ageing gentlemen were often called—than they could reasonably be reckoned to cope with. The problem was spotted by Douglas Haig and at least one of his staff—Charteris — who in 1914 observed of some higher commanders that: 'They are almost all too old for their jobs of fighting like that which we are having. I was told of one general who insisted on his own guns stopping firing for at least one and a half hours after his lunch time so that he might enjoy undisturbed his afternoon siesta.'[31] Some élite battalions chaffed at the caution of such higher commanders, and the 2/Royal Welch by March had labelled their brigade commander 'Old stick in the mud' because 'the active minds had found him slow to move'.[32] In May 1915, however, G.H.Q. imposed an upper age limit for brigadiers,[33] and the 2/Royal Welch had a new brigade commander. But Haig's concern was with the higher as well as the lower levels of high command. In his diary of June 1915, he wrote generally of the need for 'young capable commanders' at the front and, more specifically, of majors to command brigades. In July 1915, when with Asquith and Kitchener, Haig urged that young officers should be promoted to the top levels of high command and proposed that older generals should be removed. He wrote of the meeting, 'we went down through the lists of Major Generals, etc., in the army list. I said it was important to go down low on the list and get young capable officers'.[34] Kitchener and Asquith agreed with Haig's thinking, but others did not; nevertheless Haig remained doyen of the thrusters throughout the war, and his policy of appointing young, abrasive officers to all levels of high command was, according to one authority, 'a fixed idea with him'.[35]

The experience of the Royal Welch shows the workings of this policy in respect of promotions to brigade level; for several thrusters, either of the 1st or 2nd battalions, were regimental officers at the outbreak of war, and subsequently became brigadier generals; these included Major O. de L. Williams, Captains C. S. Owen, C. Stockwell, and J. R. Minshull-Ford. In 1915, Major Williams commanded the 2/Royal Welch and afterwards the 92nd brigade (31st division) and, from the first days of trench war, he had insisted the battalion controlled no-man's-land and had encouraged active patrolling. Robert Graves draws an unsympathetic picture of this officer.[36] Certainly, Williams was authoritarian , but such was the style of command at that time, and whether he was more or less severe than his peers, which is the real question, one does not know—my impression is that he was not. He was respected within his battalion, and in the unit history, to which many members contributed, Major Williams appears as an abrasive but civilised soldier, with a dry and intelligent sense of humour.[37] Captain Owen was adjutant of the 2/Royal Welch in 1915 and after commanded successively a New Army battalion and the 37th brigade (12th division). He was an efficient and respected soldier with a genius for colourful comment, which amazed all and was envied by many, 'we all admired the adjutant very much', wrote a voice from the ranks approvingly, 'he could give us all chalks on at swearing, and beat the lot of us easily'.[38] Old soldiers were not easily beaten at this game, but others also remarked on Owen's virtuosity; for instance, an officer of his New Army unit recalled, 'the colonel was known as "The Fireater" . . . [he had] . . . a tongue as sharp as a razor, and a command of language that a sailor would have envied'.[39] Robert Graves has preserved one of Owen's gems, which expressed the acrimony between the Royal Welch and the Scottish battalions of the brigade, 'The Jocks are all the same; both the trousered kind and the bare arsed kind: they're dirty in trenches, they skite too much, and they charge like hell—both ways'.[40] Captain Stockwell was an efficient and brave soldier, but not the first choice of his men, it seems; Private Richards commented, 'I never remember him having any favourites; he treated all men in the same way—like dirt'.[41] Stockwell served with the 1st and 2nd battalions of the Royal Welch and later commanded the 164th brigade (55th division). Captain Minshull-Ford was with the 1st battalion and made one of the first experimental raids of the war in November 1914; in 1916, he commanded the 91st brigade of the élite 7th division.

But exactly how did thrusters move men to action where others could not? In the first instance, they operated upon the complex tactics and technology of phase two, constantly constraining trench fighters, by oral and written orders, to maximise aggression as per manual, that is, to accelerate the machine's motion. Such pressure had profound and pervasive effects for several reasons: all thrusters were committed to the active front policy; all were energetic by inclination and administered the policy accordingly; some— especially brigadiers and their staffs—organised trench war not only from theoretical but also from practical knowledge and knew from personal experience what was and was not possible in the trenches. In short, thrusters were the innovators of 1915 and, in 1916, administered techniques they had previously helped to evolve.

These men maintained pressures towards aggression from each level of the high command hierarchy. At the highest level, that is, G.H.Q., Douglas Haig, the thruster in chief, clearly conveyed the ethos of active trench war in his first dispatch, which summarised events of the first six months of his command—from December 1915 to May 1916—and which was itself an authoritative statement of how trench war should be conducted. Haig reported that:

> On the British front no action on a great scale . . . has been fought during the past five months; nevertheless our troops have been far from idle or inactive. Although the struggle . . . has not been intense, it has been everywhere continuous . . . Artillery and snipers are practically never silent, patrols are out in front of the lines every night, and heavy bombardments by the artillery of one or both sides take place daily in various parts of the line. Below ground there is continual mining and counter mining . . . All this is taking place constantly at any hour of the day and night, and in any part of the line . . . In short although there has been no great incident of historic importance to record on the British front . . . a steady and continuous fight has gone on, day and night, above ground and below it. The comparative monotony of this struggle has been relieved at short intervals by sharp local actions . . . One form of minor activity deserves special mention, namely, the raids . . . which are made at least twice or three times a week against the enemy's line.[42]

Haig pursued this active front policy throughout the war. The popular and current image of trench war corresponds closely, I suspect, to Haig's representation, which is also found in official and semi-official works. The latter include battalion and divisional histories, most frequently written by combatants, yet these works usually refer to the undertone of war, although often in anecdotal form. However, in at least one divisional history by a non-combatant historian, Haig's summary of active trench war is assumed to describe the state of affairs upon all, and not merely some, sectors. For instance, the 62nd divisional history reads: 'The Flanders offensive had begun . . . and the attentions of both of the allies and the enemy were turned to the northern battle front, comparative peace reigning from Arras southwards. And yet, there was no real peace, for as Sir Douglas Haig said in one of his dispatches of another phase of the war, but which applied to all periods of trench warfare';[43] the author then quotes Haig's first dispatch.

In the high command hierarchy, G.H.Q. was immediately above

the several army commanders, and immediately below these were corps commanders and their staffs. Army and corps were concerned not merely with the plans and conduct of large battles but also with trench war, especially when no battle was in progress on their fronts, which was most of the time for most commands. Army and corps commanders presssured trench fighters to harass the enemy in direct and indirect ways: directly, by initiating raids at specific times and places (a raid destroyed live and let live and usually stopped the latter reappearing for some time); indirectly, by establishing schools for specialist instruction and publishing warlike pamphlets for circulation throughout the command. In respect of the latter, trench fighters found a non-combatant staff's incitement to violence absurd and reacted contemptuously with a sometimes bitter humour. Thus, the ambiguity of a pamphlet from an army school thirty miles behind the line asking the question, 'Am I offensive enough', was quickly exploited: 'It is for the subaltern to ask himself each morning as he rises from his bed,' an infanteer wrote, 'Most laudable! But, as the Lewis Gun Officer remarked today, it is one of the paradoxes of war that the further you get from the battle line the more offensive are the people you meet!'[44] Nor were fighting men slow to voice this mood to high command in a more public way, as the following shows:

> Our brigade was in a comparatively quiet part of the line . . . and the Boche seemed content to keep it so on the principle of live and let live. Unfortunately our generals were not so pacifically inclined but persistently exhorted the troops to assume an offensive spirit. At about this time a cartoon appeared in a regimental magazine showing a foul looking temporary gentleman (second lieutenant) with a long cigarette holder and purple socks, above the caption: 'Am I as offensive as I might be?' This was a lampoon of an official circular which stated that every officer and man should ask himself this question.[45]

Finally, army and corps harassed the front line with memoranda demanding that divisions within their area demonstrated an offensive spirit against the enemy. General Haking, commander of XI corps, sent all divisions a memo about trench war:

> The Corps has been distinguished since its formation for the constant offensive action it has been called upon to carry out, and

a fine offensive spirit is apparent in all units. It is of vital importance that every effort should be made from the highest to the lowest to foster and increase this spirit throughout the winter months . . . by constantly harassing the enemy . . . we can greatly improve the morale of our own troops and wear out and depress the enemy . . . the offensive spirit of the troops must be carefully encouraged throughout the winter months and the natural desire of the troops to have a quiet time in the trenches must be discouraged in every possible way.[46]

This was the winter before the Somme. Haking was a most aggressive corps commander, asserting that no-man's-land did not exist on his corps front because the latter extended right up to the German line.[47]

Division was directly under corps and this unit with its constituent brigades was responsible for the detailed and immediate conduct of trench war, transmitting onwards and downwards to brigade more specific versions of corps orders. Thus upon receipt of Haking's memo, Lord Cavan, divisional commander of the Guards, sent his own specific proposals for harassing the enemy to brigades, namely, 'that lanes from 50 to 100 yards wide were to be cut by the artillery through the wire at various points in the enemy's wire, and kept permanently open; and (2) that raids were to be carried out from time to time during the hours of darkness on one or other of these selected points'. The memo continued, 'Lord Cavan was confident . . . that aggressive action of this kind would keep up the morale of the troops and be of good antidote to the inevitable slackness resulting from life in the trenches; and finally, that if the enemy were continually harassed the spirit of his troops would deteriorate'.[48]

All this echoed the official manual which held that harassing the enemy raised the morale of troops and gave them 'a healthy interest and wholesome topics of conversation'.[49] However, even in the élite Guards division and despite the historian's disclaimer, 'Nor were the corps commander's (Haking) warnings against the hibernating habit required by the Guards Division',[50] some battalions probably hibernated; for some were less aggressive than others and occasionally content to let sleeping dogs lie. Such seems to have been the case in the 1915 summer when the 1/Grenadier Guards, commanded by the notoriously aggressive Lord Gort, relieved the Scots Guards, who were peacefully coexisting with the Germans 80 yards away, for two officers of the Scots Guards remarked that 'now Gort had arrived this agreeable scene and sector would certainly lose its character';[51] (they were right, for Gort was never passive, affirming that the purpose of being there was to fight the enemy). Likewise, another Guards officer intimated his unit sometimes held peacetime sectors: 'I honestly believe that our Commanding Officer looked upon trench duty as a period of idleness to be drastically remedied immediately the Battalion was behind the lines'.[52] Nevertheless, there is no doubt that élite divisions were generally more active than others, and, in the winter of 1915/16—the time of Haking's memo—the Guards division was aggressive enough to elicit from the army commander, Sir Henry Rawlinson, a special letter of commendation which referred in particular to the division's raiding patrols, 'This shows that a commendable spirit of enterprise exists . . . It is evident that the division has established a moral ascendancy over the enemy which is of the highest value, and I desire to compliment them on their good work'.[53]

But other divisions were less impressed by the official view of health and wholesomeness and were more pressured by their commanders. In the 9th division during spring 1916, Winston Churchill noted the quiet of the line and, further, that the general, 'means to stir them up';[54] the divisional history recorded of the time that:

> General Furse strove to foster the offensive spirit throughout the division, so sections were known as 'fighting' sections, to impress upon each man that his principal duty was to fight. He exhorted all the battalions to make 'No-Man's Land' 'Ninth Division Land' . . . Every night the area in front of the battalions in the line was actively and persistently patrolled. But this was not enough for the G.O.C.; he wanted the men to secure prisoners; 'Corpses are more important than acres' was his constant injunction . . . All ranks realised and never forgot that on taking over trenches it was not their job to sit still and wait for things to happen, but to devise enterprises to worry the enemy as much as possible.[55]

In the same way the 55th divisional commander ordered his men 'To harass the enemy as much as possible, to keep him ever on the alert, to lose no opportunity of inflicting casualties upon him';[56] while in the 41st division an officer watched while a truce disappeared after the 'Divisional commander issued one of his periodical orders that the enemy must be harassed and allowed no rest'.[57]

Divisional commanders had more opportunities than army or corps commanders for personal contact with fighting men, and the spoken word, either in informal or formal situations, often supplemented the written order. For instance, the commander of the 24th division gave a lecture to gunners in which 'The idea he emphasised was that . . . we must kill every armed German on every possible occasion'.[58] More informally, the 48th division commander gave impromptu pep talks during his trench tours:

> Every soldier in the division got to know that 'Fanny' spent more days in the front line than any of them. He was easy and pleasant spoken and liked to drift into a trench wearing an old raincoat so that men were not intimidated . . . One of his favourite gambits was to encourage sentries in the front line to complain about their discomfort. Then he would quietly chip in: 'The Germans over there have got very good dugouts. You can go and take them as soon as you like'.[59]

Some divisional commanders and other higher commanders offered money rewards for acts demonstrating the offensive spirit; thus the commander of the 63rd division held out a prize of five pounds to the first man to take a prisoner—a sum which the battalion commander of the 2/Honourable Artillery Company, an infantry unit despite its name—promised to double.[60]

An infantry officer himself, the historian of the 33rd division declared that brigadiers were regimental soldiers, promoted from command of companies and battalions and, further, that 'nearly every action proves it was a Brigadiers' war'.[61] Whether he was referring to battles, trench war, or both is not clear; but certainly some brigadiers—especially thrusters—had both a profound influence upon trench war and, in some divisions, a special responsibility for stimulating the offensive spirit.[62] Brigadier General Studd was a typical thruster, and impressed upon his brigade, before it went into the line for the first time, a firm idea of what trench war was all about. According to a battalion history, Studd:

> Laid down very clearly the object which all ranks must definitely set before them as long as they were in the line. That object must

be obtained at whatever cost. The Boche must be made to feel his moral inferiority. No opportunity must be lost of impressing on him that he was only there on sufferance, and until such time as we chose to advance and drive him out. No-man's-land must be denied to his patrols. His miners must be outwitted and outmanoeuvered; weak spots in his trenches must be covered by our snipers; his machine guns must be located as soon as they fired and must be knocked out by our artillery; his gunners must be put in mortal terror of our bombardments. His very life must be a burden to him. And all the time, by active patrolling and work with the Lewis gun, rifle and bomb, we must be cultivating in ourselves the aggressive spirit . . . Only second in importance to aggressive morale—and in a sense contributory to it—unceasing work in our own trenches, dugouts . . . There was no illusion, either in the mind of the Brigadier or in the minds of the men, as to what the translation of these two objects into practical soldiering would mean. So long as the battalion was in the line there could be little sleep or rest for anybody, and the men would need . . . to have a weapon in the left hand . . . [and] . . . a shovel in the right.[63]

As we have seen, all higher commanders could, and did, issue such orders, although perhaps in less vehement tone, but Brigadier Studd as a brigade commander was better located than army, corps and divisional commanders to ensure orders were carried out. Being the least of higher commanders, brigadiers had the narrowest span of control, and therefore more opportunity than others for personal supervision and scrutiny of front lines. For example, Brigadier Crozier, another model thruster, quickly found out, by frequent face-to-face contact, the inactive among company officers and battalion commanders in his brigade, and just as quickly replaced them with thrusters;[64] Crozier, moreover, made a practice of personally patrolling no-man's-land.[65] Such personal constraint was used not only by brigadiers but also by brigade staff officers, such as the brigade major who was the leading spirit behind raids made by units of the 76th Brigade.[66]

Brigade was part of high command's system of impersonal control since, with little personal contact, it transmitted orders to lower fighting formations; at the same time brigade control was relatively personal since brigadiers and their staffs more than other higher commanders mixed with trench fighters in face to face situations, as we have seen. Neverthless, all high command control meant non-combatants issuing orders to combatants, where the lives of the latter but not of the former were endangered by execution of these orders. Trench fighters viewed this arrangement as not only impersonal but also inhuman and unjust.

So far in this chapter several elements of the impersonal system controlling aggression in phase two of trench war have been identified, namely, specialised technology; the greater force of high command directives after the technology was installed; the energetic administration of trench war by thrusters positioned at all levels of high command. Statistical records were another part of this system of control. Combatants were required to keep exact accounts of the aggression of their own as well as enemy units, and these records were then channelled upwards and rearwards to the mandarins. Statistical records were a mechanism of control, because they were collated by generals who compared the fighting activity of one battalion, brigade or division with another. Where records revealed offensive spirit lacking in a unit, it was pressured still further. Reports had been sent to high command throughout 1915, but these were not always frequent, detailed or mandatory and were therefore deficient as a means of control. But the system changed radically in 1916 when high command decreed 'periodical situation reports are required from units in the trenches at stated hours, usually at morning, noon and evening '.[67] In respect of reports, an officer of the 49th division described the difference between the first and second phases of trench war thus, 'the highly organised system of reports, which in later days was a perpetual worry to luckless adjutants and company commanders, had not yet developed. If a company commander wanted to sent out a patrol he simply sent one; he never dreamed of informing battalion H.Q. much less of asking its permission or submitting a report after the event'.[68] This referred to trench warfare in summer 1915, and exactly how organised reports were in the 33rd division in 1916 was told by a Royal Welch Fusilier: 'the company commander had to make daily returns to brigade: a.m.—3.30, one; 8.30, one; 11.30, one; p.m.—3, one; 7, three; 10, two indents. Besides daily battalion returns, occasional returns and reports were called for by both brigade and battalion'.[69] In autumn 1916 in the same division, the 5/Scottish Rifles grumbled that 'Intelligence reports set in with their usual intensity . . . the brigade intelligence officer insisted on having more material for his flights of deduction than the laconic and customary report of "enemy quiet"'";[70] an 11th division officer concurred that in 1916, 'Great stress was laid on the necessity for full intelligence reports', and added, 'enquiries were instituted when companies sent in "nothing to report"'.[71] 'A case of trench feet', an officer of the 16th division remarked with irony, 'will provoke far more correspondence and censure than a heavy casualty list, which provokes none at all'.[72] A trench foot was swollen, sometimes frost-bitten, but always painful, yet it indicated low morale and possible inertia to high command; whereas a high casualty list indicated a battalion's fighting spirit.

Written reports from the front line were therefore frequent, imperative and had to contain detailed accounts of affrays under-taken, otherwise sanctions followed. It was the same on the other side of the wire, and a German historian argued that the soldier's zeal for fighting diminished when he had to write out reports after action;[73] but this view neglected the control function of reports. No doubt the fighting efficacy of élite units like the 2/Royal Welch was not helped by what they termed 'wind'; for units inclined to live and let live, however, such reports were one more constraint towards aggression.

The present chapter has suggested that the personal, regimental control of aggression typical of trench war of the first phase was replaced in the second phase by an impersonal control. The change was from local to central regulation where the producers of violence no longer directed its disposition. Non-combatants had alienated control of violence from combatants who perceived them as an external, alien group, unaware of the realities of trench war, and uncaring of trench fighters' needs. What this centralised constraint meant in actual events such as raiding and patrolling, can be seen in the diary of General Jack. It will be recalled that in 1915, raids and patrols were *ad hoc* tactics, often originated at battalion level; but at the start of 1916, raiding was judged by Douglas Haig as a primary tactic of trench war, and thus subject to special scrutiny. Jack, a company commander in January 1915, wrote then in his diary: 'Tonight my lance corporal and I perform another minor recon-naissance. When the nights are suitable the company sends a small patrol into No-Man's-Land, always with a definite, even if unimportant mission'.[74] The company's choice to patrol was spontaneous and local and made where an alternative—to remain inert—was possible; patrolling was the response of a good battalion, expressing and reinforcing its sense of honour. But eighteen months later, that is, in the second phase, no alternative existed. 'We have orders to patrol actively', wrote Jack, now a battalion commander, 'My patrol leaders understand that I trust them to do their best, but nothing stupidly rash. When they are going in front with their men on important missions I take post in the advance trench . . . to be responsible if high command are dissatisfied with the endeavour'.[75] There was no choice here. The order was not only to patrol but to patrol and get results, else high command wanted to know why.

Jack's diary also illustrates the centralisation of control over raiding. In December 1914, his battalion was ordered to raid the enemy, but conditions were so unfavourable that the battalion commander and the brigadier protested with vigour to higher authority, who thereupon cancelled the raid.[76] Probably, such a protest would not have been successful in and after 1916, or if it had, the protester would have been sent home for lacking the aggressive spirit; for instance, in summer 1916, high command ordered the 11/ Royal Sussex to raid, whereupon the battalion commander, a Colonel Grisewood, 'demurred, was disposed of, and another battalion was forced to lose the lives which ignorance and arrogance cost'.[77] High command inflexibility in respect of raids is shown by an entry in Jack's diary, describing a raid which occurred in 1916 when he was a battalion commander: 'At 9.30 p.m. the raiding party of 24 . . . assembles in the front trench, where I take post . . . the group proceeds noiselessly in single file through a gap in our wire until its head is about 30 yards from the German gap to be entered'; at this point the raiding plan went awry, and the raiders sent back one of their number to Jack, who had then to make a quick decision: 'It is intensely difficult to decide what to do next. The operation has been especially ordered by high command, and prepared. If we make no attempt we shall likely have to carry it out on another night, perhaps under peremptory orders and under less favourable conditions.' Jack decided on a hazardous *ad hoc* scheme which also aborted and he entered in his diary, 'This wretched affair concludes at 2 a.m. . . . I do not finish my reports on the operation till 3 o'clock'.[78] This account shows clearly the diminished discretion of front line commanders with respect to raiding in 1916. According to Jack, the raid was ordered by high command; was planned by high command; could not be cancelled by a battalion commander, even where unexpected and adverse circumstances arose; finally, detailed reports had to be prepared immediately.

As we have shown, centralised constraints were unique neither to

Jack's battalion nor to division but prevailed throughout phase two, applying indiscriminately to élite and other units. From early in 1916, raiding became an ordinary duty of battalions,[79] or, as a Royal Welch Fusilier put it, 'Every self-respecting battalion will want to raid, the others will be ordered'.[80] The pressure to raid came from the very apex of high command, and was conveyed onwards and downwards to combatant level. Shortly after assuming command of the B.E.F., Haig instituted a weekly army commanders' conference, which not only furthered good understanding between Haig and army commanders but also was a control whereby G.H.Q. made sure armies conformed to the raiding policy. In turn, army and corps pressured divisions. During winter 1916–17, the 5th division historian affirmed, 'Higher authorities ordained that all through the winter the Germans were to be harassed in every possible way. Constant patrolling on no-man's-land and at least two raids in each division every week was the order';[81] of spring 1916, the historian of the 17th division disclosed that 'a division that did not report a number of raids each month was regarded as showing slackness and want of zeal'.[82] Likewise, brigades were pressured by divisions, and Brigadier Croft was urged to make raids by visiting staff officers, who invidiously compared his brigade's raiding record with that of other brigades.[83]

5

A sequence is now emerging in the narrative. At the start of trench war, live and let live often occurred as overt fraternisation and orally arranged truces. But these were highly visible and thus vulnerable to high command, who countered with legal action against identifiable persons involved in identifiable truces. Live and let live, however, adapted to these counter-measures, by evolving from an overt to a covert form, namely, inertia. The meaning of inertia among antagonists, that is the choice of non-aggression where aggression was possible, was something like: we'll forgo firing if you'll do likewise. Such a choice was simultaneously an act of peace and communication and, further, a background assumption of quiet fronts, shared and understood by all seasoned soldiers. It evolved spontaneously, not conspiratorially, as adversaries with like interests in like situations interacted in trenches. Inertia was a simple yet subtle truce but difficult to counter; nevertheless during 1916, and after, high command managed, in the words of Charles Sorley, to 'bang together' the heads of reluctant fighters. The specialisation of the means of violence, the theme of Chapter 3, and the centralisation of control over violence, the theme of the last chapter, were counter-measures which hemmed in trench fighters with constraints making aggression ever more difficult to avoid. The bureaucratically controlled specialised technology of the second phase diminished the discretion of trench fighters, rendering inertia a less likely, and aggression a more likely, choice of action. The machinery of violence was now installed, and the war experience assumed a new dimension.

The next question is clear: does the sequence end at this point? Was the effect of technology and central control enough to prevent peace once and for all? Or did live and let live adapt to the new conditions of 1916? My theme is that men were not puppets of war, quite powerless before events; but active against events, over which some control was sought. Moreover, the constant search for control partly answers the problem: how did men endure the war? Thus I shall argue that live and let live did not disappear but re-emerged in yet another form.

The present chapter divides into three parts: firstly, I shall discuss the general principle behind the new form of peace; secondly, this will be illustrated in respect of two different types of weapons and activities; finally, I shall try to estimate the size of live and let live, that is, the ratio of peace to war exchanges—of active to quiet fronts—for the war generally.

The term 'quiet' or 'cushy' applied to a sector could mean either a lack of aggression or of its animating spirit or of both. Mutual aggression was sometimes zealous and sometimes not, and where it was not, the sources characterise fighting as 'perfunctory', 'desultory', 'spasmodic', 'conventional', or routine. This distinction concerns the somewhat puzzling comments made by trench fighters about certain sectors, for example, one reads of the disturbance or interruption of the 'even tenor' and rhythm of trench war; but fire exchanges are disturbing and unpredictable since surprise is usually sought. Or consider a soldier describing a trench tour: 'We had shot a few hundred pounds of ammunition at each other but neither side had shown any real animosity or malice',[1]—if shooting at each other is not malice, what on earth is? Similarly, another soldier describes a German bombardment, 'He [the Germans] means business this morning . . . not the usual morning strafe . . . there's been a smell of real spite in the air this morning'.[2] Is it possible that some shells are spiteful and some not? Real 'animosity' or 'spite' denoted earnest aggression as on active fronts, but 'desultory' aggression was something different; in both cases, weapons were fired but in the latter case fired in a 'routine' way only. Edmund Blunden referred to this perfunctory aggression of quiet sectors as 'ritual',[3] and the process of ritualisation was both an undertone of war and an adaptation of live and let live to the changed conditions of the second phase. The ritualisation of aggression is defined as compliance with official patterns of fighting activity, either with deliberate disregard of, or without due regard for, its intended purpose—to inflict loss upon the enemy.

Although social factors in phase two constrained soldiers to harass the enemy more than before, the situation was not a simple dilemma where a combatant reasoned: either I aggress the enemy and suffer retaliation, or I remain inert and risk high command sanctions. There was a third choice—ritualisation—where trench fighters acted on the assumption that: if I aggress the enemy in a way which causes him no harm, he will probably return the favour. Where such tacit expectancies were collectively held on a front, a milieu emerged like that depicted by an officer of the 38th division, 'The firing could rightly be described as desultory, for there was little desire on either side to create trouble; some rounds must of course be fired, otherwise questions would follow'.[4] The author elsewhere wrote of the same time and sector, 'Despite the fulminations of the Generals, the infantry was in no mood for offensive measures, and it was obvious that, on both sides, rifles and machine guns were aimed high'.[5]

Ritualised aggression was superficially consistent with the letter but certainly not with the spirit of high command orders; moreover, front line commanders could exchange peace with the enemy, who reciprocally ritualised his retaliatory fire, while simultaneously sending records of fighting activity to high command. In one sense, such reports were truthful, accurate accounts of bombs and bullets shot off but in another were misleading because non-ritualised and ritualised fire were not distinguished.

According to the weapons and tactics involved, ritualisation was manifest as one of two general types: either it was perfunctory tactic and weapon use, or routinisation; the former was connected with small arms and close combat, and the latter with artillery and trench-mortars, and each, in turn, will be examined below.

Ritualised aggression was, of course, a means of communication among antagonists as well as a form of live and let live. Communication had occurred in other truce types, either by written word and word of mouth or as certain actions acquired a new meaning when antagonists interacted in trenches, such as when inertia emerged as a symbol of peace in 1915. It seems logical that inertia might come to mean peace, for one's actions when inert correspond more to peace than war; but it appears illogical, if not impossible, that one could convey to another a wish for peace at the same time as assaulting him with bullet and bomb, for by its nature a bursting bomb seems unable to symbolise benevolence. Paradoxically, ritualised aggression achieved precisely this, for it functioned as a communication system, comprising a continuous series of reciprocal acts among antagonists, where each seemingly hostile action symbolised peace not war.

The principle underlying such communication was simple. All experienced trench fighters knew that weapons could be used either lethally or superficially, and one antagonist could infer from the way another operated a weapon, whether the latter preferred war or peace. For instance, if A persistently fired a weapon at B without regard for range and accuracy, that is, with no 'real animosity' or 'malice', without 'real spite' and perhaps 'aimed high', then B attributed A's lack of zeal to choice not chance, for the choice of accurate fire was always possible. By ritualised weapon use, A signalled a wish for peace to B, and if B was of the same mind as A, he reciprocated and ensured that A was not harmed in the subsequent exchange of ritualised fire. Thus, with the most unlikely of means, either adversary could communicate the inclination to live and let live to the other, which, if and when required, established a mutually reinforcing series of peace exchanges. What an outsider might perceive as a small battle, entirely consistent with the active front policy, might be in fact merely a structure of ritualised aggression, where missiles symbolised benevolence not malevolence, and where the constant flow of ritualised bombs and bullets caused neither anxiety nor harm but, on the contrary, gave to each antagonist constant reassurance of the other's peaceful disposition.

Of course, this account of the principle of ritualisation over-simplifies the reality, inasmuch as trench war comprised many different weapons, and to each of these there corresponded a particular ritual as well as proper usage, although, as stated above, two general types of ritualisation can be discerned. Ritualisation appeared in many forms, and while the ways of mishandling weapons varied with their nature, the meaning of mishandling was everywhere similar to trench fighters, namely, the disposition for peace. In the rest of this chapter the different modes of ritualisation of infantry and artillery are illustrated, and these illustrations will show that ritualisation was endemic to trench war, constantly recurring at different times and places on the western front. The analysis starts with that general type of ritual associated with small arms and close combat—perfunctory tactic and weapon use—and examines how fighting patrols were ritualised.

A battalion commander declared that the principle impressed upon patrols was, 'Always engage the enemy when he is close at hand', and his battalion certainly practised what he preached; for instance, one patrol set out to capture a prisoner from either a German patrol or working party but could find neither so, undeterred, it crawled to a German trench and bombed that instead.[6] Many patrols were

models of initiative and aggression, such as the daylight patrol in the
42nd division whose members were rewarded by high command
with four days leave for capturing a hostile German mortar and its
garrison.[7] But other patrols were of a different sort, and contact with
the enemy was deliberately avoided. Such patrol avoidance was a
form of ritualisation—the perfunctory performance of a tactic—
and is mentioned in several sources as a general practice. Avoidance
assumed two main forms: firstly, the avoidance of hostilities when
patrols encountered each other in no-man's-land, and secondly, the
avoidance of situations where such encounters were most probable.

The first form was described by Charles Sorley of the 12th
division:

> All patrols—English and German—are much averse to the death
> or glory principle; so, on running up against one
> another . . . both pretend that they are Levites and the other is a
> Good Samaritan—and pass by on the other side, no word spoken.
> For either side to bomb the other would be a useless violation of
> the unwritten laws that govern the relations of combatants
> permanently within a hundred yards of each other.[8]

These 'unwritten laws' were also observed by a battalion of the 41st
division, 'Patrols were now constantly out under junior subalterns
in no-man's-land examining the enemy's wire . . . occasionally
similar Boche patrols could be detected by our own. Each would
give the other a wide berth'.[9] Even in the élite 7th division, we find
Sassoon, himself an aggressive patroller, commenting that 'patrols
had a sensible habit of avoiding personal contact with one
another';[10] in the 6th division, however, the skill of a patrol
specialist was noted, 'Mostyn was always aggressive; the policy of
"crossing to the other side of the road" on sighting someone whose
looks were not liked was not his',[11] yet mention of the custom
showed awareness of its existence and practice.

The cases above, which refer to night patrols, suggest both British
and Germans on quiet sectors assumed that should a chance face-to-
face encounter occur, neither patrol would initiate aggression, but
each would move to avoid the other. Each patrol gave peace to the
other where aggression was not only possible, but also prescribed,
provided, of course, the gesture was reciprocated, for if one patrol
fired so would the other. Such assumptions also operated during

daytime; for instance, Herbert Read, serving with the 21st division, was on patrol with two men:

> we suddenly confronted, round some mound or excavation, a German patrol . . . we were perhaps twenty yards from each other, fully visible. I waved a weary hand, as if to say: what is the use of killing each other? The German officer seemed to understand, and both parties turned and made their way back to their own trenches. Reprehensible conduct, no doubt.[12]

Read saw this as a sign of war weariness on both sides, which is consistent with our interpretation; for war weariness was a complex of attitudes and actions, both individual and social, of which live and let live was one form. But high command would have found less fault with Herbert Read than with soldiers of the 33rd division, who evolved an intricate plan of avoidance on a sector where a straight road crossed no-man's-land, intersecting both British and German front lines; on either side and parallel to this road was a ditch. The British patrol crawled along one ditch and the German patrol the other, and, when both reached the middle of no-man's-land, one or other patrol raised up a helmet on a rifle, which signal was repeated by the other patrol. Avoidance thus established and understood, both patrols sat down and waited, repeating at intervals the signals of reassurance. After a credible time had elapsed, both patrols returned to their respective trenches, and no doubt the Germans—like the British—reported all was quiet.[13]

The second type of avoidance, namely, avoidance of areas where hostile patrols were most likely to meet, involved a simple manoeuvre which diminished chances of encounters: a patrol went forward into no-man's-land for a few yards only, and it then turned to either left or right, and moved parallel with its own trenches, thus avoiding the middle of no-man's-land and the area in front of enemy trenches. Ian Hay said that at night, 'there exists an informal truce founded on the principle of live and let live', and, further, that enemy patrols were ignored unless they behaved 'too boldly' and came close to the British line, when 'there is a little exuberance from a machine gun'.[14] Similarly, a private soldier of the 47th division wrote, 'At night . . . I saw figures moving out by the enemy trenches . . . we never fired at those shadows, and they never fired at us; it is unwise to break the tacit truces of the trenches'.[15]

Patrol avoidance was not, however, always this simple, especially if patrol leaders were either new officers, or determined to attack; nevertheless these were sometimes managed by old soldiers. As one sergeant wise in such matters explained:

> You get your orders, an' they make up . . . a plan; but that's all eyewash. You've got to forget all that . . . an' make your own arrangements . . . I've taken out quite a lot of officers now . . . pretty decent chaps as a rule. They draw up a plan, an' they ask me . . . an' see if its all right. It's all right, sir, I always say to 'em; you just bring it in at th' orderly room, an' we'll do what's possible. Only one officer gave me any trouble . . . 'e were a bastard, . . . Military Cross an' bar; regular pot hunter; an' we lost one of the best corporals we ever had through that bloody man. Wouldn't be told, 'e wouldn't.[16]

Some idea of what seasoned trench fighters 'told' such officers, and how conspiracies were hatched so that 'unwritten laws' remained intact, is given by an N.C.O. of the 55th division:

> More new officers came. The patrollers had no compunction in curbing their enthusiasm in a way that usually made the sergeant grin and turn a blind eye. The whittled stumps that had once been a hedge . . . were pointed out as the wire in front of the German trench. Parties of the enemy working in front were invented; at prearranged signals messages of caution passed from both forward flanks to the officer in the centre . . . most subalterns tempered their pugnacity with discretion . . . on their return to the front line the officer would sometimes throw out a feeler: 'What does one say on these occasions?' . . . (the patrollers) . . . would reply: 'Well sir, I should suggest there was a strong wiring party out mending the wire, and that on ascertaining their strength you withdrew the patrol and asked for a Lewis gun strafe'.[17]

The same N.C.O. told of an amusing event where an officer decided against the judgement of his men to make a retaliatory patrol. The patrol had set off into no-man's-land when one of their number— the N.C.O.—noticed the absence of another—his friend Walker; shortly after this, a cough was heard, and the patrol stopped, listened but was waved on by the officer. The N.C.O. continued:

Another cough, almost peremptory. A stoppage; a whispered conversation. The idea came to me, as we stood there undecided, that a lonesome Jerry lurked . . . afraid of engaging us, yet urgently desirous of turning our head. And turn we did. A retaliating fighting patrol, purpose defeated by two coughs! Before we had reached our wire again, Walker gained my side. I heard him chuckling, but not until afterwards did it dawn on me what he had done: the biggest spoof ever.[18]

Just how widespread was patrol ritualisation? One can only speculate, but my impression is that it occurred in all except élite units for some of the time. Unfortunately, the question cannot be answered by official records, since ritualised patrols entailed ritualised reports as the following makes clear: an order to patrol was given to a subaltern of the 17th division, who thought it a 'plain invitation to suicide'; he talked with his sympathetic company commander, and they jointly decided, 'I'd better go out and make a show, and together we'll cook the report'. The subaltern duly returned after a ritualised patrol and, 'Down in the dug-out Rowley [the company commander] and I write a report that is as near as lying as can be without falsehood'.[19] The cooked report would have been sent to battalion H.Q. and transmitted in summary form to brigade H.Q. Brigadier Crozier of the 40th division confirmed that in 1917, 'It became increasingly difficult as time went on, to obtain correct reports from officer patrols',[20] and he took measures against ritualisation, 'it was my habit to order samples of German wire to be cut and brought back by officers on patrol . . . [thus] . . . one would know that the German wire had been visited;[21] similarly, in the 55th division, the brigadier 'insisted that samples of the German wire be brought back . . . [as] . . . proof that a patrol had crossed no-man's-land'.[22]

But these measures could be evaded, as in the anecdote told by one private soldier to another of the 14th division going to the front for the first time. The first soldier had been a member of a patrol ordered by an officer to bring back a piece of enemy wire as proof of its zeal. In no-man's-land the patrol found a coil of German wire which was brought back and placed in a sap just in front of the British line, and the patrol leader snipped off a piece of wire and gave both this and a cooked report to the officer. The next night the order was repeated, and the patrol sloped off to the nearby sap for a smoke and chat, after which genuine wire and fictitious report were again given to the officer. The old soldier concluded, 'That went on every night and the old man never knew we had a coil of Jerry wire on our side'.[23] Such a tale rings true in the context of our theme, but hearsay must be treated with caution; on the other hand, anecdotes may concern more general practices, and such could have been the case here, for Brigadier Crozier confirms that a similar custom existed in his command where some officers kept a coil of German wire in a dug-out and sent a piece to Crozier when he asked for proof of patrol efficiency.[24] The German army had its troubles as well, and A.F. Vieth von Golssenau, an experienced company commander and regimental adjutant, affirmed that the custom of cooking reports was a symptom of the rift between front and rear.[25]

We now move on from patrol to weapon ritualisation. Previously, it was observed that the nature of a weapon determined the manner of its ritualisation, and weapons are grouped for purposes of analysis into small arms and others. Small arms here include machine-guns—Vickers and Lewis; rifles—sniping and ordinary; and hand-grenades. The common circumstance which each shared, and which produced a similar mode of ritualisation, was that small arms were lethal only against exposed persons, and not against persons protected by trenches; whereas larger weapons—artillery and mortars—could be deadly against persons whether protected by trenches, dug-outs or whatever. The ritualisation of small arms is described first and that of large weapons later.

We have examined the potential fire power of specialised small arms technology along a battalion front, and it was massive. On active fronts the least exposure of the body—or part of it—during daytime resulted in almost certain death or injury: 'none save the very rash would dare to thrust his head over the top, for the snipers on both sides were appallingly quick',[26] said a soldier as noted above, and similar comments emphasising the danger of revealing one's body outside of the trenches abound in war literature. On the other hand, on quiet fronts, disclosure to the enemy's view, whether by chance or design, was by no means deadly, for the rules of active and quiet fronts were quite different. The principle of small arms ritualisation was as simple as it was effective: the weapon was fired either with intent to miss the target or in such a perfunctory way that a hit was more a matter of chance than decision. On quiet fronts , 'rifles and machine guns were aimed high',[27] as happened after an abortive 1915 Christmas truce, and this form of ritualisation appeared in the war at least as early as the 1914 Christmas truce. For instance, on the 4th division sector a truce had been prolonged for a week, during which time the German high command visited the line, and in order to prevent generals from discovering the truce, the Germans told the British of the visit and explained they must open fire with machine-guns, 'but would aim high well above our [the British] heads'; at the appointed time a British soldier witnessed, 'the flash of Spandau machine guns well above no-man's-land'.[28] In the 8th division one unit struck up a truce with the enemy and arranged 'that the truce should be ended at midnight by the simultaneous firing, very high, of all rifles so that there might be no casualties'.[29] But whatever its origin, this form of ritualisation recurred throughout 1915 and increasingly thereafter, and in the second phase of trench war, the most frequently found form of live and let live was a mixture of ritualisation and inertia.

Small arms ritualisation is indicated by two types of evidence: firstly, the sources directly refer to either the general practice of ritualisation, or a specific act; the second type—of which there are two subtypes—consists of descriptions of sectors where the degree of unrestricted movement by soldiers both within and without the trenches was entirely inconsistent with zealous weapon use by the enemy. It must be stressed that where these weapons were used properly with but a modicum of skill, trench fighters could neither leave nor show themselves above ground in front or support trenches, nor walk in areas in between without risk of death or injury. On the other hand, unrestricted movement in and out of trenches can be explained by one of several reasons: where a truce had been arranged verbally for a specific purpose such as aiding the wounded; where a shortage of small arms ammunition existed;[30] where in the half-light of daybreak one side remained above ground unaware they were visible to the enemy. But where a source records unrestricted movement and gives none of these reasons—nor any other—it can be assumed that free movement was related to either ritualisation or inertia or both.

Let us look at the direct evidence first. While inspecting the front line, two officers of the 41st division witnessed what was termed an 'experienced piece of window dressing'. The battalion history describes the incident in detail:

> All was quiet . . . when suddenly . . . [there was a] . . . terrific
> bang of split air . . . They [the officers] heard a cockney voice

announce in tones of disgust 'B . . . it, missed him'. Looking around, they discovered one of the battalion's snipers peering ostentatiously through his glasses from the parados at the Hun front line . . . a month or two later, the effect of this little piece of eyewash was nullified.

Some time then elapsed during which hostilities damaged both British and German lines. The history tells that while inspecting the damage with his officers, the colonel:

> much to his disgust discovered that not a shot was being fired at the enemy as they dodged across the gaps in their trench. They in their turn, . . . were allowing our men to cross the gaps in our trench without molestation. This was too much for the colonel . . . The first sentry he came across happened to be the sniper . . . now . . . returned to duty with his company. He received the full blast of the colonel's indignation: 'Man alive, what are you there for? Don't you see these Huns?' To which the sentry diffidently replied: 'I ain't a sniper now, sir'.[31]

This anecdote directly refers to the 'eyewash' function of ritualised aggression, namely, to convince authority the front line was active and not inert. In the illustration, the attempt was immediately perceived as ritualisation, although the term was not used; however, it is possible that brigade might have been deceived by a written report claiming a fictitious victim as real.

But the dual function of ritualisation was to convey not only aggression to high command, but also peace to the enemy. How the bullet of our sniper was construed by the Germans is not known for certain, but the meaning of bullets fired by German snipers at other times has been recorded by British trench fighters. 'The one enemy activity with which the battalion had to contend was sniping . . . Not all of it was in deadly earnest. On the left the Germans amused themselves by aiming at spots on the walls of cottages, and firing until they had cut a hole. Our men said, Fritz had to be chummy, he had a brewery working just behind him'.[32] The meaning of ritualised sniping, namely, that bullets did not symbolise animosity, was clear to the British. Moreover, the explanation was not merely facetious, for it referred to the exchange among antagonists: on the one hand, the British were threatening, if you snipe too much we'll bust your brewery; on the other, the Germans were reasoning, if you

leave our brewery be we'll keep on shooting badly. Always an acute
observer of undertones, Ian Hay, soon after his arrival at the front,
commented on the discrepancy between the acknowledged skill of
German snipers, and the degree of unrestricted movement allowed
to British soldiers working on trench maintenance at night:

> No one was hit, which was remarkable, when you consider what
> an artist a German sniper is . . . possibly there is some truth in
> the general rumour that the Saxons, who hold this part of the
> line . . . conduct their offensive operations with a tactful blend of
> constant firing and bad shooting, which while it satisfies the
> Prussians causes no serious inconvenience to Thomas Atkins.[33]

Machine-gun fire was also ritualised, 'all was quiet save the
stammer of a Lewis gun firing at the enemy's rear lines to conceal
our lack of activity'.[34] In this example the dual role of ritualised
aggression is again clear: the eyewash is explicitly acknowledged,
and one understands how ritualised fire conveyed to Germans the
British wish to exchange peace. The next illustration shows that not
only was hand-bombing ritualised, but ritualisation also occurred
on both French and British sectors: 'Some of our saps are less than
ten yards apart. At first we threw bombs at each other, but then we
agreed not to throw any more . . . If a Frenchman had orders to
throw bombs several times during the night, he agreed with his
German "comrade" to throw them to the left and right of the
trench.'[35]

The indirect and circumstantial evidence for ritualisation consists
of material indicating a degree of personal movement around and
within trenches, incompatible with proper small arms use by the
enemy. Where a source records such movement without explanation, except that it occurred on a quiet front, one can infer that
either ritualisation or inertia or both existed. In 1915 such
movement might have meant inertia only, but later probably
revealed a mixture of ritualisation and inertia, since, in phase two,
inactivity must be concealed and some shots had to be fired: 'It is all
quiet, so much so that we are told to develop the offensive
spirit . . . Each man must fire twenty rounds per noctem'[36] wrote a
platoon commander in 1916; most likely these shots were fired
either in a desultory way, or to miss the enemy, thus allowing him
freedom of movement and preserving the peace meanwhile.

The sources show that the degree of free movement each

antagonist allowed the other varied between sectors, although on individual sectors the freedom given by British to German—and conversely—was roughly equivalent, because a stable exchange relationship requires each party to give and take in roughly equal proportions.[37] Two types of indirect evidence signified ritualisation: firstly, where antagonists are described as walking openly above trenches, one can infer that each side deliberately and reciprocally fired either high or wide to cause no injury to the other; secondly, where combatants clearly had a degree of free movement, safety and comfort in trenches, far exceeding that on active fronts, one can likewise infer that weapons, while not deliberately aimed to miss, were fired in such dilatory fashion that any injury to the enemy was caused by chance and not design.

The first type of evidence is found in an account of a divisional relief where the 20th replaced the 40th division in the line. The narrator, a 20th-division brigade staff officer, made a preliminary tour of the line accompanied by his brigadier, and both walked for a mile along a deep communication trench which led into the front line. The staff officer remarked:

> we were astonished to observe German soldiers walking about within rifle range behind their own line. Our men appeared to take no notice. I privately made up my mind to do away with that sort of thing when we took over; such things should not be allowed. These people evidently did not know there was a war on. Both sides apparently believed in the policy of 'live and let live'.

During their return both officers ignored the communication trench and walked over the top. Witin a few days, the author's brigade was in the line:

> the front was so quiet that it was difficult to restrain the men from walking about on the top . . . Time passed very peacefully, as the Germans were very quiet. My battalion snipers had the time of their lives . . . We literally kept a game book of hits for the first three days; after that the Germans did not show themseves so much; also they started to retaliate. Wiring was carried out every night, but not on the style we were accustomed to . . . Our men did not creep through the wire carrying coils of wire, stakes etc., instead a general service wagon was driven into no-man's-land with materials on board, which were dumped out . . . at first we

expected bursts of machine gun fire . . . but, nothing happened.
It must have become a well established custom, as the enemy did
the same thing themselves; we did not interfere.[38]

There is little doubt that ritualisation and inertia comprehensively prevailed before the 20th division took over. Each side
probably fired some shots, as a matter of form, and in such a way
that the other was not harmed. The above excerpt has interest for
other reasons. Firstly, it suggests live and let live meant different
things to different units; for despite the author's disclaimer, the
20th, as well as the 40th division, exchanged peace: the two divisions
differed not in respect of whether the practice was permitted, but in
which activities the practice was allowed. The 40th division
ritualised small arms fire across the board by night and day, whereas
the 20th did so at night, and only in some activities. Officially,
however, truces in respect of any activity at any time or place were
forbidden. For example, while the 20th division carried on
customary nightly truces with enemy working parties, in similar
circumstances the élite 7th division harassed the enemy: 'our patrols
succeeded in discovering that the enemy made a practice of working
whenever we had working parties out . . . One night therefore after
our parties had started working they were quietly withdrawn, fire
being then opened by rifles and machine guns, apparently with
excellent results'.[39] Secondly, the former illustration shows the
mutually contingent nature of live and let live: when the British
ended ritualised sniping, the Germans did likewise and retaliated—
exchanges of peace became exchanges of war.

The sectors where ritualisation concealed inactivity were not as
infrequent as might be supposed. For instance, in the 24th division,
a gunner, taken by an infantry officer to the front line, was

rather horrified to hear that it was . . . only twenty yards from a
German post. However, the subaltern . . . assured me that they
had a complete understanding with the Hun infantry, and that
we should not be sniped . . . we quickly reached the
place . . . and . . . my guide, pointed out a tree 30 yards off, and
said that the Hun sentry was there . . . neither side has any sign
of a trench—both are sitting in shell holes a few yards apart,
separated by nothing but a few yards of open ground.[40]

Obviously, the 'complete understanding' included all small arms—

rifles, machine-guns, and hand-bombs. On the 25th divisional front, it was neither foolhardiness nor *sang-froid*, but simply a wish to avoid discomfort that caused two horses and their riders to appear near no-man's-land one day. One horseman, a gunner officer, wrote:

> It is so peaceful that the other afternoon, having to go to Battalion H.Q. in the trenches and not wanting to push my way up a long communication trench, my groom and I rode together . . . [to] . . . H.Q. and though it is barely 500 yards from the Boche front line, not a bullet or shell came near us. But the infantry were rather surprised as they gazed up at us from below ground level. It was a funny feeling to be riding over trenches and through gaps in belts of barbed wire, knowing that hundreds of men, friend and foe, are there: yet with no sign of anything but a thin wisp of smoke rising from the Hun lines where someone is presumably frying sausages for tea.[41]

Of course, the two acts, that is, riding horses and frying sausages, were related, for both were concrete manifestations of the underlying exchange of peace.

Incidentally, this material well illustrates the two-way exchange between adversaries where each allowed the other to go about his business in safety, provided the other gave the same in return—exactly what this business was on the quiet front, we shall later examine. The two sides of exchange, that is, the give and the take, are sometimes explicit in war books but more often reciprocity is left implicit. For instance, give and take is fairly clear above, where the 20th-division officers returned over the trenches in full view of Germans, who were conforming to a commonsense rule of everyday life with which readers are familiar, namely, one should not harm persons who do one no harm. Similarly, in the second illustration, mutuality was explicit: the German sentry allowed the British to move freely, and the British in return did not aggress the German; the same applies to the sausages and the horses.

But some war books mention merely the take, that is, safety conferred by the enemy, and omit to mention the give—the reciprocal safety given to the enemy, and a one-sided account of war or peace then emerges. Thus in some sources frequent references to safety and quietness on one side are recorded, but nothing is said of the other side of the line. For instance, a 12th-division officer wrote:

'Early in October we left the Somme and took over the line north of Arras . . . We had been in some pretty quiet sectors in our time, but never in one so quiet as this . . . Even when we showed ourselves on the parapet no one fired at us'.[42] Nor did the enemy fire on the 15th-divisional front when 'fatigue parties walked along the parapet of Posen Ally in broad daylight'.[43] But had the British made themselves a nuisance the story would have been different.

Again, on the 30th-division front the German was 'quiet; he hardly ever did any shelling to count and all . . . were walking about with the greatest impunity. There were lots of places where you did not dare show yourself a month before . . . we had working parties of a hundred or more working in broad daylight and in full view, but he did not pay the slightest attention to them';[44] but this situation might have been very different if the British had paid attention to the Germans. On the front of the 56th division, not only could trenches be approached in daylight, but 'even when the enemy were able to detect a solitary vehicle they never took the trouble to fire at it';[45] and one officer of the 37th division recorded, 'I had the as yet unusual experience of relieving trenches in broad daylight . . . I led the No. 10 [platoon] . . . along a ridge in the full view of an uninterested German audience. But it did not matter. Nothing ever happened in this sector. It was so quiet'.[46] No doubt it was quiet, but if the British had begun to take an interest in German reliefs, it would have been reciprocated and the quiet shattered. Lord Reith wrote of another type of trench relief with complete personal exposure, 'while superintending the erection of . . . wire I was suddenly taken short . . . instead of going back to the trench, I went about 20 yards further out into no-man's-land'.[47] In conclusion, the point is that many war books assert that the front was quiet, and one must be mindful that fronts comprised two opponents, and quietness was part of the mutual exchange of peace, involving ritualisation and inertia; otherwise a background expectancy or undertone of war will elude the reader.

Earlier we distinguished two types of circumstantial evidence signifying ritualisation: unrestricted movement, and movement which, while restricted, was far more free than on active fronts where, 'you could not show a finger by daylight'.[48] The difference between unrestricted and partially unrestricted movement corresponds to the very quiet 'paradise',[49] or 'absolutely peaceful'[50] sectors   and   the   merely   quiet   sectors   mentioned   in

the sources. Hitherto, we have seen how ritualised aggression—
meaning deliberately firing high or wide—allowed unrestricted
movement on very quiet fronts, and next we shall look at how
ritualisation—meaning perfunctory weapon use rather than careful
misuse—allowed partial movement on quiet fronts. This occurred
where each side merely avoided provocative active front tactics,
seeking neither to create opportunities for aggression, nor to exploit
those existing; consequently, neither side needed to exercise
scrupulous care in trenches in order to avoid harm. Partially
unrestricted movement meant one could move quite freely within
front, support and communication trenches knowing the enemy
would not take advantage of accidental exposure or weakness in
trench defences. One could also crawl out of the trenches into the
grass behind to read a book, as did Blunden,[51] and it was safe
enough to show a finger or two and more. At the same time neither
side indulged the other so much that combatants could safely walk
along the parapet as on very quiet sectors. For instance, when two
Germans were seen digging in their line on a quiet front, an officer
commented, 'Their appearance was regarded as an impertinence
asking for target practice which promptly followed';[52] certainly, the
Germans thought it impertinent when Americans attached to the
41st division for instruction, 'exposed themselves unnecessarily even
to the extent of attempting to play cards on the parapet',[53] for their
guns fired though the front was quiet. Generally, on quiet fronts
movement was neither wholly restricted nor wholly unrestricted.
One trench fighter put it neatly, 'Our predecessors seem to have
had some arrangement with the Huns not to fire, for at first they
were very cheeky, and their working parties came out right into the
open in broad daylight. A shot or two put that right, however, and
afterwards neither side troubled the other over much'.[54] That was
the essence of peacetime sectors, namely, neither side troubled the
other over much provided each kept out of sight and avoided
blatantly unwarlike behaviour. Weapons were fired, of course, but
mostly as a matter of form.

Perfunctory weapon use was the most common form of ritualisation, and the pervasive undertone of war, but it was sometimes
difficult for an outsider to identify. Such weapon use is simple
enough to grasp in principle, but its concrete expressions are not
comprehended, unless one is familiar with the exemplary use of
weapons on active fronts. For instance, machine-guns—Lewis and
Vickers—were weapons of opportunity; instructors impressed upon

trainees, 'the opportunity to inflict moral and material damage upon the enemy must be looked for'.[55] Such opportunities occurred by night and day, but especially by night, when front line sentries often stood head, chest and shoulders above trench level, so that the enemy could not surprise the garrison. As a routine duty, machine-gunners swept the enemy front line with fire, and whether traversing fire was lethal depended on a simple variation in the gun's operation: either fire moved evenly along enemy trenches from left to right or it moved unevenly, looping back at sudden and irregular intervals. The former method of fire was predictable, and did not disturb seasoned sentries, who bobbed down and up as the fire approached and passed; but the other method was unpredictable and caused casualties when sentries bobbed down, up, and down again for all time, as looping fire took off their heads. A New Zealand officer described such fire: 'The enemy machine gunner . . . with his fine judgment of elevation . . . had the height of the parapet to an inch, and was able to cut the bags along an arc of 200–300 yards; sometimes he would make his spray of bullets suddenly switch back to catch any unwary head'.[56] Likewise, a Guards officer on an active front noted it was unsafe to get up after machine-guns had traversed as they nearly always swept back again.[57] On the front of the 51st division, German machine-gunners using initiative fired 'a series of bursts into a particular portion of breastwork until it became non-bullet proof';[58] exploiting the weakness thus created, the guns then fired bullets at irregular intervals into the trench and caused many casualties.

Machine-gunners showed less concern for range, accuracy and the creation of opportunities for lethal aggression on quiet fronts, and weapon use was not only dilatory but occasionally light-hearted as gunners, each firing perfunctorily at the other's line, rapped out rhythms of popular tunes in concert: 'Machine guns chattered and were answered by machine guns. One ingenious machine gunner could "loose off" to the time of the well known line in "Policeman's Holiday" and a dozen machine guns, on both sides, would answer with two shots—"Bang-Bang"'.[59] Musical machine-guns were commonplace on quiet fronts, and some gunners developed a personal style and were named accordingly by their adversaries. Thus in front of the 41st division, the German gunners were known as Duck Board Dick, Fritz, Peter the Painter, Parapet Joe and Happy Harry: 'As for "Happy Harry", he came to be quite liked, even as he was much admired. His skill at producing recognisable tunes in his staccato manner was a great incentive to our own gunners to get so familiar with their own guns as to be able to emulate his example'.[60]

The infantryman's fighting time was taken up with 'minor offences',[61] that is, sending over rifle-grenades, sniping, patrolling and bombing, and on active fronts rifle and bayonet men were 'generally asking for trouble';[62] but on quiet fronts 'the war was not waged very furiously',[63] and rifle fire was ritualised in much the same manner as machine-gun fire. Thus a soldier of the 3rd division observed, 'the senior officer in charge wished to annoy the Huns and ordered five rounds of rapid fire at dawn. Of course we fired at nothing in particular and except by accident can have done no damage';[64] on the 16th division front, a German sentry visible to the British had an 'exemption card' and, according to an officer, 'He is not allowed to be shot at, because that would spoil the picture'.[65] Like ritualised machine-gun fire, humour attached to ritualised sniping, regarding which a soldier of the 27th division wrote, 'We have been having some "sport" with . . . [a] . . . sniper. By means of a bayonet periscope we spotted his loophole, and have been taking more or less unaimed shots at it. He indicates a miss each time by waving a spade from side to side. We do the same',[66] and in the 16th division a similar incident was recorded by a battalion commander, 'My . . . sniping officer tells me he had a shot this morning, but his would-be victim signalled a "miss", raising and lowering a stick above the parapet. I have known them do this before with a shovel. Our enemy . . . has some humour'.[67] Indeed this practice was not uncommon on quiet fronts where neither side devoted all energy and skill to the serious business of sniping.

On active fronts hand-bombs were passing constantly and mutually between trenches where these were 50 yards or less apart, and where distances were greater, zealous trench fighters were 'forever puzzling out the best possible ways of slinging over bombs with hand made catapults',[68] on quieter fronts, however, these machines were sometimes used for more peaceful purposes, as a sergeant of the 12th division explained: 'One of these uncertain weapons . . . was placed just outside my shelter. However, it caused a lot of fun. The great thing was to make a quick "getaway" after releasing the spring, as the bomb was liable to fall back into the trench . . . Tins of bully beef, however, always seemed to make beautiful flights into the German lines ninety yards away'.[69] Where adversaries were within throwing distance of each other, hand-bombing was probably ritualised in the way already described. Concerning hostile use of grenades when trenches were close, an officer of the 14th division wrote: 'the trenches are so close that they run through the remains of the same houses. In consequence nobody thinks of throwing grenades about—a case of "those who live in glass houses" ';[70] nine months later and in the same sector, another officer commented:

> good bricked up trenches they were . . . and your footsteps could easily be heard as you walked along them. So could those of the German sentries as they paced along their trenches, which . . . were no more than ten or fifteen yards from ours. The closeness of the two lines was a good insurance against strafing on either side. The mildest exchange of hand grenades or bombs . . . would have made life intolerable.[71]

Obviously live and let live had prevailed here perhaps for several months, and though grenades were very probably thrown during this time, they were thrown to cause no injury, in the way described by a 47th-division soldier who, with another, occupied a sap only 25 yards from the Germans; 'When Jerry sends a couple of bombs over after he's had his supper we'll send one over just to let him know we're still awake'; this duly happened, and, 'Apart from two small explosions nearby and our reply, the night was comparatively safe'.[72] Thus, where antagonists were separated by small distances or inhabited trenches which ran through the same house, each could easily have thrown bombs at the other; however, while such opportunities were exploited on active fronts they were foregone on quiet fronts, where bomb-throwing was ritualised.

Between rifle and machine-guns on the one hand, and artillery and trench-mortars on the other, there was a difference which affected the way each weapon type ritualised aggression: small arms fired bullets effective merely against persons; larger guns fired explosive shells effective not only against persons but also against trenches. Even on active fronts bullets could not harm trench fighters who kept well under cover; but most shells destroyed most defences in some degree, and some shells penetrated the deepest dug-out; thus soldiers were never entirely safe from artillery and trench-mortars. The difference was important; for while both forms of small arms ritualisation were consistent with truces, larger guns could neither vaguely spray shells over trenches, nor fire wide to miss some persons without causing harm to others. Even if shells were fired casually, chance ensured some dug-outs and garrisons were shattered; yet if shells were fired deliberately to miss persons, some trenches and their tenants were hit likewise by chance. Consequently, neither mode of small arms ritualisation was suited to the large guns which, moreover, could not preserve peace by inertia, since a lack of shelling was perceived more easily than a lack of other fire.

The trench-mortars and artillery, however, evolved at least three other variations on the theme of ritualisation, and one of these concerned no-man's-land. Although large guns could not fire onto the enemy trenches without causing casualties they could fire into no-man's-land, thus avoiding casualties and preserving peace. For example, a private soldier of the 2nd division wrote: 'We observed a Canadian battery of mine throwers at work, and watched them off and on for about an hour. All this time they were firing shots off at very frequent intervals . . . every single one of them fell about 100 yards away from Fritz's front line, and exploded in "No-Man's-Land", doing no harm to anybody'.[73] The infantries of each side often complained to their respective artilleries that shells fell short and dropped into friendly trenches, and such short shelling was usually attributed either to faulty equipment or bad shooting, but some might have been caused by gunners attempting to drop shells short of German trenches but over the British.

To comprehend the second mode of ritualisation evolved by large guns, one must know something of exemplary artillery and trench-mortar tactics. In general, artillery and mortars were expected to search enemy lines, either for targets of opportunity, that is, single soldiers and soldiers in groups, or more permanent targets, such as all trenches and especially communication trenches along which men and materials moved constantly in and out of the line. They also sought out offensive and defensive strongpoints in the trenches; trench-mortar, machine-gun and artillery emplacements; mine-workings; company and battalion H.Q.s and roads and road junctions behind the trenches, leading into communication trenches. According to its nature, a target once located was either destroyed or registered; thus, gunners immediately shelled an enemy working party, but they registered a communication trench or supply road for future use. Some targets were frequent and vulnerable venues for concentrations of men and materials and shelling caused large losses; these were termed 'tender spots' and

included communication trenches during a changeover of garrisons, and supply roads with troops, ammunition and rations in
transit. On active fronts opposing artilleries pounded away at
opposing trench systems with ingenuity and zeal, and while neither
side neglected targets of opportunity, each paid particular attention
to the other's tender spots. A good example of German artillery
exploiting a vulnerable supply road is described by a British officer:

> Food, water, ammunition, guns, wire, and everything else which
> the linesman needs, must pass along this solitary lane and the
> Germans know it. The shell fire is seldom heavy . . . but it is
> persistent, wearing and of the most deadly accuracy. A very
> favourite trick is to shell some point on the road and thus compel
> traffic to wait. In five minutes they know that there will be a solid
> column of wagons on the far side of the block, and then they
> lengthen the range—preferably with shrapnel. Then it is like all
> hell let loose. Half a dozen among those crowded limbers can do
> the most terrific damage.[74]

A similar exploitation occurred on the 12th division front and took
the form of:

> artillery crashes, which consisted of two minute concentrations at
> irregular intervals on the various tender spots; two of these were
> the road junction at the church and the crossroads . . . These
> crashes proved disconcerting and expensive in casualties, but it
> was a game at which two could play, as no doubt the Germans
> found to their cost.[75]

The German fire was expensive not only because it occurred on
tender spots but because it came at irregular and unpredictable
intervals.

Where live and let live prevailed, the strategy was different: the
guns of each side carefully registered the other's tender spots, not in
order to shell them, but to avoid shelling them by chance. 'With
regard to all shelling there would appear to have been conventions',
commented an officer of the 36th division, 'Those who have seen
German shells at Mailly-Maillet dropping at dusk, the hour when
the transport started for the line, on to the Sèvre and Auchonvillers
Roads, but never closer than one hundred yards to the first houses of
the village will agree with this opinion'.[76] In this illustration the

exchange between adversaries is a taken for granted assumption, but the reciprocity of these 'conventions' is clear enough elsewhere, for instance, according to a unit of the 61st division: 'The nights at Laventie were distinctly noisy, since eighteen pounder batteries, not to mention a fifteen inch railway gun, surrounded the village. But the place itself was seldom shelled: it seemed to be a case of live and let live. If the Germans shelled Laventie, the British retaliated on Aubers';[77] and an Australian unit taking over trenches for the first time on the western front, was surprised that, 'by a mutual understanding it had become the custom for both sides to refrain from shelling villages and billets in the rear areas'.[78] Similarly, the 2/Royal Welch observed that, 'from Cuinchy the rattle and clatter of the enemy limbers on the *pavé* road, bringing up the rations at dusk, was plainly audible. The artillery on both sides respected the enemy's ration limbers'.[79] The mutual respect of the gunners sometimes included the enemy's trenches as well as his stomach, as Lord Reith observed:

> I slept through another shelling . . . the artillery F.O.O. came up and observed from the trench while his battery retaliated, reporting back by telephone. Funny business this. Enemy throws some shells at our trench: 'We've got your range accurately, you see. No monkey tricks'. Home Battery replies: 'we've got yours— trench line and battery both. So no more nonsense. Live and Let Live.'[80]

Reith put into words the meaning of a structure of ritualised aggression, which was well enough understood by the initiated, like an officer of the 1st division who noted: 'Thirty six "Jack Johnsons"[81] spread over an hour and twenty minutes were dropped upon us, the enemy started with our fire trench, of which he showed that he had the range, repeatedly only just missing it'. The message was clear: the Germans would continue 'just missing' the trench only for so long as the British behaved themselves.[82]

Unrestricted movement in trenches was indirect evidence for small arms ritualisation as well as artillery, and sometimes trench-mortar, ritualisation. On an active front, artillery and sometimes mortars not only sniped at enemy soldiers moving openly in their lines but also registered communication trenches, crowded with men and materials as one garrison relieved another. These were very tender spots indeed. Thus daylight reliefs (reliefs usually occurred at night and even then on active fronts were hazardous) indicated a tacit agreement that neither side would shell the other during this vulnerable time. For instance, on the 41st divisional front, the Germans ignored such reliefs, no doubt as part of a reciprocal deal, 'Spoils Bank sector had one great advantage— reliefs could be carried out in daylight, although only by kind permission of the enemy, who, from his point of vantage, could not fail to see what was going forward';[83] and, similarly, on the 48th division's front, it was noted that trenches could be relieved, 'in clear distant view of the enemy'[84] without the latter exploiting the situation.

In general, mortars like artillery avoided aggressive tactics on quiet fronts, but two opinions existed concerning trench-mortars as lethal weapons. The first, namely that mortars were deadly weapons on quiet and active fronts, was held by inexperienced soldiers or soldiers in non-solidary battalions (by non-solidary units, I mean units where informal networks of five to ten men had either not emerged, or had emerged but involved a relatively small proportion of total unit personnel. When informal networks had not developed, men were mostly held together by formal, bureaucratic rules). A private of the 2nd division explained why mortars were lethal:

> *Minenwerfers* . . . of all projectiles, are, I think, the most nerve-racking. The trouble is we can see them. They are sent from trench mortars, and their path therefore is at first almost a vertical one in the air, and after reaching a very great height, they descend on their target in a long curve. The moment they reach the highest point in their path, they become visible . . . and in their descent, the course becomes very erratic, and it is impossible to judge exactly where they will strike the ground. When they do explode, the explosion is simply terrific.[85]

The author was an inexperienced trench fighter and a member of a battalion apparently lacking solidarity, and whereas he thought the visibility of mortar shells nerve-racking, experienced trench fighters of solidary units used visibility to advantage, organising themselves so that no casualties occurred during bombardments: 'As the flight of a minnie is slow, C Company soon learnt to look out for them. When one was spotted the direction was called out and everyone made a rush down the trench in the opposite direction'.[86] This

1. Sentry of the 1/4th Royal Berks watching through a periscope in the trenches near Ploegsteert Wood, Spring 1915. For many trench fighters Ploegsteert was for long periods of time a 'rest cure sector'

2. German soldiers carol during the Christmas of 1914. On both western and eastern fronts, mutual musical entertainments between enemies were not infrequent through the war on very quiet fronts

3. Two Germans set up a small kitchen in their dugout, and almost certainly, the enemy opposite had made similar cooking arrangements

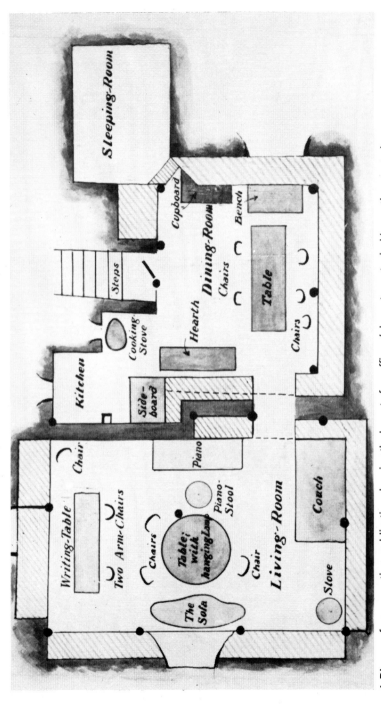

4. Diagram from a wartime publication showing the layout of an officers' dugout on a typical 'peacetime sector'

5. German officers of the 27th Infantry Regiment in their dugout

6. A French officer shaves in the front line. On some 'cushy' sectors it was even known for soldiers to take baths

7. A machine gun in British trenches

8. French officers' mess in the trenches August 1916. Flowers are in a German shell case. Clearly 'mutual understandings' were well developed on this sector

9. Portuguese in the trenches. Arrival of hot rations in a carrier strapped to a man's back near Neuve-Chapelle, June 1917. The Portuguese were great believers in the 'principle of laissez-faire'

10a and 10b. Trench life on 'cushy' sectors

11. One synonym for 'live and let live' was 'let sleeping dogs lie'

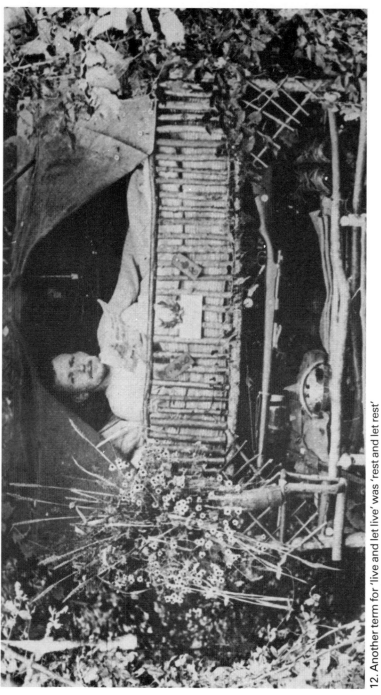

12. Another term for 'live and let live' was 'rest and let rest'

13. Afternoon tea in the trenches

14. Sometimes animals appeared in the trenches. Here the Germans hold a lion cub mascot; elsewhere milking cows were kept in the front line

15. A German trench household only 40 yards from the French. This household could have been destroyed by one enemy hand grenade but for the tacit truce

16. British troops make puddings in the trenches

17. Soldiers eat dinner in the trenches, Arras, March 1917. Possibly an 'egg and chips sector'

18. German trenches in the Vosges sector where live and let live prevailed for long periods throughout the war

19. British troops in France

20. British soldiers frying bacon in a reserve trench. On an active front, smoke from the stove would have attracted instant and lethal enemy gunfire

21. French soldiers eating in the trenches

22. An immaculate German trench a few yards from the French line

23. The 9th Battalion, the Cameronians (the Scottish Rifles) make a daylight raid. More than anything, raids destroyed live and let live. This was the other face of trench warfare, and life could be nasty, brutish and short on active sectors

method also worked at night when a trail of sparks marked the mortar's flight, and most sources—including the German[87]— agreed that, 'if warning was given in time, these bombs were easily avoided by moving up or down the trench'.[88] But mortar crews were aware of this weakness and on active fronts countered infantry evasion: thus a soldier of the 47th division agreed it was possible to dodge minnies, 'but if two came over together, aimed at different spots, then it was difficult', for in avoiding one a person ran into the other.[89] Moreover, zealous mortar crews knew avoidance meant movement, and therefore fired when their opponents' trenches were knee-deep in mud and escape was impossible. Evasion was also countered by mortar strafes which 'took place just before dusk, where it was too dark to see the shell, yet too light to see the burning fuse'.[90] Further mortars coordinated their fire with other weapon groups so that the enemy could not exploit the visibility of shells, and thus avoid them. For instance, against a unit of the 48th division 'the Boche started firing rifle-grenades before each mortar, so that we should stoop to avoid the former and so miss seeing the flight of the latter'.[91]

In conclusion, both artillery and mortars avoided aggressive tactics on quiet fronts. The nature of artillery aggression was summed up briefly by a gunner officer of the 11th division when asked by a new colleague what · shooting was done: 'Damned little . . . as little as possible. Sixty rounds a day for the battery is the approximate allowance for ordinary strafing purposes. We don't shoot up the trenches unless he shoots up ours. We sometimes put a few over on a minnie. We use up the sixty rounds on hidden roads and that sort of thing'.[92] The general picture is familiar. But exactly how were the sixty rounds used up, and what precisely was 'that sort of thing'? Some clues are found in our analysis of the third and final method of artillery and trench mortar ritualisation, namely, routinisation.

The third mode was, perhaps, the most typical, and its underlying principle was as simple as it was effective. The general idea with small arms ritualisation was to fire to miss the enemy, whereas the idea behind artillery and trench-mortar routinisation was to fire so that the enemy could dodge the missile. We have seen how trench fighters evaded mortar shells because the latter moved slowly and visibly along a high trajectory. According to their type, artillery shells moved over a high or flat trajectory but, either way, shells travelled too quickly to be wholly visible. How then could such shells be evaded? Simple: the guns of each side fired upon the other's trenches every day, at the same time, at the same place, and with about the same number of shells. Both artillery as well as trench mortars did this. As successive days passed without deviation, such routinised aggression became predictable and thus avoided, as an officer of the 63rd division explained in respect of trench-mortars:

> at a fixed hour each day the Germans blew the same portions of the line to dust with *minenwerfers*, our men having departed half an hour previously, according to the established routine from which neither side ever diverged. Our guns were very busy by spasms, and every day destroyed small portions of the thick red masses of the German wire which every night were religiously repaired.

—on an active front, of course, repair work was prevented by machine-gun, mortar or artillery fire. Of this 'normal', 'peacetime' sector, the author concluded, 'It was all very gentle and friendly and artificial, and we were happy together'.[93] Trench-mortar routinisation was widespread on quiet fronts, for instance opposite the 11th division we find, 'The enemy was very quiet; only his trench mortars were offensive, but even these paid scant attention to strictly limited localities, with the result that our casualties were very light'.[94] In front of the 9th division:

> the enemy . . . contented himself with trench mortar bombardments. He stuck to fixed periods . . . one could wander about peacefully in the sector except between the hours of two and four p.m.—the time of the trench mortar interlude. The type used was the 'rum jar'—a huge unwieldy bomb that was thrown high into the air—and a man was absolutely safe if he used his eyes and wits. Sentries with whistles kept a lookout, and when a mortar was on the way a whistle blast gave warnings.[95]

Where trench fighters could both see mortar shells and knew the time of firing, they were, as the source indicates, 'absolutely safe' provided they were experienced.

Both field and heavy artillery routinised aggression in the same manner. Gunners fired each day the same number of shells, at the same target, at the same time, and, as this pattern persisted, it became a fixture of the front, more or less predictable to trench fighters, who either left or avoided the target area before shelling started. Such a pattern might remain unchanged for a long time, for instance, a German officer, returning to a sector after a lengthy absence, noted, 'the front line has not changed at all. The guns fire on their appointed targets, at the appointed time, with the appointed ammunition'.[96] Such routinised shelling was a form of ritualised aggression fully compatible with live and let live. Additionally, gunners proved their offensive spirit with statistics of the number of shells fired against the enemy; but routinised shelling was inconsistent with the ethos of the active front and specific instructions which laid down that shelling should be at irregular intervals.[97]

A few illustrations will show how combatants easily evaded routinised shelling. On the 30th division's front it was recorded that the Germans 'practically always shelled the same place, which we had got to know and which we carefully avoided';[98] likewise in the 19th division an officer commented, 'the Boche gunner is meticulously methodical; we get to know the very minute any one fieldpiece wakes up, its target for the day and the number of shells likely to come our way. Thus counter measures are taken'.[99] Churchill, when a battalion commander, also noticed 'the artillerymen—particularly the Bosche artilleryman—is a creature of habit and sticks to the targets he sets his fancy on';[100] another battalion commander thought that in the matter of habitual shelling, 'Fritz seemed very wanting in "nous" because his daily strafe hardly ever touched our positions . . . he always strafed at the same time of day, usually from noon to one o'clock, so that we could quite easily arrange our day's work without being interfered with by his nuisances'.[101] But it was the commander, not Fritz, who lacked understanding, since such shelling was probably reciprocal; anyhow it caused so little trouble that another officer of the battalion had leisure enough to pen a report to battalion H.Q. thus:

> Twelve little Willies at noon to the tick,
> Got our heads down, and got them down quick,
> Peaceful and calm was the rest of the day,
> Nobody hurt and nothing to say.[102]

Routinised shelling was sometimes so predictable that not only was it unnecessary to get one's head down but, according to an

officer of the 48th division, 'one could on most days . . . watch with
a feeling of complete security a variety of shells bursting . . . a few
hundred yards away'.[103] Nor need ritualised shelling interrupt
mealtimes:

> The trenches were not often shelled, and in general the holiday
> atmosphere was only disturbed . . . at four o'clock in the
> afternoon, with comic regularity, by a few shells on Arras
> cathedral, we were usually having tea at that time . . . but we
> had complete confidence that the efficiency of the German
> artillery would prevent any shells falling short and hitting our
> headquarters by mistake.[104]

Routinisation sometimes allowed trench fighters to get one up on
high command—whose discomfort always hugely delighted the
front line—as a unit of the 48th division recorded:

> So regular were they (the Germans) in their choice of targets,
> times of shooting, and number of rounds fired, that, after being in
> the line one or two days, Colonel Jones had discovered their
> system, and knew to a minute where the next shell would fall. His
> calculations were very accurate, and he was able to take what
> seemed to uninitiated Staff Officers big risks, knowing that the
> shelling would stop before he reached the place being shelled.[105]

The practice occurred on French and American as well as British
sectors, for example, a war correspondent visiting the front of the
U.S. 42nd division was surprised that soldiers moved about openly
except between the hours of 2.00 and 4.00. An infantry officer
explained: 'the officer in charge of the German battery just over the
hill . . . probably has instructions to shoot so many rounds a day
into us. So in order to simplify the matter he, being a true German,
starts at two and quits at four, when he has used up his supply of
ammunition'.[106] The phrase 'being a true German', refers to the
methodical German character, which some believed explained
routinised shelling, and in so far as this explanation referred to
methodical German observance of unwritten rules, it was true; but
then British, French and Americans were equally methodical in this
matter, which is a fact not always pointed out. Alternatively the
assumption that Germans were methodical and others not creates
more problems than it solves, for instance, why did the Germans

choose to comply methodically with rules of peace and not with official rules which specified aggressive tactics and irregular fire? The answer seems clear from an exchange perspective, namely, the Germans chose to routinise shelling since this choice was reciprocated by the foe. Two types of evidence support this interpretation: firstly, German narratives show that British and French shelling was routinised; secondly, some combatants recognised the reciprocal nature of shelling. British artillery routinisation is recorded in Junger's diary: 'Lieutenant Boje told me that he had only had a single casualty for a long while as the British shelling was so methodical that it allowed them to sidestep and avoid it each time'.[107] Likewise a German gunner commented on 'the evening gun' fired by the British, 'At seven it came—so regularly that you could set your watch by it . . . it always had the same objective, its range was accurate, it never varied laterally or went beyond or fell short of the mark . . . there were even some inquisitive fellows who crawled out . . . a little before seven, in order to see it burst'.[108] Both Remarque and Renn observed on routinisation: the former wrote of British guns which usually 'start punctually at ten o'clock'; but which one day 'started an hour too soon';[109] Renn also wrote of a sector where 'there are four shells daily at eleven o'clock, always at the same time and in the same place'.[110] Another German infantryman also described artillery routinisation in a manner leaving no doubt of its reciprocal nature:

for weeks we had been at the front: second line, first line, rest, first line, rest—and so the routine continued with unbroken monotony. During that period there hadn't been a single show, merely a few unexciting patrols led by the 'old hands' . . . the way the war was carried on in the Champagne was really ludicrous . . . At 7.22 a.m. half a dozen coal boxes of the six inch variety landed in a bunch on our front line; at 7.25 six of ours returned the compliment. Promptly at noon each side sent over a heavy mortar shell. By way of an evening blessing there was a mutual exchange of coal boxes beginning precisely at 7.22 . . . when the exchange of compliments was due, we retired . . . to our famous concrete shelters . . . On the other side of No-Man's-Land things were presumably just the same. It was all very comfortable.[111]

In this case, it was not only methodical Germans who routinised aggression; both German and French were equally meticulous in observing the rules of live and let live.

Of course, the Germans were not alone in grasping this, and Ian Hay saw the mutuality of routinisation and, further, showed it ended abruptly when one side broke the rules. Hay described a situation where some officers were in a front line dug-out, and the British artillery fired unexpectedly on German support lines. One officer: 'sighs resignedly . . . why can't they let well alone?'. Another commented that the Germans would object since the British did not usually fire at that time of an afternoon; moreover, he guessed the Germans would reciprocate, and sure enough, 'in five minutes the incensed Hun is retaliating for the disturbance of his afternoon siesta'.[112] As a private soldier put it, artillery routinisation was 'quite a give and take business . . . if we were quiet, Fritz was quiet. If we became noisy, then Fritz would show his teeth. Consequently our artillery was called some very pleasant names whenever they set the ball rolling'.[113]

6

In the last chapter we saw how truces adapted to the conditions of trench war's second phase by ritualising aggression, and examined forms of ritualisation in various fighting activities. The theme for this and the following chapter will be the social structure and social change of live and let live, but the direction of enquiry changes. Until now, we have shown how peace persisted, that is, neither dispersed nor deteriorated, despite external counter-forces such as threats from high command, specialised technology and the centralised administration of violence. From this point, however, attention focuses upon the internal rather than the external forces counter to live and let live. Internal forces are the constituent parts of live and let live itself, for example, trench fighters and weapon groups; while external forces are environmental conditions which impinge upon truces. Concerning the former, we want to know exactly why trench fighters conformed to live and let live, and, further, how potential deviants, such as aggressively inclined soldiers, were prevented from destroying the peace, for it took many men to make peace but only one man to break it. The enquiry is about social sanctions, the rewards and punishments which made peace rather than war the preferred choice of action for some soldiers and weapon groups, despite the fact that high command prescribed and rewarded aggression. We want to know the nature, range and organisation of these sanctions, and precisely how sanctions reinforced tacit truces and deterred deviance from them.

The system of sanctions is analysed thus. Two different situations are distinguished: the first concerns rewards and punishments used by one *antagonist* to induce the other to comply with—not deviate from—the rules of live and let live; the second refers to rewards and punishments used by one *compatriot* to make another compatriot comply with the rules of peace exchange. Both situations are similar in as much as each concerns sanctions which maintained live and let live. In this chapter we shall deal with the workings of sanctions *between* antagonists, that is, British and German as well as French and German, or, alternatively, what can be called *interarmy* as distinct from *intraarmy* sanctions. Firstly, we shall look at the exchange of rewards between enemies, and secondly, the exchange of punishments.

We have seen that the live and let live relationship was a mutually contingent exchange between enemies, where each rewarded, or positively sanctioned, the other by restricting aggression to a level mutually defined as tolerable. From the fighting man's point of view the benefits received in return for those bestowed were the motives underlying the ongoing sequence of exchange. The range of rewards was wide and varied, but one prime benefit which each antagonist gave to the other and which underlay most exchange was, of course, survival. Obviously, to restrict aggression was to increase chances of survival, since aggression and survival were inversely related: as the volume of bombs, bullets and shells passing reciprocally between the trenches increased, so the chances of avoiding death and injury decreased. The most general motive of exchange was the interest in staying alive common to all combatants, who, as Charles Sorley put it, 'found out that to provide discomfort for the other is but a roundabout way of providing it for themselves'.[1] First and foremost then, live and let live was, as its name implies, an arrangement whereby antagonists maximised life chances and minimised death chances.

A further benefit accruing to trench fighters was the diminution of other deprivations of trench life. These discomforts were of different types. For instance, mental strain and stress were maximised on active fronts, for the rhythm of aggression, while more or less continuous, was also irregular and unpredictable; on the other hand, ritualised aggression on quiet fronts was predictable, and consequently anxiety decreased as trench fighters were not continuously fearful for their lives.

Officially a tour of trench duty was spent harassing the enemy and improving trenches. On quiet fronts, however, the time and energy of trench fighters was free for the creation of a style of trench life which, if not exactly gracious, brought benefits enough for soldiers to think twice before provoking the foe. Often the day was spent making life more comfortable, and while comfortable meant different things to different combatants, all would agree comfort concerned food and drink. On cushy fronts soldiers arranged that the variety and amount of food if not ample at least exceeded official rations. For instance, hares and partridge and the like were shot in no-man's-land and retrieved by daylight,[2] and during one trench tour some units of the 5th division, 'had a most peaceful time—so peaceful indeed that in the millpool at the Moulin de Farguy, which was in our front line, fishing was indulged in'.[3] A meal is not complete without vegetables, and the green-fingered among a battalion of the 18th division were said to have 'very good potatoes from a patch in no-man's-land';[4] elsewhere a gunner noted of a cushy sector, 'There are even seed cabbages in no-man's-land. They are not actually cultivated there but I'm sure the infantry don't let them go to waste'.[5] Breakfast is better with fresh milk, and milking cows were occasionally kept in trenches. There are five recorded cases of trench cows, each in different divisions— the 5th, 18th, 30th, 48th and 51st—and on different sectors near the Somme.[6] Usually, each cow had its own dug-out and was grazed at night; during a relief the outgoing battalion handed over cow together with official trench stores, to the incoming battalion. One private soldier of the 30th division was a full-time but unofficial cowman for two months.

On quiet fronts there was time for men to cook food and brew tea: 'We . . . often see the smoke of their [the Germans] mealtime fires ascending in blue grey spirals . . . under quiet conditions it is only common courtesy not to interrupt each other's meals with in-termittent missiles of hate',[7] wrote an officer of the 19th division. Sometimes a battalion shop was sited in the line for food, drink and other comforts; for instance, a unit of the 49th division set up a canteen at battalion H.Q., 'and a hawker went round the front line daily to sell cigarettes, etc. to the men, within 200 yards of the enemy';[8] similarly a unit of the 15th division had a canteen in the trenches, and a soldier remarked, 'It was so quiet that Jimmy Hay [the quartermaster] made ovens in the rearward areas, and sent hot food forward'.[9] If neither food nor milk was available from battalion, other arrangements might be made, as a private soldier of the 33rd division indicated: 'Sometimes the trenches were cushy, as at Pommiers, where their front line dugout had wire beds, and where the line was so quiet that each afternoon one of their party slipped down to the village for eggs and oats, and fresh milk and fruit. Every morning they had freshly made porridge for breakfast.'[10]

Comfort involved more than adequate food and drink, however, and another unpleasantness of trench war was the ubiquitous louse.

Out of the line combatants could visit a delousing station, which gave a bath and change of clothing, but on active fronts soldiers were molested by both enemy and lice. On the other hand there was plenty of time for delousing or chatting on quiet fronts where, 'chatting became a social occasion where groups of men gathered in either a dugout or the open cracking jokes and lice together'.[11] Trench fighters could adapt most things to a useful purpose given the time, and a unit of the 18th division solved the problem of hygiene and lice by modifying a defunct brewery as a bath. There was nothing so unusual about this, except that 'men had their periodic baths in the Brasserie of Moy in the actual front line positions', and, further, it seems, 'the sector was so quiet that . . . the officers keep their valises in the line'.[12] Opportunities for outdoor bathing were pehaps more frequent, and Blunden remembered a canal in the British support line where parties of men were taken for baths, 'with the Germans probably aware but unobjecting a few hundred yards along'.[13] He also described a sector peaceful enough for reading, 'in daytime we sometimes got out of the trench into the tall sorrelled grass behind, which the sun had dried, and enjoyed a warm indolence with a book [not Infantry Training, I think]. The war seemed to have forgotten us in that placid sector'.[14] But it is more likely that both sides had forgotten the war. The benefits of live and let live included not only books but music also, and a unit of the 50th division affirmed that 'In one trench there was a piano actually in the front line, and the men had many good sing songs. The Germans did not object to this as a general rule';[15] similarly a battalion of the 31st division, 'boasted a piano'[16] at company H.Q. in the front line. Briefly, the benefits of quiet fronts were many and varied, and, as an officer of the 49th division commented, 'little wonder that men hated working parties and usually preferred the comparative peacefulness of advanced posts'.[17]

Until now live and let live has been shown as a sequence of instrumental exchanges which emerged and were maintained to satisfy survival, security and comfort needs, common to all combatants. Conformity to live and let live was thus a matter of expedience, not of morality: one restricted aggression and gave the foe greater survival chances merely because the reciprocal act increased one's own survival chances. At first trench fighters defined exchange as neither morally good nor bad but just a technically efficient means to an end. I will argue below, however, that instrumental exchange was supplemented and reinforced during trench war by moral sanctions, that is, rewards and benefits of an ethical kind. The evolution of live and let live, from an instrumental social structure to a structure sustained by utilitarian as well as moral sanctions, involved several related factors, which included the attenuation of hostile feelings and simultaneous emergence of a consciousness of kind among antagonists; the growth of an indigenous trench contra-culture, that is, a design for trench life evolved and shared by antagonists, which both reflected their own needs and, additionally, opposed official needs and policies. One must emphasise, however, that this process concerned some, not all, or even most, antagonists. Some neither exchanged peace nor developed solidarity with the enemy, but fought with zeal and felt either hatred for the foe, or nothing. In this chapter, I want to suggest that certain social processes and attitudes, namely, social exchange and social solidarity respectively, were causally related in such a way that the former determined the latter. However, the war comprised other processes and attitudes, and elsewhere a similar connection between conflict enmity will be suggested.

Firstly, one must demonstrate and explain the decline in mutual hostility among antagonists, and secondly, show how, in the absence of enmity, a consciousness of kind developed. Concerning images which men at war have of each other, Glenn Gray distinguished between the abstract and the concrete.[18] In the former, propaganda abstracts from the complex whole of an enemy's culture and behaviour some negative items, and from these alone creates a simple stereotype, biased against the enemy. For instance, British propaganda represented German soldiers of 1914–18 as aggressive, barbaric huns, destroyers of culture, violators of the aged and young and so forth. From persons exposed to it, such an image evokes hatred for the foe and, further, enmity gives a justifiable motive for killing and inhibits guilt feelings, which otherwise would emerge at thoughts of homicide. On the other hand, concrete images of the enemy are produced not by propaganda, but by reflective minds contemplating the war experience. Gray asserts that concrete images of the enemy are relatively rare among combatants; but then he wrote from personal experience as a combatant of the Second World War, and I will suggest that soldiers of the First World War often had such concrete images. The essence of the concrete image is the realisation that the enemy is neither entirely evil nor entirely different from oneself—as portrayed in simple abstract images—

but a complex being of both good and bad impulses. The abstract image stresses dissimilarities between self and foe, whereas the concrete image, which derives from experience and reflection, underlines similarities.

On arrival in France the newly trained British soldier had either an abstract image of the enemy, inculcated in training, or none at all; but in any case he was immediately exposed to the abstract image as high command assiduously attempted to build up the offensive spirit. Yet despite official policy, some soldiers experienced the weakening of this stereotype before the realities of trench life. The attitudes of adversaries cannot be exactly known now, but the sources give some clues, and these are here divided into material written in the war and retrospective material. With respect to the latter, hostile sentiments are relatvely rare, and references to lack of hatred between enemies are quite frequent. For example, Read,[19] Mottram[20] and Burrage[21] refer to lack of hostility towards the enemy, and Lord Moran, a battalion medical officer for much of the war, recalled only one expression of feeling against the Germans, and 'soon it was forgotten; men spoke again of "Fritz" with amusement and tolerance'.[22] Purdom, who examined over 300 personal narratives of the war, found hardly any hostile feeling against the enemy.[23]

Concerning material written during the war, the picture is somewhat different, and expressions of hatred and bitterness are more frequent; at the same time, it would be wrong to conclude that an attitude of hostility prevailed. Houseman, who edited letters written from the front by British soldiers later killed, found hatred of the enemy seldom mentioned;[24] and in Germany a selection of letters by middle-class students who also lost their lives was published in 1928 and a student of these letters observed that abuse and hatred of the enemy was rare.[25]

Writing after the war, an experienced private soldier commented on the attitude change which occurred during trench war: 'hatred of the enemy, so strenuously fostered in training days, largely faded away in the line. We somehow realised that individually they were very like ourselves, just as fed up and as anxious to be done with it all. For the most part, the killing that was done and attempted was quite impersonal'.[26] This soldier is conscious that his image of the enemy changed, and this change concerned his war career. But his account of the process of change is vague: 'we somehow realised . . .', yet it is like that of others who refer to the same variation and give no explanation. There is a problem here, however. Things do not change without cause or reason. The social scientist must distinguish the social from other causes of human behaviours. Social processes determine some mental phenomena, and our argument is that the process of cooperative exchange eroded abstract images of the enemy, and provoked the growth of concrete images; the latter then replaced the former. Exactly how this happened—how, 'hatred of the enemy . . . faded away in the line', is examined below.

The basic premise of this argument is that the more frequently persons interact with each other, the greater will be their sentiments of mutual friendship.[27] Thus cooperative exchange among persons causes an increase in sentiments of liking amongst them. While live and let live was a relationship between persons formally designated as enemies, it was nevertheless cooperative exchange. Therefore live and let live was accompanied both by an increase in sentiments of liking among antagonists and a decrease in sentiments of enmity. Let us spell this out a little more. The instrumental exchange between enemies was based upon shared needs for survival, safety and comfort, and a corollary of this was mutual awareness by antagonists of their similarities. Awareness was inconsistent with abstract images of the enemy but could not be ignored, since it derived from actual war experience, and reflection upon that experience. Moreover, awareness was a developmental thing. From the earliest stages of trench war, each side observed specific and temporary truces, and, as an unintended consequence, such truces revealed to each antagonist that a wider range of needs and values was shared with the enemy: brief truces to collect wounded showed to each side that the other was compassionate and not essentially cruel; temporary weather truces showed to trench fighters of both sides that each reacted in the same way to a common adversity; as nightly ration carts clattered up to the trenches, and neither side aggressed the other, each adversary was aware of his enemy's hunger as well as his own; as live and let live diffused throughout fighting activities, each antagonist inferred from the behaviour of the other that the enemy's sole purpose was not to commit death and destruction, as the abstract image represented. This discrepancy between the abstract image of the enemy, stressing dissimilarities, and the emergent concrete image, stressing similarities, was resolved as the former was replaced by the latter, which was consistent with the reality of antagonists' cooperation throughout the routines of trench war and life. The stage was now set for the appearance of other direct and tangible expressions of the developing consciousness of kind among trench fighters.

Before looking at this common consciousness, we must first note that all exchange is influenced by a universal value, namely, the moral norm of reciprocity.[28] At all times, in all cultures, exchange relations are constrained by this ethic which evokes obligations towards others on the basis of their past behaviour. Specifically, it prescribes that you should give benefits to those who give you benefits, and, further, that you should not harm those who have given you benefits. The moral norm of reciprocity effected live and let live in several ways, forming an ethical matrix which facilitated the origin of exchange and both stabilised and reinforced exchange once it had emerged.

Concerning the origin of live and let live, a time existed at the onset of trench war when peace exchange was not customary; though each antagonist might wish to exchange peace, he still looked upon the other with suspicion, and regarded exchange as hazardous. The norm of reciprocity eased the emergence of exchange during this time: it was internalised and shared by both sides, and constrained trench fighters, who first received benefits from restricted aggression, to reply in kind, thus giving real grounds for confidence to soldiers, who initially restricted aggression, that their action would be requited. Because antagonists shared this value, there was less apprehension about initiating exchange, and consequently the latter emerged more readily.

With respect to the persistence and stability of exchange, the trench fighter had learned during childhood that social life conformed to rules of give and take, which affirmed not only that give and take was a fact of life but also that it was morally right. Further this basic behavioural constraint was not eradicated by military training and thus was brought to the battlefield. The rules of reciprocity are diffuse not specific; it is a general rule of conduct which applies to countless *ad hoc* situations and transactions, for example, where a peacefully inclined soldier thought his enemy had restricted aggression, he might reply in kind from habit, without reflecting whether the response was appropriate to war situations. When they went to war, antagonists had already learned and had experience of reciprocity which had only to be applied to a new, if novel, context. The longer the exchange of peace persisted, the more confident each adversary grew of the other's intention; for each was manifestly conforming to the rules of reciprocity, and, consequently, live and let live became more stable.

From the start of the war the instrumental exchange concerning the needs for survival and comfort was embedded in a framework of familiar moral rules. In a real sense, trench fighters took the assumptions of peace into war. As exchange proceeded, antagonists realised their similarities concerned not merely survival needs but also moral factors: the enemy was perceived as a proper sort of person who, like oneself, could be trusted to keep his side of a bargain. The effect of the reciprocity ethic on exchange, reinforced the process whereby the latter generated sentiments of liking, and contributed to the emergence of a consciousness of kind among antagonists to which we now turn.

Cooperative exchange was the core element in the growth of trench fighters' consciousness of kind, or solidarity. Exchange released energy and time otherwise used in aggression for alternative pursuits, such as the creation of a style of trench life, more comfortable than that of the active front, and, further, exchange eroded enmity and increased good will. As a result there developed another type of non-instrumental exchange which symbolised the antagonists' common consciousness. We can distinguish primary and secondary exchanges: the primary exchange was of services, where each provided a service for the other, namely, the restraint of aggression, from which derived the benefits associated with the life-style of quiet fronts; the secondary exchange was of attitudes, and comprised the exchange of expressive behaviours symbolic of goodwill. If the primary exchange was instrumental and concerned self-interest, secondary exchange concerned socio-emotional feeling states. The two types of exchange were, of course, interrelated, for the primary exchange of service made possible the secondary exchange of attitude, and, at the same time, the latter fed back into and reinforced the former. Secondary exchanges assumed various forms: humour, banter, conversations, reciprocal singing and so forth. Previously, examples of these were given to illustrate live and let live. Interest here, however, lies in the origin of secondary exchange and its role in both the growth of a common consciousness and a trench contra-culture, where live and let live appeared as a social system supported by moral as well as utilitarian sanctions.

Intertrench gossip is mentioned in many sources and its content and function for trench subculture is commented on by some soldiers. Montague saw humourous exchange as the great solvent of ill-will affirming that 'it was impossible to suppress laughter between men within earshot of each other along a line of some hundreds of miles'.[29] But he neglects to mention that enemies have temper and time for laughter only when not killing each other, and, further, tacit cooperation usually existed where enemies did not fight. No laughter occurred on active fronts. Although Montague did not look at the underlying social process making humour possible, he was aware of the results of humourous exchange in reducing hostility and aggression and wrote:

> There was, in the Loos salient in 1916, a German who, after his meals, would halloo across to an English unit taunts about certain accidents of its birth. None of his British hearers could help laughing at his mistakes, his knowledge and his English. Nor could the least humourous priest of ill will have kept his countenance at a relief when the enemy shouted: 'We know you are relieving', 'No good hiding it', 'Good bye, Ox and Bucks', 'Who's coming in?' and some humourist in the obscure English battalion relieving shouted back, with a terrific assumption of accent: 'Furrst Black Watch' or 'Th' Oirish Guards!' and a hush fell at the sound of these great names.[30]

Similarly, it could not have been easy to respond lethally to the German who announced his arrival on sentry duty by shouting across no-man's-land, 'It is I Fritz the Bunmaker of London. What is the football news?'.[31]

Verbal exchanges were made easier as some Germans spoke English, having lived and worked in Britain before the war, as the following makes clear: ' "Hallo Tommee", cried a German voice, "Are you soon going home on leave?" "Next week" the Englishman shouted. "Are you going to London?" was the next question. "Yes". "Then call at 224 Tottenham Court Road and give my love to Miss Sarah Jones". "I'll go all right and I'll jolly well . . . her".'[32] All verbal exchanges whether humourous or not contained an element of farce in both senses of the improbable and ridiculous as an officer of the 48th division observed when describing night truces:

> Every night the picks and shovels of 300 or 400 men could be heard merrily at work with the inevitable undercurrent of conversation . . . When the moon was bright the enemy could be

seen peacefully attending to his own wire, while we were reminded that the hour had come to break off by a voice from opposite calling out 'Time to pack up sappers; go to bed'. Every morning a new length of enormous breastwork invited shells, which never came. On such occasions the thought arose that we must be taking part in the most expensive farce in the history of the world.[33]

Aside from the farcical element, some exchanges were neither humourous nor instrumental but of a straightforward conversational kind, and these included casual good morning greetings, comments on the weather and other topics of mutual interest. On the 18th division front, twenty yards separated the trenches, and the Germans called out, 'Good morning, Tommy',[34]—greetings no doubt returned; in a similar way, one sentry in a sap might call out to his opposite number, 'It's a cold night Jock'.[35] Further, like Fritz the Bunmaker, not a few Germans were interested in British football, as a private soldier of the 47th division described, 'a voice called across, "What about the Cup Final?" It was then the finish of the football season. "Chelsea lost" said Bill, who was a staunch supporter of that team. "Hard luck", came the answer from the German trench and firing was resumed. But Bill used his rifle no more . . . "A blurry supporter of blurry Chelsea" he said "E must be a damned good sort of sausage eater" '.[36] The connection between the realisation of common interests and the weakening of aggression is clearly shown here, and it is the more interesting as elsewhere the author shows Bill as the most aggressive man of his section, constantly firing at the enemy until stopped by the section's collective disapproval. Of another sector and time, the 47th division's history recorded, 'The enemy, used to a policy of live and let live, exposed himself very freely, and made efforts at friendly conversation. The 18th battalion unbent so far as to give him *The Times* in answer to a request for news'.[37]

The growth among adversaries of a shared consciousness was stimulated not only by verbal exchange but also by musical exchange of various sorts. John Brophy wrote of tacit and reciprocal singing arrangements sometimes existing between British and German,[38] and Adams witnessed nightly interludes of nonsense conversations, clapping and laughter ending with a sing-song where the Germans yodelled and sang, and British reciprocated with Tipperary.[39] On both sides also instrumentalists were appreciated.

Richards remembered a German violinist who played selections from operas, 'In the summer evenings when a slight breeze was blowing towards us we could distinguish every note. We always gave him a clap and shouted for an encore';[40] and a German soldier remembered anticipating with pleasure regular evening trumpet recitals by a British soldier, hoping that no harm had come to him when one night all was quiet.[41] In the 30th division, it was recorded, 'Our life certainly had its humourous side. One of the things which was done on Christmas eve was a patrol of an officer and about ten men of the 19th battalion who went out and established themselves in shell holes just outside the German lines and sang Christmas carols to them'.[42]

In addition to verbal and musical exchanges, the everyday routine of quiet fronts was expressed in a variety of incidents which, while not part of a direct exchange in the sense that a British song was reciprocated by a German, were nevertheless similar in as much as both incident and direct exchange affirmed and reinforced the common consciousness of trench fighters. An infantry officer described such an event: 'two lads in this regiment got fed up with each other in the trenches, so in broad daylight they got up on the parapet and fought. After a quarter of an hour one was knocked out, but all the time the Germans were cheering and firing their rifles in the air to encourage the combatants. Who says the Germans are not sportsmen?.'[43] The Germans were an appreciative audience of another incident involving the daily British ration of rum. This was misappropriated by a Scottish soldier who staggered drunkenly into no-man's-land and lurched along the battalion's front, all the while taking frequent swigs from a stone jar containing the rum. The inebriated Jock was in full view of the Germans who not only refrained from fire, but also laughed and cheered him along.[44]

On quiet fronts, then, primary instrumental and secondary expressive exchange occurred, the former continuously, the latter more intermittently; but each type of exchange systematically strengthened the common consciousness of adversaries, stressing their similarities while weakening their differences. But no account of these similarities is complete without mention of the aversion towards high command shared by trench fighters of all nations. Fault is found with high command in personal reminiscences and battalion histories; in British, German and French material; in writings of officers, N.C.O.s and private soldiers; among the personnel of all weapon groups; among those who practised live and let live and those who did not; with respect to the British army, condemnation is found among regular, territorial and New Army soldiers; it occurs in the literatures of disenchantment and qualified disenchantment; it is found in authors of all temperaments, for example, Jack, a conscientious and cautious regular soldier given neither to overstatement nor superficial judgement, makes no less than thirteen adverse comments on high command in his diary.[45]

Neville Lytton, of the 39th division, voiced this attitude concisely and in essentials comprehensively:

> we were all of us regimental officers and we had the true natural antipathy to the general officer and his staff. When one is in the front line one cannot help having a fairly deep sympathy for the wretched fellow in the other front line across 'no-man's-land'; one knows that he is going through just as many dangers and discomforts, and that he is simply carrying out the orders of some general whose dangers and discomforts are infinitely less, and the hatred that you both have towards these generals breeds a common sympathy that is irresistible.[46]

As Lytton asserted, hostility derived from two factors; firstly, the front fighters' comparison between their own, and high command's, dangers and discomforts, and the power over combat activities held by a non-combatant high command. Concerning comfort, the front line felt aggrieved that high command, especially army and corps, had the most comfortable billets in the most pleasant places, and, further, that they sometimes excluded all but army or corps personnel from these areas.[47] The front line thought of high command as a prolific source of trivial orders and demands, 'sometimes they are like a flood',[48] complained Jack. Such orders often seemed irrelevant and harmful, such as the one changing Jack's 'carefully drawn up system of trench routine',[49] and they would come at awkward moments, as when a battalion held the line. Equally resented were high command's criticisms of small shortcomings in dress, appearance and weapons of men fresh from the front.[50]

Secondly, and concerning power, both high command and trench fighters had authority to initiate aggression, but their positions differed radically with respect to the consequences of the exercise of authority. When a member of high command initiated aggression, he thereby exposed neither himself nor other members of high command to death or injury; but when a trench fighter initiated aggression, he exposed himself and his fellows to some degree of risk from retaliatory fire. All combatants were aware that the probability of retaliation was a constraint against the use of aggression, and many believed immunity from retaliation made high command more liberal with the lives of fighting men than would have been the case if generals shared the risks of aggression. Moreover trench fighters believed high command was not sufficiently accountable for the use or misuse of power; for instance, they often felt that generals lacked practical knowledge of trench war, and, further, they knew that ignorance neither stopped high command from arbitrarily altering plans for raids made by combatants, who knew local conditions and carried out the raids, nor from planning and initiating raids at times and places which combatants knew involved high risks. One trench fighter referred to such interference as 'the caprice of the abstract tactician who from far away disposes of us',[51] and the issue of accountability was raised, but with more passion, when following a costly minor attack, Blunden heard 'conversations fiercer than Bolshevik councils against the staff concerned'.[52] Some believed lack of accountability was connected with base motives, for instance, Westman, a German N.C.O. commented of a minor operation costing many lives, 'this is just to gratify the whim of an irresponsible general'.[53]

All this shows the existence of a consciousness of kind shared by trench fighters, antagonists and compatriots, associated with differential distribution of life and death chances, determined by high command; a collusive exchange where life chances were increased, and an expressive exchange which symbolised benevolence, not malevolence. Trench fighters wrote of this consciousness both during and after the war. As we have seen, Lytton referred to an irresistible, 'common sympathy', between antagonists; David Jones dedicated his classic of war experience 'To the enemy front fighters who shared our pains against whom we found ourselves by misadventure';[54] another soldier wrote:

> Across no-man's-land there were men sharing trouble with us, fighting the same losing battle against water, powerless before the sudden storm of bursting metal, and longing to be home again with their children. Were they the enemy? A scrap of song floating across at dusk . . . were we to freeze into hatred at these manifestations of a life so like our own?[55]

While during the war a soldier wrote in his diary, 'At home one abuses the enemy, and draws insulting caricatures. How tired I am of grotesque Kaisers. Out here, one can respect a brave, skilful, and resourceful enemy. They have people they love at home, they too have to endure mud, rain and steel'.[56] Moreover Brophy and Partridge noted that the British soldier talked of the German as 'Jerry' which was, 'a familiar expression, almost of affection . . . used constantly by private soldiers';[57] likewise Westman wrote that Germans called British 'Tommies'.[58]

Not only trench fighters but commentators and historians have also remarked on this consciousness of kind. Pfeiler observed that a common theme of German and other war literature was the fellow-feeling of all soldiers which transcended nationalities, and which was brought about by their common war experience;[59] and a distinguished yet apparently puzzled military historian wrote of the 'curious sense of kinship',[60] among opposing trench fighters. I have tried to show this solidarity was not odd, curious or chance (unless by curious one means at variance with official policy, which it certainly was) but was systematically related to other social processes and attitudes which together comprised the contra-culture of the trenches. Moreover, solidarity was the precondition of moral sanctions, and the next step of our argument is to examine the latter's emergence.

When a consciousness of kind evolved within live and let live, a new social bond, sustained by both moral and utilitarian sanctions, replaced the old instrumental tie between antagonists. The enemy now was not just a trading partner nor was the relationship with him merely one of self-interest. The enemy was not only a person with whom one exchanged services but someone for whom one also had fellow-feelings. A truce was no longer only an instrumental arrangement, for the restraint of aggression was simultaneously an act of expediency and symbolic of fellow-feelings. A series of reciprocal aggressions might be a communication system between enemies where each told the other both of his wish to trade and of his feeling that the other was a fine fellow. Originally, German soldiers did not shoot British soldiers for reasons of self-interest, and *vice versa*. But when Jerry identified with Tommy, to shoot him was not merely inexpedient but also morally wrong: if an enemy was a fellow sufferer, with whom one sympathised, then one ought not to harm him; and to act otherwise violated one's conscience. On the other hand, to act according to one's conscience brought rewards not only to oneself, for virtue was its own reward, but also to the enemy, who liked to feel his fellow-feelings reciprocated. Thus the infusion of the instrumental by the moral changed and strengthened live and let live, which was then supported by both moral and utilitarian sanctions. Moreover, this consciousness of kind was systematically reinforced in a ritual way. One has seen how ritualised aggression functioned among adversaries as a means of indirect communication, involving perfunctory weapon use, which conveyed the disposition to live and let live. But a structure of ritualised aggression had another and quite distinct ritual function. A ritual is a recurrent social event where the participation of persons and groups in ceremonial practices simultaneously symbolises and reinforces their shared commitment to abstract values. In trench war, a structure of ritualised aggression was a ceremony where antagonists participated in regular, reciprocal discharges of missiles, that is, bombs, bullets and so forth, which symbolised and strengthened, at one and the same time, both sentiments of fellow-feelings, and beliefs that the enemy was a fellow sufferer. Thus the ritual function of periodic and perfunctory firing was to develop and maintain the consciousness of kind among antagonists which, in turn, was related to moral sanctions underlying live and let live.

Sources confirm the existence of moral sanctions against aggression, for instance, the diary of a brigadier reads:

> When going round the trenches, I asked a man whether he had had any shots at the Germans. He responded that there was an elderly gentleman with a bald head and a long beard who often showed himself over the parapet. 'Well why didn't you shoot him?' 'Shoot him' said the man; 'Why, Lor' bless you sir, 'e's never done me no harm'. A case of live and let live, which is certainly not to be encouraged. But cold-blooded murder is never popular with our men.[61]

If our soldier had not shot for fear of being shot at in return, restraint could be interpreted as means to an end, namely survival. But this restraint was not merely instrumental. The soldier believed it morally wrong to kill another who had not harmed him and defined the situation in terms neither of expediency nor of technical possibilities, but as one where fellow-feeling existed and moral constraints applied, which made irrelevant the fact that the other was an enemy. The moral norm of reciprocity rules that persons ought not to harm those who have done them no harm, and, further, that persons should repay one benefit with another—the restraint above probably requited an earlier benefit. Moreover, the brigadier's comment about the unpopularity of cold-blooded murder indirectly acknowledges the influence of this ethic even in wartime, for otherwise there were few reasons (given safety from retaliation) why cold-blooded murder should not be popular. Indeed, as many reasons as rewards existed for killing to be popular, since murder was meritorious conduct and rewarded amply by high command.

Another commander noticed his men's belief that the enemy should not be harmed unless doing or planning harm and described the working of moral constraints in the line:

> Killing human beings is not dear to the hearts of Englishmen . . . they would sometimes show a great disinclination to fire on Germans walking in the open behind the enemy lines. It seemed as though the idea was that the particular German in question was not trying to injure them—he might have been carrying a plank or a bag of rations—and so they would watch him and no one would attempt to shoot unless there was an old soldier with them.[62]

Whether the German carried a plank was irrelevant from the military view, and fire was the correct response. Neither was restraint merely a matter of expediency since the German's power to retaliate was impeded by the plank he carried (although others might have avenged his killing). But it is clear that restraint was partly moral from what the men said at the time: as the German was harming no one, he should not be harmed. The same morality is seen again in the act of a private soldier recorded in the diary of his friend: 'Fred . . . told his sergeant that he had just seen a Fritz show his head over the parapet and asked if he fired at him said, "No, I couldn't kill him, for he ain't done me no harm" '.[63]

Some similar accounts do not refer directly to moral motives, whose influence can however be inferred on the grounds that events described are otherwise unintelligible. For instance, after heavy rain flooded the trenches, an officer wrote: 'The wretched Huns opposite are even worse off, being deeper down in the valley. They were seen this morning quite openly on top of their trenches throwing up mud and water. Our men did not shoot although ordered to do so'.[64] If this situation was one where self-interest operated, the men would have fired for at least two reasons: to refuse an order to fire when in action was to risk a massive legal sanction; secondly, the Germans had no weapons and were vulnerable in as much as they were fully visible, and the British overlooked their trenches and thus could fire with impunity. The fact they did not fire is most plausibly explained by 'common sympathy' and 'sense of kinship' or what is here called consciousness of kind, which rules that one ought not take advantage of another's misfortune. Moral constraints also operated in an incident described by an officer:

> I was having tea with A Company when we heard a lot of shouting and went out to investigate. We found our men and the Germans standing on their respective parapets. Suddenly a salvo arrived but did no damage. Naturally both sides got down and our men started swearing at the Germans, when all at once a brave German got on to his parapet and shouted out 'we are very sorry about that; we hope no one was hurt. It is not our fault, it is that damned Prussian artillery'.[65]

Moral constraints appear in the Saxon apology for behaviour which violated a situation of goodwill and trust; the Saxon concern that someone might have been injured; finally, the Saxon affirmation that they were not responsible for repaying goodwill with injury.

So far I have tried to show that the original instrumental exchange between antagonists generated a consciousness of kind entailing the reinforcement of truces by moral sanctions. However, the argument was not that either all, or most, adversaries developed sentiments of common sympathy; on the contrary, it was assumed that attitudes of malevolence, benevolence and indifference existed amongst them. It was not assumed, however, that the distribution of attitudes was random, and the problem has been to relate specific attitudes to trench fighters involved in specific social processes. Cooperative exchange was associated with consciousness of kind, and elsewhere enmity will be related to other social processes. This view denies neither that other social factors determined some solidarity, enmity or indifference, nor that non-social factors, for instance, psychological and physiological, determined some sentiments.

Incidentally, this argument throws light on the puzzling fact that the prevailing civilian attitude towards Germans corresponded to the abstract propoganda image whereas the attitude of soldiers did not. Trench fighters on home leave noticed the difference. For example, an officer of the 32nd division commented, 'Among the fighting men the bitterness was least; it increased steadily through the various degrees of security until genuine ferocity was achieved by non-combatants who had neither part nor lot in the war';[66] and Robert Graves commented, 'England looked strange to us returned soldiers. We could not understand the war madness that ran wild everywhere, looking for a pseudo-military outlet. The civilians talked a foreign language and it was newspaper language. I found serious conversation with my parents all but impossible'.[67] Montague noted the same phenomenon while observing that the British soldier, 'grew more and more sure that the average German was just a decent poor devil like everyone else'.[68] The difference between the civilian and combatant attitudes does seem odd, for both were exposed to propaganda, but soldiers suffered more severely and directly at the enemy's hands than civilians, yet civilians were more hostile than soldiers. But the problem is perhaps partly resolved when one realises that civilians, unlike soldiers, did not cooperate with the enemy, and if cooperative exchange erodes enmity, it follows that hostility to the enemy would be more frequent and intense on the home than on the war front.

The first part of this chapter dealt with the system of interarmy positive sanctions, that is, material and moral benefits gained directly and indirectly by antagonists. Interarmy sanctions included not only rewards for conformity but also negative sanctions—punishments—which one antagonist inflicted on the other for deviance from live and let live, and these are our subject now.

The system of interarmy sanctions involved ritualised aggression where each side accepted from the other a certain amount of perfunctory aggressive activity as each knew the other, like itself, must fire weapons to satisfy high command. The informal rules regulating ritualised aggression could be highly specific, such as where the 5th division allowed Germans to fire two shells per day on each battalion sector,[69] but more often they were general as the following incident shows:

It was very still. 'Has the war stopped?' one felt inclined to ask.

No, there is the sound of shells exploding far away . . . Then a 'phut' from just opposite . . . and a rifle grenade burst with a snarl about a hundred yards behind. Then another, and another, and another . . . I waited. There were no more. It was just about touch and go whether we replied. If they went on up to about a dozen, the chances were that the bombing corporal in charge of our rifle grenade battery would rouse himself and loose off twenty in retaliation. But no . . . and the afternoon slumber was resumed.[70]

The rules, it seems, were not broken by the arrival of four to twelve grenades, which were regarded as routine, but if twelve were exceeded, 'the chances were', retaliation followed. Despite this imprecision in levels of permissible ritualised aggression, combatants generally had a good idea of what was, or was not, compatible with live and let live, and if one side deviated the other meted out punishment by returning to officially prescribed levels of aggression.

The principle underlying the process of negative sanctions is seen by comparing retaliation on active and quiet fronts. On active fronts, the response to aggression was escalated counter-aggression based upon the high command precept: give the enemy three for one, that is, bombs, bullets, shells or whatever; whereas on quiet fronts each side received from the other an amount of ritualised aggression varying within predictable limits and merely responded in kind. But if the volume or manner of delivery of weapon fire was inconsistent with limits imposed by live and let live, the response conformed to the official three-for-one principle. On active fronts escalated aggression functioned to prime and maintain the war, whereas on quiet fronts it re-established truces by severely punishing the enemy for deviance.

Instances of escalated aggression used either to maintain war or restore peace are not infrequent in the sources. On an active front, a gunner wrote in his diary, 'I have discovered that whenever I fire at Belvarde Island the Hun at once retaliates; it is evidently a tender spot, so I shall frequently shell it now';[71] obviously, the enemy defined this shelling as violating any tacit concordat and responded unequivocally by retaliating in earnest. Nevertheless, the gunner was determined to escalate aggression and in so doing acted strictly according to military precept, namely, an aggressive gunner should search out and shell soft spots despite retaliation. What is and what should be, however, are often different things, and things were managed otherwise on quiet fronts. For instance, on the front of the 42nd division, the artillery well knew the location of the enemy's tender spots which were shelled only to preserve the peace, 'A selection . . . was made of those targets which would cause the enemy the most immediate damage and inconvenience. These were registered and when the enemy shell fire exceeded what was considered the limit of normal harassing, prompt and effective retribution was dealt out to him by guns of all calibres'.[72] Elsewhere the 42nd divisional history makes clear this sector was quiet—there was a village 2000 yards from the trenches where civilians provided light lunches for the troops, who called the sector, 'the egg and chips front'.[73] Apparently where the enemy was most vulnerable, he was least harassed, and aggression functioned as a negative sanction to maintain truces, for targets were attacked only when the enemy 'exceeded . . . the limit of normal harassing', which was not, of course, defined by official policy but by unofficial rules. The 42nd divisional artillery was not alone in this practice; for instance, in another quiet sector, the German artillery was described as 'always peaceful and gentlemanly during the morning', but as waking up in the afternoon, whereupon the guns of the 50th division, which all the time knew the enemy's soft spots, opened fire, 'so that in a short time he [the German] wished he had kept quiet'.[74] Briefly then, in each case the motive for escalated aggression is not so much to sustain or prime violence, as to diminish or contain it by making deviance from live and let live a painful choice of action for the enemy.

The infantry as well as the artillery escalated aggression as a sanction to maintain truces, and an officer of the 48th division clearly and candidly described the system in respect of rifle-grenades:

> We go out at night in front of the trenches . . . the German working parties are also out, so it is not considered etiquette to fire. The really nastly things are rifle grenades . . . they can kill as many as eight or nine men if they do fall into a trench . . . But we never use ours unless the Germans get particularly noisy, as on their system of retaliation three for every one of ours come back.[75]

This sector was plainly quiet, and the rules of live and let live operated in respect of at least two activities: working parties and rifle-grenading. It seems neither British nor Germans used rifle-grenades to initiate aggression, but the British did use them to restore truces and deter Germans when the latter were 'particularly noisy', that is, when they exceeded levels of aggression defined informally as tolerable. Similarly the Germans used rifle-grenades on the three-for-one principle as a deterrent to British provocation, and it seems mutual understanding existed, neither side bothering the other unduly.

Sometimes an ace in the hole strengthened a system of sanctions. This was a target of extreme vulnerability which was scrupulously avoided so that if the enemy broke the rules, he could be instantly aggressed and intensely injured. With respect to artillery, an ace was a tender spot, but for the infantry it might be any one of many tactical advantages, for instance, knowledge of the time of the enemy's relief in the trenches as well as the route taken by incoming and outgoing battalions. In this connection, a soldier of the 1st division compared the aggressive qualities of Saxons with those of Prussians and Bavarians: where the two latter held a sector, 'dingdong warfare', usually occurred, whereas the Saxons were a 'quiet lot', and to prove the point he described a sector where the Saxons 'used to inform the battalion when their relief was due and who were to relieve them, so, in their own words "Save your ammunition" '.[76] The Saxons wanted the quiet life, but in case the British did not they explicitly threatened to use their ace and attack during the British relief; in this context, the Saxon remark, 'save your ammunition' means: don't fire at us during your trench tour, else we'll reply when you are most vulnerable. Perhaps the Saxons thought it expedient in this case to verbalise what was otherwise tacit, for the narrator's battalion alternated in the trenches with the 1/Gloucester Regiment, an aggressive battalion little inclined to exchange peace.

Another ace in the hole situation was recorded by a gunner officer who was taken by an infantryman to a concealed post only a few yards from the German line. From this post both the interior of German trenches and numerous Germans could be clearly seen, and, further, the infantryman suspected a large dug-out existed nearby. From the military point of view it was an ideal target—a tender spot, and the gunner offered to shell it; but the infantryman declined and asked the gunner to say nothing to anyone about the target, since it was being kept as a sanction against German aggression, 'the old man [battalion C.O.] wants to keep it up our sleeve, just in case'.[77]

The analysis of positive sanctions in the first part of this chapter showed how combatants found conformity to live and let live either expedient or morally rewarding or both; and the study of negative sanctions in the second part showed that combatants defined conformity expedient since to choose aggression was not only to relinquish rewards but also to incur punishments. Now I shall suggest that a morality existed with negative as well as positive sanctions. In respect of the latter, morality laid down that benefits received ought to be repaid in kind, and, further, benefits ought not to be repaid with injury or harm. Soldiers thus thought of fire restraint in respect of fellow sufferers as ethically correct. With negative sanctions, the moral law concerned the exchange, not of benefits and gratifications, but of deprivations, that is, negative reciprocity. The primordial *lex talionis* prescribes an eye for an eye and a tooth for a tooth, and holds that punishments received ought to be repaid in kind; thus retaliation is not merely expedient but ethical.

Occasionally, the soldiers defined the enemy as inhuman and morally reprehensible and thus meriting punishment. We have already seen that the nation sought with no great success to inculcate sentiments of revenge among soldiers, and irony lies in the fact that, whereas neither propaganda nor training developed hatred for the foe, it emerged readily enough upon violation of the unofficial rules of live and let live. Combatants felt strongly that punitive retaliation was morally right where benefits bestowed by their compliance with truce rules were requited with injury and harm. Some soldiers found the official war and its rules neither meaningful nor legitimate; but the rules of peace had evolved in response to their felt needs and experience, and violation of these rules evoked strong sentiments of anger. The peace unlike the war was not an alien thing. Blunden describes an incident where angry retribution followed the breaking of truce rules, which injured several members of his battalion:

The Germans about this time also fired *minenwerfers* into our poor draggled front line; this inhumanity could not be allowed, and the rifle grenades that went over in reply for once almost carried out the staff's vicarious motto: give him three for every one. One glared hideously at the broken wood and clay flung up from our grenades and trench mortar shells in the German trenches, finding that for once a little hate was possible. To throw minnies into that ghost of a front line.[78]

In terms of military tactics the bombardment was absolutely rational, and no question of its humanity or otherwise existed; but in terms of the ethical undertones of war, it was inhuman and thus merited moral outrage and retribution. This theme will be further explored in the last chapter.

7

In the last chapter we examined how live and let live was sustained by a system of sanctions, which was mutually administered by antagonists, and which comprised rewards and punishments for compliance and deviance respectively. But truces were maintained not only by British sanctioning Germans, and Germans sanctioning British, but also by British sanctioning British and Germans sanctioning Germans. The former was an interarmy process among antagonists, and the latter an intraarmy process among compatriots, and it is this system of sanctions, administered by and between compatriots, we shall now analyse.

The sanctioning process occurred at two different levels: the interpersonal dealing with the relationships of individuals within their military primary groups, and the intergroup concerning relationships among different weapon groups, such as infantry and artillery. I shall look at the interpersonal level first. One might think that the rewards to individuals from the interarmy exchange of peace alone accounted for the persistence of truces; but the problem of persistence was more complex, since further benefits accrued to soldiers as primary group members. Among members of military primary groups, such as an infantry section of 5–10 soldiers, the exchange of benefits concerned two areas: firstly, exchanges to do with physical survival during combat; secondly, exchanges concerning economic, expressive and emotional aspects of trench fighters' lives. Exchanges affecting life and death are examined first.

During combat the aggression of a trench fighter endangered not only the enemy but also his compatriots—especially members of his section; for aggression meant retaliation, and retaliation harmed both the instigator and other trench fighters. During live and let live, however, each section member relinquished his choice of aggression, on condition all others did likewise, and consequently, the whole section was protected from potential retaliation. Truces implicated clique compatriots in tacit understandings where each exchanged peace with all others by transferring individual rights of aggression to the group, which supported peace not war; thus aggression was socially and not individually controlled. In other words, a general exchange of rewarding services existed among compatriots, not dissimilar in principle to that among adversaries. To spell out more exactly the meaning of a social relationship of generalised exchange,[1] consider a hypothetical group of trench fighters: A, B, C, D and E. At each and every point in time, A simultaneously rewards B, C, D and E by giving up aggression, as B simultaneously rewards A, C, D and E, as C simultaneously rewards A, B, D and E, as D simultaneously rewards A, B, C and E, and as E simultaneously rewards A, B, C, D. Moreover, these exchanges are not only synchronic but successive, that is, one set of exchanges follows another at immediately consecutive points of time. Throughout the combat period where clique members have the choice of aggression, the exchange of rewards is an ongoing, contemporaneous and sequential process. Both frequency and intensity of exchange are extremely high and promote strong feelings of fellowship among group members, since the certainty of each that he can rely on every other not to harm by rash action either his or the group's chances of safety and survival, grows with the passage of time. Probably the process of intense, synchronic and successive exchange is related to the comradeship which many trench fighters experienced as a positive thing offsetting other negative aspects of war. At an interpersonal level, then, live and let live involved group members in networks of exchange where each benefited the other by yielding his choice of aggression in exchange for the other's relinquishment of the same.

Concerning élite units and active fronts where missiles were fired in earnest, the safety of each soldier depended on the alertness of all others, and each trench fighter watched out not only for his own life but for every other's. On quiet fronts each gave up the right of attack and received the same in return from every other; on active fronts each gave vigilance to the rest and received the same in return. Thus on both active and quiet fronts trench fighters were bound together in systems of generalised exchange concerning life and death, and exchange generated solidarity in each case.

With respect to the second type of interpersonal exchange, the individual as a civilian exchanges emotional and material benefits within primary groups such as the family, friendship cliques, neighbourhood networks and the like but is separated from these in war, which simultaneously subjects him to long periods of stress. Research into the military, however, has shown the existence of small, informal friendship cliques which provided for their members emotional and material welfare not forthcoming from the formal military organisation. The literature[2] shows the widespread presence of these groups within all ranks of combatant and all types of weapon group. Friendship groups evolved spontaneously from formal groupings to which soldiers were assigned on completion of training. In the infantry, soldiers joined a section where the military division of labour defined their mutual interrelationships. As time passed, however, they developed common needs, faced similar problems and built up a unique collective experience, all of which generated informal social relationships which Brophy and Partridge called, 'a set of mucking-in pals . . . the true social unit of the army'.[3] Mucking-in pals formed 'trench households',[4] which Montague likened to the 'jealously close, exclusive, controlling life of a family house in an urban cellar'.[5] Trench households were highly solidary groups bound by ties deriving not only from the formal division of labour but also from shared experience, values, trust and reciprocal services. These groups were small welfare states, which guaranteed each member's wellbeing provided he in turn contributed to the wellbeing of others. Individual members specialised in providing particular services while receiving other services in return, and still other services were arranged by rota, or rendered by whoever was in the right place at the right time.

This informal organisation satisfied needs unfulfilled by the formal military structure and constituted a design for trench life: rations were received, cooked and divided by the household for its members; tea was brewed collectively; the distinction between individual and collective ownership of property was often ill-defined, for example, individuals receiving food parcels from home were expected to share some of their contents, and, further, the group received letters and parcels for absent members; mucking-in pals defended each other's property against scroungers from other households—a vital service where possession was nine-tenths of the law. Like families, trench households were sources of emotional welfare: it was expected that should one member be killed, another would supplement the official notice to next of kin with a personal and particularised account; if a combatant was wounded he was looked after by another of his household until medical help arrived—this despite orders forbidding soldiers to stop during an attack to help wounded.[6] The ties between combatants were stable and strong, for as one trench fighter observed, 'no one could have any doubt about the moral and physical failings of his pals, since everyone's life depended on the reliability of each'. Membership of a household gave individuals a degree of security which made tolerable an often uncertain and disastrous world. The exclusiveness and intimacy of such groupings was vividly conveyed by a soldier of the 47th division:

> How many nights have we marched under the light of the moon and stars, sleepy and dog weary, in song or silence, as the mood prompted us or the orders compelled, up to the trenches and back again. We have slept in the same old barns . . . we have sung songs . . . of love and lust, of murder and great adventure. We have gambled, won one another's money and lost to one another again, we have had our disputes, but were firm in support of any member of our party who was flouted by any one who was not one of WE. 'Section 3, right or wrong' was and is our motto.[7]

Among infantry officers similar cliques were found at company level. When in trenches company officers—a company commander and four platoon commanders—worked, slept and ate together usually in a dug-out. Robert Graves noted the egalitarian ethos of a company H.Q. and was impressed by the way day-to-day administrative decisions of the company were made informally at mealtimes by officers;[8] in addition to their decision-making function, informal cliques supplied welfare for officers in much the same way as section cliques did for others. Such primary groups were widespread not only among infantry but all types of weapon group, and their existence is amply documented in the literature.

In passing, it seems to me that whether individuals were members of friendship cliques or not, greatly influenced their evaluation of the war experience. Comradeship redeemed war from absolute condemnation even where combatants were extremely critical, and I suspect many trench fighters would agree with the opinion of a company commander of the 20th division: 'Though I hated the war intensely, I hope I have indicated my respect and admiration for my brother officers, my pride in my own company, and my very real attachment to the Somerset Light Infantry'.[9] Some units, however, remained merely formal associations, where members were held together by functional rather than friendship ties. In such cases fellowship did not alleviate the stress of war, which was then more likely experienced by individuals as total deprivation. It is perhaps no coincidence that the more extreme anti-war literature was written by combatants who, it seems, were not members of primary groups but were either outsiders or belonged to battalions where informal groups did not develop for one reason or another.

The benefits of clique membership need no more elaboration here, for they are particularised in many personal accounts of war. But one must emphasise that benefits were neither unconditional nor available to individuals without reciprocity on their part. A combatant was involuntarily ascribed to a formal unit after training, whereas he voluntarily achieved informal clique membership by complying with group norms. The reward for conformity was full participation in group social life together with all benefits entailed. But the punishment for deviance was either group disapproval at best, or rejection at worst, and these are powerful sanctions always, but especially in trench warfare, where life could be hazardous, and no alternative primary groups existed. Group norms regulated much of the trench fighter's life, and particularly that part concerned with aggression: on active fronts informal cliques of élite battalions supported the offensive spirit and rewarded belligerence with approval and inertia with disapproval; but in other battalions clique norms supported live and let live, and the clique rewarded passivity with approval and punished deviance — aggression — with disapproval.

As we have seen, approval was expressed by mutual exchange of benefits within the group, and the latter also managed the disapproval which followed aggression. The ultimate sanction was, of course, rejection, but milder sanctions induced conformity in many otherwise aggressive individuals. Sometimes company officers expressed disapproval with the collective suggestion that bellicosity was a temporary aberration, and a British officer described this form of sanction while commenting on a war memoir in which a German officer, after dining in the company mess, suggests to his fellow officers an unrehearsed raid on the British that same afternoon:

It was not a suggestion which one can imagine being made in a British company mess in those days. We were ready enough . . . to take part . . . in an organised raid if we were ordered to do so. A good battalion prided itself on aggressive patrolling and on being in command of No-Man's-Land at night. But, apart from that, most people were disposed to live and let live and to appreciate a quiet afternoon . . . as a heaven-sent opportunity to read a book or write a letter. Had anyone proposed an impromptu raid, 'officers only', in such circumstances, he would have been suspected of punishing the brandy too freely and advised to lie down.[10]

In the 1st division the same type of sanction was noticed by Graves when his company clique defined the voluntary patrolling of no-man's-land as 'a mad escapade'.[11] In each case the clique's collective view, that zealous aggression consistent with official norms was abnormal behaviour, restrained officers inclined to use their skills and weapons with lethal effect.

Where mild ridicule was ineffective, informal cliques used more decisive sanctions against deviants who broke the peace, and individuals were either directly told to be less aggressive or labelled by the clique. In the former case, a soldier acting as group spokesman would tell another off for his offensive spirit in a way described by one private soldier whose section was standing-to at dawn:

> We could see the German trenches distinctly now, and could almost count the sandbags on the parapet. Presently on my right a rifle spoke. Bill was firing again. 'Nark the doins, Bill, nark it', Goliath shouted, mimicking the Cockney accent, 'You'll annoy those good people across the way.' 'An' if I do!' [replied Bill]. 'They may fire at you!' said monumental Goliath with fine irony.[12]

If the individual persisted with aggression, however, he was labelled. Labelling is a stronger sanction where a group defines as undesirable certain behaviours and beliefs which are then identified often with a derisive and graphic term;[13] group members then avoid all behaviours consistent with this label, for to do otherwise is to invite group rejection. A battalion history refers to labelling when examining the attitude of soldiers towards battle:

> The troops, although not generally bellicose were almost eager for the fray . . . thus it came about that members of the battalion were heard to say that they were looking forward to the battle.

This attitude was certainly a novelty . . . it had for a long time been the practice to look askance at any man who claimed to be keen on a fight. The recognised attitude in public circles, both on the part of officers and other ranks, was that of a pacifist. 'Live and let live' was claimed as their motto by some of the most zealous soldiers, simply because they hated the idea of being dubbed 'fireaters'.[14]

A fireater was a soldier whose battle behaviour was animated by the offensive spirit. This negative stereotype helped contain aggression to levels collectively defined as unobjectionable, because trench fighters knew cliques rejected undesirable persons, and fireaters were so labelled.

Negative sanctions sustaining peace operated not only through interpersonal relations, where one person sanctions another when both are members of a primary group, but also through intergroup relations, where one group sanctions another when both belong to a wider collectivity. The groups concerning us are weapon groups: field and heavy artilleries; trench-mortar; various infantry weapon groups. The wider collectivities are the British, French and German armies.

Until now one assumed all weapon groups on quiet fronts had equal interests in live and let live since all benefited similarly. Yet this was not so. Benefits were unequally distributed among different weapon groups: all benefited in some degree, but some groups had a greater interest in truces than others and suffered more if live and let live deteriorated into kill and be killed. At intergroup level, negative sanctions concern the efforts of weapon groups relatively more interested in peace to control the actions of groups less interested; moreover our account of the sanctioning process will add meaning to the phrase 'poor bloody infantry', of whom a commentator wrote: 'the immortal valour of our noble infantry, which continues to bear the greatest burden in the fight . . . It is the infantry with rifle, bomb, and bayonet that both takes and holds, endures the greatest and the longest strain, and suffers by far the heaviest losses'.[15] Doubtless few would disagree, but it is not exactly clear why infantry endured the 'greatest burden', and the 'longest strain', and the reasons will become apparent in so far as trench war is concerned from what now follows.

Many particular factors inclined a weapon group to live and let live, but one general factor influenced all groups at all times. This was a weapon group's vulnerability to attack from enemy weapon groups; and, further, this vulnerability was inversely related to a group's capability to aggress enemy groups. Each weapon group was liable to attack from either one, two or three types of enemy group. A highly vulnerable group could be attacked by three types of enemy group, for example, the infantry was attacked not only by enemy infantry but also by trench-mortars, as well as field and heavy artilleries; moreover the capability of infantry was low for it could aggress neither field nor heavy guns but only enemy infantry. In contrast, the vulnerability of heavy artillery was low, for one side's heavy guns could be attacked only by the other's; but heavy guns had a high capability, for they could attack enemy infantry and field guns as well as each other.

A weapon group's interest in live and let live varied directly with its vulnerability, and inversely with its capability: the greater a group's vulnerability, the greater its interest in peace, and the less its vulnerability, the less its interest; the greater a group's capability to aggress enemy weapon groups, the less its commitment to the quiet life; and the less its capability, the greater its interest. Thus infantry had a high commitment and heavy artillery a low commitment to live and let live. To describe the process of negative sanctions at intergroup level is largely to show how weapon groups with high vulnerability and low capability discouraged groups of low vulnerability and high capability from aggression. But one must first show how weapon technology determined a weapon group's vulnerability and capability, thereby imposing a pattern upon trench war.

Trench war occurred on a long strip from the Swiss border to the English channel. This strip was divided along its length into two mutually hostile substrips, each with inner and outer boundaries: the inner was set by no-man's-land, the outer by the extreme range of the enemy's heavy guns. Both substrips contained three contiguous and parallel zones, which extended back successively from the substrip's inner boundary. Starting from the innermost zone and moving rearwards, these zones are here numbered 1, 2 and 3. Zone 1 was bounded on the inner side—the side facing the enemy— by no-man's-land, reaching rearwards to an outer boundary set by the extreme range of enemy small arms fire; zone 1 accommodated infantry and trenches. Zone 1's outer boundary was the inner boundary of zone 2, which stretched rearwards to its outer boundary set by the extreme range of enemy field artillery; zone 2 contained field guns. Zone 2's periphery was the inner boundary of zone 3, which reached back to its outer boundary fixed by the greatest range of the enemy's guns; the periphery of zone 3 was one boundary of the whole battle area, and the other was the periphery of hostile zone 3. The heavy guns were sited in zone 3.

These zones differed in terms of their vulnerability both to volume and type of enemy fire: in zone 1 vulnerability was at a maximum, decreasing in zone 2 to a minimum in zone 3. Zone 1 was roughly 2000 yards in depth and contained infantry which could be aggressed by weapon groups of all three hostile zones. The infantry suffered small arms fire from its counterpart, and fire from other weapon groups which, while not directly controlled by enemy infantry, were sited in hostile zone 1, such as trench-mortars. One might think that infantry and trench-mortars were equally vulnerable since both fired from zone 1 into hostile zone 1. But this was not so, for infantry were static whereas trench-mortars were mobile, often departing with speed from the trenches after shelling the enemy, who then retaliated upon infantry. The infantry was vulnerable also to field and heavy artillery from hostile zones 1 and 2. Moreover, the tenants of zone 1 had a low attack capability, for they could neither aggress nor counter-aggress the enemy in hostile zones 2 and 3, as the range of infantry weapons reached only the periphery of hostile zone 1. The 'poor bloody infantry's' high vulnerability and low capability was unique among weapon groups and its parlous position is even more obvious when compared with weapon groups of zones 2 and 3.

Field artillery occupied zone 2, the depth of which was determined by several factors. All field guns were located out of range of enemy small arms fire, and therefore no guns were found less than 2000 yards from the inner boundary of hostile zone 1 (2000 yards was the maximum range of small arms fire). The field gun's range was about 6000 yards; therefore field guns could fire over their own zone 1 (2000 yards), into hostile zone 1 (about 2000 yards), and into hostile zone 2 for a depth of 2000 yards, which was hostile zone 2's periphery and the field gun's greatest range—6000 yards. Field gunners were vulnerable to fire from hostile zones 2 and 3, that is, from enemy field and heavy guns but not to fire from hostile zone 1, that is from enemy mortars, machine-guns, rifle-grenades and rifles. But field gunners could attack infantry (which could not retaliate) and other targets in hostile zone 1 as well as field gunners and other targets in hostile zone 2; but they could not attack heavy guns in hostile zone 3.

Heavy guns were placed in zone 3 out of range of field guns for the same reasons as the latter were sited beyond the range of small arms fire. Most heavy artillery had a range of 10,000 yards and was able to fire over two friendly and two hostile zones—a distance of 8000 yards—and into hostile zone 3 to a depth of at least 2000 yards. Heavy artillery had least vulnerability and greatest capability of any weapon group, for it was vulnerable only to the fire of heavy guns in hostile zone 3, and it could attack infantry, field guns and other targets in hostile zones 1 and 2 without direct retaliation.

If fire exchanges between zones had been symmetrical, that is, field guns fired on field guns, trench-mortars on trench-mortars, and so forth, the infantry would have suffered no more than any other weapon group. But fire exchanges were often asymmetrical, since weapon groups had targets in other than their corresponding zones, for instance, medium and heavy artillery were frequently ordered to destroy enemy fortifications in hostile zone 1; moreover, weapon groups had a tendency to fire upon groups which could not directly retaliate. Discriminatory fire was the curse of the poor bloody infantry, which, of all weapon groups, was most vulnerable to aggression and least capable of retaliation. Weapon technology imposed a pattern on trench war in which infantry benefited most from live and let live and therefore was the most assiduous guardian of the peace.

The narratives of the infantry abound with instances of, and bitter comment about, asymmetrical aggression: 'If our guns opened fire the Germans did not attempt to silence them by a counter battery demonstration, but put down a *minenwerfer* barrage on the infantry',[16] declared an infantry officer of the 32nd division, and Ian Hay stated that each afternoon British and German infantry went to ground while their respective gunners had what was humourously called an artillery duel; the humour was ironic, deriving 'from the fact that they fire, not at each other, but at us'.[17] Hay also voiced the widespread infantry view that in trench war artillery fire should be limited to the shelling of gunners by gunners,[18] and this view was expressed with some bitterness by an officer of the 38th division: 'If we improved one place, the enemy artillery, responding to our gun-fire, would bring our work to naught . . . let the guns fire at their own true opponents, the enemy artillery. Thus spake the infantry, and I am quite sure that across No Man's Land, Saxon and Bavarian spoke the same words'.[19] Of course he was right. For instance, a German gunner affirmed that enmity existed between the infantry and artillery and described the sort of incident which generated it:

> He [a gunner officer] made our battery register for no reason whatsoever. Thank God no incidents occurred; the enemy did not reply. The infantry groused, of course, at our eternally drawing the enemy artillery on them with our accursed registering . . . the following remark I overheard is typical: 'It's always the same. Along comes the artillery Johnny and swaggers about registration, and then goes calmly home. And ten minutes later we've got to pay for it'.[20]

Asymmetrical aggression also concerned other weapon groups, for instance, a sniping instructor commented that infantry officers were sometimes reluctant to improve the skill of their snipers because: 'a too successful bout of British sniping sometimes drew a bombardment. The activity of snipers was therefore not always welcome to short-sighted officers, who . . . objected to the enemy riflemen calling in the assistance of *minenwerfers*'.[21] But what was short sight to the sniping expert was long life to the infantryman.

Trench-mortars, however, aroused the strongest feelings among infantry. According to Brophy and Partridge trench-mortars caused as much trouble to their own infantry as to the enemy's and 'were everywhere unpopular',[22] and this is amply confirmed in the literature. The vivid if verbose view of the 33rd division's historian is not untypical:

> We feel sure that if Sir William Stokes, when he so patriotically offered his wonderful drainpipe [the Stokes Trench Mortar] to the British Government, had known what a volcano of unpopularity and lava flow of oaths he would call down, not only upon his own head, but upon the heads of those unfortunates who were called upon to manipulate his weapon, he would have confined his inventive genius to something which irritated the Hun less.[23]

Similarly the 5th division historian observed of trench-mortars, 'owing to the retaliation provoked by their use, those operating them were very unpopular with the occupants of the various trenches',[24] while in the 34th division, mortars 'were looked on with ill-disguised mistrust by the garrison of the front line'.[25] An officer of the 48th division wrote of 'trench mortar experts trying to get permission to fire their beastly little guns',[26] and another asserted, 'nobody loves T.M. officers'.[27]

The tension between infantry and trench-mortars is the theme of an amusing short story by Wyndham Lewis, who was a gunner. The tale concerns an eccentric and aggressive trench-mortar officer—Polderdick—who persistently breaks the rules of live and let live; the reader is told that Polderdick had a:

> restless spirit of haunting adventure [which] would sometimes make him mischievious. He would come up from the billet into a quiet world, a local truce reigning throughout . . . a few lonely shells sang or creaked overhead . . . Butterflies drifted here and there. German and English, Fritz and Tom, read the newspaper, slept, wrote to Gretchen or the lovely Minnie—Polderdick would gaze around at this idyllic scene with a dissatisfied and restless eye . . . He put up his periscope . . . 'I see a Hun's back in that . . . sap to the left. Swelt my bob if I don't see two having a shave, the bastards, large as life'. As fast as they could be loaded, he sent his Flying Pig hurtling in all directions. All the peaceable warriors in the trenches were filled with amazement which rapidly turned to fury when they realised what was happening . . . Infantry officers rushed up to Polderdick, shaking their fists in his face. But flourishing his stick mysteriously, he hastily retired down the communication trench and was seen no more till the next day. Meantime the *riposte* had come and a furious bombardment had fallen on the trench. In the rear the Field [field guns] started, the heavies joined in, layer behind layer, until the enormous guns . . . were shattering the air with their discharge.[28]

Although this story is dramatised fiction, there is neither irony in 'idyllic scene' and 'peaceable warriors', nor farce in 'Fritz's shave'. The incident described was possible and plausible, and the issues concerned were real and common enough: asymmetrical aggression; the manner in which violence escalated until weapons in all three zones were involved; the fury of the infantry. All are well illustrated.

Concerning the maintenance of truces, the infantry could not order artillery or trench-mortars to stop shelling, thus the infantry's problem was to establish informal control over autonomous and deviant weapon groups, where little, if any, formal control existed. Further factors exacerbated the problem. Firstly, as we have just seen, most weapon groups were less committed to truces than the infantry—to say this, of course, is not to say other groups had no interest. Secondly, the members of specialist weapon groups tended to be individually more aggressive than the infantry. Thirdly, at the interpersonal level, aggression was controlled within a primary group where one individual sanctioned another in direct, face-to-face situations; but at the more impersonal, intergroup level—where pressure passed from group to group among groups, and not from persons to persons within groups—the control of aggression was more problematical, for functional not personal ties bound weapon groups together; consequently, both range and types of available sanctions were correspondingly reduced.

But what could the infantry do about it? How could the rifle and bayonet men prevent other weapon groups breaking the peace? The short answer is that the infantry used various means, such as persuasion, harassment, hindrance and power to bring deviant groups into line with their interests. Firstly, let us see how the infantry managed trench-mortars.

The historian of the 5th division commanded the division's guns and mortars and would have had a good knowledge of infantry ploys which made life difficult for trench-mortars. He states that mortars 'were very unpopular with the occupants of the various trenches, and considerable cunning was needed before the officer in charge could get them into action'.[29] This is confirmed by the 9th division's historian, who maintained 'all trench mortar officers were unpopular', and that trench garrisons treated 'trench mortars with disapproval if not hostility, and it was usually only by stealth that the T.M. officer was able to fire at all'.[30] But mortar crews neither had a monopoly of stealth and cunning nor held all the cards because, firstly, mortars got some of their targets from the infantry, who could keep these from mortars, and thus preserve peace; secondly, where trench-mortar officers already had targets, they were expected if not ordered to inform infantry commanders from whose trenches mortars were to be fired. For instance, in the 32nd division a mortar officer wrote: 'General Tyler, the C.R.A. of the Division, came around the line. He asked me to fire as much as possible . . . he ordered me to see the infantry battalion and company commanders about my firing as mortars were cordially disliked by the latter'.[31] Of course, an enterprising and experienced infantryman could find many convincing reasons why mortars could not be fired from his part of the line, for instance, the historian of the 15th division recorded that a brigadier ordered an 'enthusiastic' T.M. officer to find the best position for a shoot; upon arrival in the line the latter was directed to the company fronts by the battalion C.O., who soon afterwards joined the T.M. officer, who was meanwhile watching a heated dispute between two infantry captains, each claiming the other's sector was more suited than his own as a mortar site. The infantrymen appealed to the C.O. to settle the matter. After careful consideration, he decided neither site was as suitable as another, which was one hundred yards outside of the battalion's area, and to which the T.M. officer proceeded, much to the relief of the others.[32] One can be fairly sure the infantry judged site suitability not only in technical terms but also in terms of their vulnerability to enemy retaliation. Briefly, then, the infantry was in a position both to keep targets from mortars, and mortars from targets, and did so not infrequently.

Where mortars would not let sleeping dogs lie, relations between infantry and T.M. crews deteriorated rapidly, for instance, one mortar officer—Scott by name—enquired after targets at a battalion H.Q. and saw the battalion commander who 'was after my blood at first sight', for a mortar had dropped a shell short of enemy lines, and 'had ceased firing before enemy retaliation had commenced'. The infantryman didn't care that this mortar was not in Scott's command (all T.M. men were the same to him) and he wanted his pound of flesh, ordering Scott to find the officer responsible. Scott refused, asserting, 'I was not under his orders but those of the Brigadier and C.R.A., and that I only visited him to enquire what shooting he wanted done . . . and on receiving the expectedly tempestuous NO, saluted and left his headquarters. Inwardly, I rather funked thinking of what might happen on the morrow. Would I be court-martialled or not?'.[33] Scott was not court-martialled but he could have been, and it is no surprise that, rather than face such hazardous encounters, mortar crews bent on aggression resorted to stealth and did not always tell the infantry of an intended shoot. The infantry, however, were equally enterprising and mobilised instantly to eject intruders, and the 9th division historian cites Ian Hay's informal dispatches for an account of a mortar officer's attempts to get a weapon into action. Hay first passes a general comment on trench-mortar personnel:

> the most unpopular man in the trenches is undoubtedly the Trench Mortar Officer. His apparatus consists of what looks like a section of rainpipe, standing on its legs . . . This he discharges over the parapet into the German trenches . . . Then he walks away . . . For obvious reasons, it is not advisable to fire trench mortars too often . . . But the whole weight of public opinion in our trench is directed against it being fired from anywhere at all.

Hay then describes how infantry opinion was translated into action: a junior mortar officer with his 'gang of pariahs' was stealthily searching for a firing site among the front trenches, but was discovered by a platoon officer who guessed his game, and with initiative instantly quoted, 'an entirely imaginary mandate from the C.O. that no retaliatory shell fire should be attracted here'. Thus thwarted the T.M. crew removed to another likely site which, unknown to them, was in charge of a senior officer, and Hay commented, 'Field officers have no need to employ the language of diplomacy when dealing with subalterns'. Ejected this time in a peremptory way, 'the abashed procession' continued its trek until a trench commanded by a mere corporal was found; before help could be summoned, the T.M. officer seized his chance and hurriedly hurled three bombs over the parapet and then retired. Probably, the bombs fell harmlessly in no-man's-land, but in any event infantry harassment prevented effective weapon use.[34] The absence of a commissioned officer enabled mortars to fire in Hay's account, but a platoon sergeant of the 47th division told the present author in conversation that his own authority forcefully exercised sufficed to see off offending trench-mortars.

Perhaps the most cutting affront endured by a mortar crew from an unsympathetic infantry occurred in the 41st division on whose front mortars had built new firing sites. A battalion history takes up the tale:

> It so happened that on taking over one day our right front company found a beautifully sandbagged emplacement constructed just off Old Kent Road. O.C. company, a keen opportunist . . . quickly transformed it into a new, palatial latrine, seeing that, as was no uncommon occurrence, its

predecessor had been put out of action by a minnie. Nothing could have cut poor Maconochie to the quick so effectively [the T.M. Officer]. Almost in tears he appeared [at battalion H.Q.] to obtain the colonel's intervention.[35]

The infantry neither cooperated with mortars as per text book, nor were they helpful to them generally. Where persuasion and disapproval were unavailing, the infantry did not hesitate either to invent or misuse authority to stop mortars from firing. On the other hand, mortar crews faced inconsistent demands: high command ordered aggression, while the infantry expected conformity with live and let live; however, high command's scrutiny was distant and intermittent, whereas that of the infantry was instant and continuous, and consequently, more mortars complied with live and let live than would otherwise have been the case. At the same time, trench-mortars had their own interest in peace which alone induced compliance in some instances.

Whereas the infantry's attitude to mortars was mostly negative, it was ambivalent towards field artillery. We have seen that the infantry's hostility derived from the tendency of gunners on both sides to fire not at each other but at opposing trenches. But what of the infantry's positive attitude towards the gunners? There were several factors at work here. The infantry were by no means powerless where the artillery were concerned, and in this connection the remarks of an officer of the 48th division are illuminating; 'The game . . . seems to be played this way: if "A" starts shelling "B" 's trenches, "B" phones back to his gunners to say that his rest is being interrupted. His gunners promptly retaliate on "A" 's trenches—not the battery. That upsets "A" and he tells his gunners, politely or otherwise, to shut up.'[36] In other words, infantry could often persuade the gunners, though stronger methods were necessary with other groups, such as mortars. Few gunners were as unfeeling towards infantry as the one who entered the trench area while commanding artillery transport and answered infantry protests that his presence would provoke shelling with a curt, 'that's what you're here for';[37] most gunners would agree with the one who remarked that the term P.B.I., 'was a term of respect used by gunners'.[38] Generally, field gunners felt for the infantry a sympathy produced neither by chance nor individual temper but structured by their formal relationship. Unlike T.M. officers, gunner officers lived for short but frequent intervals with infantry in the front line, either as forward observation officers (F.O.O.) that is, spotting and directing guns on to targets, or liaison officers at battalion H.Q. where they had direct telephonic communication with divisional guns. A German gunner detached from his battery to infantry trenches held that 'You get to be more of an infantryman than a gunner',[39] and a British F.O.O. confirmed this in a letter to the present author, 'When a F.O.O. or Liaison Officer had to mix with the infantry officers he came to have their point of view and their worries'.[40] Thus most gunner officers had shared trench life with the infantry; had experienced the infantry's vulnerability; were aware of its role as whipping boy, and knew the reasons for its high commitment to live and let live. Now, to say some gunners identified with infantry, that is, acted and thought like them, is to say gunner officers could easily be persuaded to conform with that form of live and let live most consistent with infantry needs. On cushy fronts, such compliance meant that neither was artillery fire aggressive nor did gunners shell each other's infantry—which could be an artillery form of live and let live; typically, shelling was desultory and spasmodic—routinised or otherwise ritualised—and, unless specific orders to the contrary existed, gunners 'fired as little as possible', at the enemy, 'until some silly B decided otherwise', as the F.O.O. from the 63rd division put it. He also remarked that an order to fire a few rounds was 'often ignored', not only because it might embarrass the infantry but because a gun once fired had to be cleaned.

Concerning infantry constraint on artillery to let sleeping dogs lie, the same gunner officer remembered that, 'One was often greeted in the front line by infantry officers and N.C.O.'s "I hope you are not going to start up trouble". To which all I could answer was "not unless *you* want" '.[41] This reply referred to the twofold role of artillery in truce maintenance: firstly, as we have seen, the gunners ritualised shellfire; secondly, the infantry relied on artillery to maintain truces by instant and massive retaliation when the enemy broke the peace. Thus the full meaning of the above gunner's response was: I will not fire aggressively unless you want retaliatory fire for truce maintenance. One has already seen that deviance from live and let live was punished by escalated aggression so that either the instigator stopped firing or another group suffered and thereupon pressured the instigator to stop. From the infantry's point of view, field guns were ideally suited for this purpose, that is, as negative sanctions to restore peace, for they brought down accurate, rapid fire upon the enemy, and, further, the gunner's response was immediate, since infantry/artillery communications were quick and efficient—F.O.O.s had telephones direct to batteries and liaison officers were linked directly to guns. On the other hand, trench-mortars were not as effective as negative sanctions, for neither were they accurate nor was their range sufficient—'pigs' were notoriously inaccurate—moreover, infantry/trench-mortar communication was not quick or efficient. Nevertheless, the infantry sometimes used quick-firing Stokes mortars as sanctions as the following shows; 'While Stokes-guns were welcomed at times as offsetting the enemy's account of "minnies", there were times, especially when things were quiet, when they were not so popular'.[42]

Briefly, then, infantry/field artillery relations were sweetness and light provided the latter did not act as an autonomous weapon group, bringing down retaliatory fire upon the infantry, and provided gunners both ritualised shelling and served as a powerful negative sanction against an enemy threatening the peace. A German gunner describes such a situation:

> So far as the infantry is concerned, our battery enjoys the greatest popularity . . . because our outfit takes liaison and contact with our Brother arm of the service more seriously than was the case with any of our predecessors; we are always there when we are wanted, every request made by the infantry is carried out, and they feel we are protecting them. That is the highest objective we can possibly have.[43]

Elsewhere he relates how:

> We'd be sitting deep in our dugouts of an evening, when one of the infantry chaps would come clattering over and call. Come along, he'd say, they had something nice for us, we were to come and get it. If they ever have any delicacies to spare, they make us a present of them, partly of course because they feel we are protecting them.[44]

However, the *rapport* existing among field gunners and infantry was less frequently found among heavy gunners and infantry, for there was little personal contact between the two arms. Siege gunners rarely came into trenches, mostly staying near their guns, which were several miles behind the infantry; further, heavy guns were army or corps units, whereas field gunners and infantry belonged to division. The infantry opinion of heavy artillery was expressed by a battalion commander, who in the trenches one day

> came upon a stranger. I asked him who he was. He said he was an officer of the Siege Artillery. Now, we do not see much of the Siege Artillery in the Front Line. They shoot off the map, from behind and seem to scorn forward observation . . . So I gave the officer in the trench a few hints on manners. I said: 'We know the Field Artillery well . . . Their officers are always with us. But your people we do not know. Indeed, all that our men know of you is that they occasionally get one of your shells in the small of the back'.[45]

This lack of communication and *rapport* was a more serious matter for infantry, whose commitment to live and let live was maximal, than it was for siege artillery, whose commitment was minimal, for the former could not easily influence the latter to comply with the rules of peace, as these were interpreted in zone 1. There is evidence, however, that opposing siege artilleries came to understandings with each other, for instance, Wyndham Lewis, who for several months had been a heavy gunner on an active front, was attached to a heavy gun battery on another sector:

> This battery seldom fired. Everything was different in this part of the line . . . Nobody fired on the Vimy front, at the time I was there. Nobody thought of war. I was told that for months nothing had happened there . . . Complete peace had reigned on both sides of the line. By mutual consent the Hun and the Canuck abstained from hostilities, except for a shot or two now and then . . . They always say that it is impossible to start a war again after an armistice. This local peace must have been very enervating for the troops.[46]

In the present and previous chapters we have been looking at the system of sanctions which supported live and let live, but at the end of this chapter I want to turn to another, but related question, namely, how widespread was live and let live? I have argued it was neither isolated nor ephemeral but endemic in trench war, and this is demonstrated in some degree by illustrations showing the existence of truces at different times throughout the war, on different sectors, and in different divisions and battalions. However, sources can be organised to show not only the frequency of truces among a multitude of units, but also the incidence of truces in the careers of single units. The most suitable source[47] for this purpose is a battalion history which is comprehensive in two senses: firstly, in giving a full itinerary of sectors held by the unit, together with dates; secondly, in that the history is not merely a record of gallant deeds but includes also a sample of those activities which, if neither heroic nor glorious, are nevertheless very human (let me say I believe all trench fighters were heroic). Such sources describe trench war in its active and non-active aspects and give enough particulars so that readers aware of undertones can judge whether a sector was cushy, and, further, they often assert explicitly that live and let live prevailed in a sector, or the line was quiet, a rest cure, or whatever.

Such histories are rare but at least three exist, although the experience these record is probably not untypical. These are histories of the 1/4th battalion The Duke of Wellington's Regiment— a territorial unit in the 49th division which served on the western front from April 1915 to the end of the war;[48] the 7th Battalion The Royal Sussex Regiment of the 12th division which served in France from June 1915; and the 10th battalion The East Yorkshire Regiment of the 31st division which served from March 1916. None of these divisions was an élite formation at any time during the war. Whether the battalions were more militant than others in their respective divisions is difficult to know; certainly, none was an élite battalion like the 2/Royal Welch Fusiliers. Not all battalions produced written histories, and one could argue that only battalions with solidarity and morale would publish histories, and since morale and fighting spirit are associated, it follows these battalions had better fighting records than others. On the other hand, solidarity operated either for or against the offensive spirit. My own view is these battalions had a high degree of solidarity which on the whole ran counter to aggression.

In the following analysis, the total number of trench tours done by each battalion was established; then narratives concerning particular tours were scanned for assertions that tours were active or quiet, and other clues from which the lines' state could be inferred. Some tours could not be identified in this way and these constitute another category, labelled not known. Thus all tours are entered in Table B as one of three types.

Table B

	11th East Yorks Regt 31st division	7th R. Sussex Regt 12th division	1/4th Duke of Wellington's Regt 49th division
Quiet tours	22	22	20
Active tours	5	17	24
Not known	14	11	6
Total	41	50	50

In the case of the 11th East Yorks more than half the tours contained some measure of live and let live; with the 7th R. Sussex and 1/4th Duke of Wellington's Regt, 44 and 40 per cent respectively of all tours were quiet. Concerning active tours, little more than 10 per cent of the East Yorks' tours conformed to the official pattern of active trench war, while for the 7th R. Sussex and 1/4th Duke of Wellington's Regt, the figures were 34 and 48 per cent respectively. Whereas we have previously shown that live and let live existed in many divisions, these figures show that tacit truces were endemic in at least one battalion of each of three non-élite divisions; further, it is quite possible that similar figures could have been calculated for other battalions of these divisions—indeed, I think it reasonable to assume that live and let live was regularly found in other units of these divisions, unless evidence to the contrary exists.

The dimensions of the undertone are becoming more clear, and the next question seems to be: if live and let live was widespread in some battalions of all non-élite divisions, what was the proportion of élite to non-élite divisions? This is a difficult problem since the élite principle was not formally instituted in the British army; yet some divisions won high renown for their fighting ability and were informally designated as élite or crack units and then used by high command as assault divisions in battles and trench war. No one questioned the existence of élite divisions, but there were several opinions as to which divisions were élite and which not. Montague believed there were few élite divisions in the British army in the latter stages of the war, and this opinion appears to have been shared by Mottram.[49] Robert Graves' view seems more discriminating and, according to him, represents the consensus of thirty seasoned trench fighters from different divisions, serving as infantry instructors. Graves, who was of their number, noted that a common topic of conversation in the instructors' mess was the reliability of various divisions in battle: 'it seemed to be agreed that about a third of the troops . . . were dependable on all occasions: those always called upon for important tasks. About a third were variable: divisions that contained one or two weak battalions but could usually be trusted. The remainder were more or less untrustworthy: being put in places of comparative safety, they lost about a quarter of the men that the best troops did'.[50] This view is consistent with my own impression. One has, then, a threefold banding of divisions: a third in the élite band, a third variable, and a third non-élite. None of the battalions here examined was in an élite division, therefore each was of a division within the second or third band. If all three divisions were of divisions within the non-élite band, and if the behaviour of each was typical of others in the division then live and let live existed during more than 40 per cent of the trench tours of one-third of divisions in the B.E.F., or, put alternatively, live and let live occurred in 13 per cent of the tours of all divisions, élite, variable and non-élite, in the B.E.F. The figure of 13 per cent assumes that units of neither élite nor variable divisions made truces with the enemy; but such an assumption is unrealistic, for, firstly, one cannot be sure no battalion of an élite division at any time sustained a truce with the enemy, and, secondly, it is most likely that some units in variable divisions sometimes entered into live and let live arrangements; moreover there is evidence that élite units in variable divisions occasionally took over and maintained truces,[51] and therefore it seems reasonable to assume that non-élite units within variable divisions acted similarly but more frequently. Thus any calculation of the frequency of truces in the B.E.F. as a whole, which is based on the 40 per cent truce rate of non-élite divisions, must take account of the above factors, and the latter must increase the 13 per cent figure, but by how much one does not know.

On the other hand, if one assumes the three divisions here considered were not non-élite but variable, then other inferences are possible. If such were the case, the percentage of quiet tours in non-élite divisions is unlikely to have been less than 40 per cent of the variable divisions; on the contrary the figure would be greater, but how much greater is a matter for conjecture. If one assumes, however, that live and let live existed for 40 per cent of the tours of both non-élite and variable divisions, that is, two-thirds of the B.E.F.—and this is the least possible figure—then on an average truces occurred in more than 26 per cent of the tours of all battalions of all divisions in the B.E.F. Further the figure would almost certainly be increased, firstly, by a small number of truces where units of élite divisions were implicated, and, secondly, by a larger number of truces, which is the difference between the number of truces made by non-élite divisions and variable divisions. Altogether it does not seem unreasonable to assert that live and let live occurred in about one-third of all trench tours made by all divisions of the B.E.F.[52] Such was the scale of this undertone of trench warfare.

In the present and preceding chapters we have looked at problems concerning the maintenance of live and let live from the point of view not of external conditions threatening its persistence, such as high command—this was a theme of the first part of the book—but of internal and potentially disruptive conditions, such as the inconsistency of the behaviours, beliefs and interests of different persons and groups actually involved in truces. More specifically, these problems were: since combatants could always choose war instead of peace, why did some choose and continue to choose peace? And why were others more likely to choose war? A partial answer to these questions lies in the working of sanctions, that is, rewards for compliance with and punishments for deviation from the rules of peace. We have examined the sanctioning process at both interpersonal and intergroup levels, and the reader should now have a general picture of how and why the various groups and persons involved in trench war related to each other to form a continuous and stable pattern of peace. The perspective of Chapters 6 and 7 has not been historical in the sense of social change, for the principles underlying sanctions were constant throughout the war. The opening chapters, however, revealed a developmental sequence in trench war comprising two successive phases during which the form of truce adapted to changing circumstances. The reader might now think the tale is told, and that peace persisted throughout trench warfare in the manner described, and this might have been true in so far as the French armies were concerned (it will be argued later that the mutinies in the French army in 1917 were an explicit form of live and let live). But the British experience was different: high command still had a move to make, and this is the subject of the next chapter.

8

In earlier chapters, our themes included the origins of live and let live, and the adaptation of truces to environmental conditions posing problems to their persistence. Concerning the latter, a sequence was described in which, firstly, events threatened a type of truce which then modified its external appearance, and where, secondly, this adaptation was countered in turn by further threats to its persistence, which caused still more modification. Live and let live successively changed its outer form but retained its inner principle: overt truces involving fraternisation were replaced by covert truces based upon inertia, which were in turn replaced by truces based upon the ritualisation of violence; all truce forms incorporated both exchanges of peace and restriction of aggression; finally, each truce form was simultaneously a means of communication among antagonists. The theme of Chapters 6 and 7, however, was not the interplay of truces and environment, but the integration of the constituent parts of live and let live, that is, the degree of mutuality and consistency between the interpersonal and intergroup behaviours of compatriot and antagonist trench fighters. The problem was to explain how and why trench fighters conformed to truces, and, in this connection, the rewards and punishments constraining diverse categories of combatant to comply with and not deviate from truce rules, were analysed. Further, it was argued that the working of sanctions not only maintained live and let live but developed it; for the exchange of rewards, between both compatriots and antagonists, produced feelings of fellowship which reinforced existing truces and increased the probability that more truces would emerge.

The analysis so far has built up a picture of a resilient social system, which was supported by powerful sanctions, and which successively adapted to threats against its existence. Consequently, at this point in the argument, the persistence of truces seems less problematical, since the image of trench war given here is of endemic live and let live when non-élite units were in the line, and active trench war when élite units held the front. No doubt this is more realistic than the conventional image of continuous conflict. But no account of the undertone of war is complete without examining the interplay between raiding and truces. Raids were quite inconsistent with truces. They were a form of agression which could not be ritualised, and thus were an ever-present threat to peace in phase two. The first part of this chapter deals with the military and political circumstances behind British high command's decision in 1916 to institute a centralised and systematic policy of raiding throughout the B.E.F.; the effect of raids upon live and let live is the theme of the second half of this chapter.

Initially, our concern focuses on the opening months of the second phase of trench war, that is the period between Douglas Haig's appointment as commander-in-chief of the B.E.F. in December 1915 to the start of the Somme battles. The thesis is, firstly, that Haig saw in the raid an eminent tactic of an active trench war, and, further, he conceived active trench war as an integral part of a wider strategy of attrition; secondly, that in his relations with the French high command in 1916, Haig was handling a problem for which the raiding policy provided a partial answer.

Haig assumed command of the B.E.F. in December 1915 and inherited a strategic agreement made by the Inter Allied Military Conference, which had decided that the Allies should make a major coordinated attack against the central powers early in 1916. The conference also resolved that until then the enemy should be worn down by minor, local and preparatory attacks, and that these should be the special responsibility of nations with abundant reserves of men. Haig was immediately concerned with the nature of these preparatory wearing-out battles. Were they to be large battles similar to those fought by the B.E.F. in 1915? If not, what form would they take? In February 1916, Haig raised the issue in a letter to Joffre, the French commander-in-chief. He agreed that the Germans must be worn down before the main offensive, but distinguished between two types of preparatory attack: firstly attacks immediately preceding the major battle; and secondly those not immediately preceding this battle. Concerning the former, Haig proposed that large-scale attacks, 'which convey all the appearance of a real effort to break through . . . with the object of inducing the enemy to engage his reserves',[1] should be made ten to fourteen days before the main battle. But Haig was against large attacks during the period not immediately preceding the main battle, on the grounds that if they occurred at this time the Germans would be able to reorganise and redeploy their reserves in time for the main battle; moreover, the Germans might score a propaganda victory and claim to have defeated a large attack. Such propaganda would diminish morale among soldiers and civilians, for neither would comprehend the true and limited aim of the preparatory battles.[2] It appears from this letter that there were three stages in Haig's strategic plans for 1916: the third and final stage was the major offensive itself; the second was the fourteen days before the main battle—for this he proposed a series of large-scale attacks; the first stage was from about February 1916 until fourteen days before the major battle, and, while Haig rejected large-scale attacks for this stage (which the French appeared to favour), he did not suggest an alternative form of attack.

The British commander opposed large battles in the first stage for at least two other reasons. Firstly, many British divisions were inexperienced at the beginning of 1916. In his diary of March 1916, Haig wrote, 'I have not got an army in France really but a collection of divisions untrained for the field. The actual fighting army will be evolved from them'.[3] Haig had no wish to commit such troops to a wearing-out process involving large battles, for as British commander at the battle of Loos in 1915, he had seen units of two divisions, lacking training and experience of trench war, leave the field in disorder. He was well aware that one function of trench war was to blood new units for large battles. Secondly, Haig believed the French expected the British to carry out most, if not all, attacks of the preparatory period.[4] In a letter of 19 January, Haig told Kitchener of his fears, contending that if the French will prevailed, the British would 'get worn out in detail', and, further, the French army's efficiency would deteriorate as a consequence of inactivity during the spring. He argued that the French should join the British in the preparatory fight and asserted, 'the losses in this wearing-out fight need not be so great as to impair the French Army in the decisive battle'.[5] Haig concluded the letter by stressing the need for activity everywhere during the spring, that is, the first stage of the preparatory period.

In respect of the first phase of the wearing-out fight, Haig's plans do not seem entirely clear. On the one hand, in his February letter to Joffre, he opposed large attacks for the first part of the preparatory period. On the other hand, in his January letter to Kitchener, Haig emphasised the need for activity everywhere in the spring. It appears, then, that he intended some form of attack for the first phase; yet this attack was not to be of the large-scale type, favoured by the French. What then did the British commander have in mind? Haig's concept of the wearing-out fight is clarified by his diary entry of 14 January 1916; moreover, the same entry shows he was beginning to think of raids as more than a mere tactic of trench warfare. Haig wrote:

At the present time I think our action should take the form of: 1. 'Winter sports' or raids continued into the Spring . . . 2. Wearing-out fight similar to 1 but on a larger scale at many points along the whole front. Will last about three weeks to draw in the enemy's reserves. 3. Decisive attacks at several points, object to break through. The amount of ammunition for 2 and 3 will be very large indeed.[6]

This shows that Haig's plan for the wearing-out fight comprised two successive stages each with a specific form of attack: the first was a series of raids; the second consisted of large attacks immediately preceding the main battle.[7] But why was the British commander attracted to a raiding policy for the wearing-out fight in the first place? The answer lies partly in Haig's rejection of large attacks; but other reasons existed, and these concerned military problems, both theoretical and practical, as well as problems to do with Anglo-French relations. We will consider military factors first.

One problem confronting high commands in 1914 was to interpret the emergent trench war of the western front. The military theory of the day mostly emphasised open wars where entrenchment of either, or both, belligerents, was a temporary and generally undesirable measure. Salient themes of military doctrine included wars of movement and the offensive spirit, and each was developed in the military manuals of the major powers. At the start of the war, the high commands of belligerent nations were not equipped in terms either of theory or experience for a static war of attrition. Yet, even though the contemporary military thought did not directly deal with the new trench war, high commands did not necessarily operate in a theoretical vacuum; for as we have already seen, some generals stressed the spirit of the offensive, and, further, trench and siege wars were similar, and the principles of siege war were contained in the military manuals of the day. However, the comparison of trench and siege warfare is useful for some purposes but misleading for others. Unlike trench war, alternative strategies existed in seige warfare, for instance, besiegers could either attack the besieged, or invest a fortress and passively await surrender of the besieged. In short, inactivity or a non-agressive policy at least might determine the outcome. During the war, however, Douglas Haig opposed any suggestion that passive defence could beat the Germans, and after the war he argued that 'ceaseless attrition'[8] had brought victory. Moreover, he suspected as early as 1915 that a policy of attrition must mostly be carried out by the British as both French[9] and Russian[10] armies were no longer capable of decisive effort. But exactly what did 'ceaseless attrition' mean to Haig?

Attrition meant different things to different persons. Joffre interpreted it as widespread and constant nibbling at the enemy with local, large-scale but disjointed attacks. To Falkenhayn, the German commander, attrition meant forcing the enemy to defend ground, as at Verdun, the symbolic value of which made tactical retreat impossible, and then systematically bleeding the enemy white. Haig's theory of attrition was formulated in his final dispatch of 1919,[11] where he viewed the war as 'a single great battle', and 'one continuous engagement'. 'Ceaseless attrition' comprised two elements: firstly, 'violent crises of fighting which when viewed separately and apart from the general perspective, will appear individually as great indecisive battles'. Haig here meant battles like the Somme, Arras and Passchendaele, each of which was a series of attacks extending perhaps over several months. Such battles were the spectacular side of attrition, and most associated with attrition in the public mind. But trench warfare was the less dramatic yet nonetheless essential other face of attrition, which wore down the enemy both in intervals between battles and simultaneously with battles, on non-battle sectors. Moreover, as far as Haig was concerned, trench warfare involved raiding, which was one important reason why raids were always prominent in his mind.

The British commander regarded raiding as a highly developed form of trench war: a specialised tactic involving special skills as well as the coordination of several weapon groups. In his first despatch of the war, Haig singled out the raid, indicating some of its functions:

> One form of activity deserves mention, namely, the raids . . . The character of these operations—the preparation of a road through our own and the enemy's wire—the crossing of

the open ground unseen—the penetration of the enemy's trenches—the hand to hand fighting in the darkness and the uncertainty as to the strength of the opposing force—gives peculiar scope to the gallantry, dash and quickness of decision of the troops engaged; and much skill and daring are frequently displayed in these operations. The initiative in these minor operations was taken, and on the whole has been held, by us; but the Germans have recently attempted some bold and well-conceived raids against our lines.[12]

Douglas Haig's first dispatch covered the period 19 December 1915 to May 1916, which included the first stage of the wearing-out process for which a strategy of raiding was planned by the British commander. The dispatch indicates this policy had been instituted and, further, mentions some infantry battalions and weapon groups for good work in respect of raids. The role of raiding changed in 1916, and the new role brought about a change in the control of raids. Before 1916, high command echelons lower than G.H.Q., for instance army and corps, ordered raids for diverse tactical purposes such as the identification of enemy troops; destruction of enemy trenches and so forth. Lower levels of authority also initiated raids: officers of élite battalions planned and executed raids on their own initiative (having first cleared their plans with high command), thereby validating and creating honour for their units. Thus, during 1915, raiding was a tactical thing, in as much as raids were determined more by local, particular authorities and conditions, than by a central authority. But from the start of 1916, that is, the first stage of the wearing-out fight, G.H.Q. exercised a central control over raiding which was consistent with its new strategic role in respect of attrition. Raids could no longer be left to local initiative and chance, and they were directed by G.H.Q. The infantry had either to obey or find good reason for doing otherwise. Infantry men soon noticed the change, and one commented of raiding in spring 1916, 'It is the mode. Every self-respecting battalion will want to raid, the others will be ordered'.[13] The strategic role of raiding in a static war of attrition, that is, to wear down the enemy both materially and morally, was not only reflected in centralised control of the frequency and manner of raiding but also expressed in an official trench war manual, published shortly after Haig assumed command of the B.E.F., which declared that a basic aim of raiding was 'to compel the enemy to keep as large or a larger garrison than ourselves, and to increase his rate of wastage compared to our own'.[14] Additionally, the *British Field Service Regulations* of 1920, which embodied the experience of trench war, emphasised that, 'It is the first principle of a raid that it should result in greater losses to the enemy than to the troops which carry it out'.[15]

In short Haig's idea of 'ceaseless attrition' made him sensitive to the need for means of attrition other than, but complementary to, large-scale attacks. As a trench war tactic, the raid was developed by November/December 1915, and, by January 1916, Douglas Haig had comprehended, quickly and with insight, that raiding could have a strategic as well as tactical role, and, further, he had defined the raid as the distinctive attack of the first of two stages comprising the wearing-out fight.

At the same time, practical as well as theoretical and strategic concerns directed Haig's attention to raids. Most probably, Haig was aware of live and let live, although his knowledge would have been of a general kind, since he lacked personal experience of trench fighting. But his concern about inertia was real enough, for he believed that inactivity led to a decline in the will to fight and the offensive spirit. As a corps and army commander in 1915, Haig had vigorously pursued an active trench war policy and had probably anticipated Sir John French's directive of February 1915, which urged commanders to aggress the enemy using all available means. For instance, on 3 December 1914, Haig wrote in his diary of the new trench-mortars extemporised by his corps and criticised other corps for not doing likewise.[16] In February 1915, Haig found fault with a higher commander, who, in his opinion, was 'useless' having 'not enough of the fighting spirit'.[17] Further, in April 1915, Haig referred in his diary to a letter from himself to Sir John French, indicating his plans for 'exploding mines and harassing the enemy during the next few weeks'.[18] All this shows that Haig tried from the outset of trench warfare to stimulate the fighting spirit in order to prevent inactivity.[19] Moreover, the British commander's awareness of and concern about inertia, is suggested by the content of the definitive manual of trench war, published within three months of Haig's appointment as commander-in-chief. Intended for infantry officers, this manual not only made the policy of active trench war explicit and mandatory, but also recognised inertia as a general and pervasive, rather than local and particular problem, asserting that:

the state of comparative inactivity, which is the normal condition of life in the trenches, is very unfavourable to the development of these qualities [the qualities the manual refers to are: initiative; leadership, and aggression] in officers and men. There is an insidious tendency to lapse into a passive and lethargic attitude, against which officers of all ranks have to be on their guard, and the fostering of the offensive spirit . . . calls for incessant attention.[20]

In addition, the revised *British Field Service Regulations* of 1920, which contained a new section spelling out the principles and problems of position (trench) warfare, clearly shows the influence of Haig's active front policy, where it affirms the necessity 'for eradicating false ideas inseparable from the comparative inertia of a prolonged period in the trenches'.[21] The manual goes on to direct that the enemy must be continuously aggressed.

Another reason for Haig defining inertia as a problem was related to his theory that the war could only be won by ceaseless attrition. Clearly, from this perspective, the final collapse of the enemy depended upon the material and moral exhaustion brought about by large battles and trench warfare; but it is equally clear that no attrition of the enemy occurred where live and let live prevailed in the line. The British commander was therefore faced with the practical problem of motivating men to fight or, to put it differently, of taking effective counter-measures against live and let live. Haig was well aware that getting men to fight was a real and complex problem, and, in an earlier chapter, we saw that he thought too simple the view that man was brave by nature and for that reason fought with vigour.[22] On the other hand, and consistent with the prevailing thought of his time, he probably assumed the existence in man of an inborn aggressive motive, which military commanders must under certain conditions cultivate in order to maintain warfare as a going concern and prevent its deterioration into peace. Douglas Haig perceived in raiding an effective method of stimulating and sustaining the aggressive spirit of the B.E.F., and, further, he most likely thought that aggression once aroused pervaded and animated all other warlike activities, which was a necessary condition for the success of the policy of ceaseless attrition. His policy of raiding provoked much controversy, for instance, some argued that raiding decreased rather than increased aggression. Whether the raid stimulated the aggressive spirit is not clear, but one thing is reasonably certain: the raid and its consequences were quite inimical to tacit truces. Perhaps more than any other factor, raiding destroyed the system of live and let live, and exactly how this occurred we shall examine later in this chapter.

The decision to establish a raiding policy concerned another problem of a political kind, which faced Haig early in his command. In 1915 and 1916, Anglo-French relations were disturbed by the French belief that the British had not taken their share of the fighting in 1915. A few days after he took command Haig wrote to his chief of staff: 'In the past there has certainly existed on the part of the French a feeling that we were not always willing to take our fair share . . . The present moment [Haig was referring to the change of command] is opportune for creating a good impression and paving the way for smooth negotiations with the French'.[23] Whether the French belief was justified does not concern us here; but it is useful to know that at 31 December 1915 French casualties numbered 1,961,687 compared with the British total of 512,420.[24] In this connection, one of the first problems with which Haig had to deal related to the British role in the first stage of the wearing-out fight. The French not only expected the British to play a major role here but also had suggested a strategy, namely, a series of large-scale attacks. Haig was faced with a dilemma. On the one hand, he was against large attacks for reasons examined above; on the other hand, inactivity would confirm the French belief that the British lacked the resolution to fight, and, consequently, Anglo-French relations would deteriorate still further. Raiding, however, provided a partial answer to this problem. When faced with French suspicions of British inactivity, Haig could and did counter that the British policy of active trench war, to which raiding was integral, resulted in heavy British, and by implication German, casualties. For instance, on 31 May 1916, after attending a meeting which included French political as well as military leaders, Haig wrote in his diary that: 'General Castelnau read over the Memorandum . . . I took exception to a para, which said "British Army had not been attacked" and pointed out that our losses since December amounted to 83,000—and 653 mines had been sprung during that time'.[25] A corollary of the British commander's assertion was that raiding had been an effective means of attrition during the preparatory stage. Thus, in so far as raiding prevented a worsening of Anglo-French relations, it was a politically expedient measure.

In conclusion to this account of the military and political

circumstances surrounding the establishment of the raiding policy, it is useful to show the extent to which raiding increased during Haig's tenure of command. Raids were infrequent before December 1915, and the official history records only one raid for that year. However, during the first six months of Haig's command, that is, 19 December 1915 to 30 May 1916, the British made 63 raids, each involving between 10 and 200 men.[26] During June 1916, the month before the battle of the Somme, three British armies carried out 43 raids,[27] and these raids, which had been substituted for large-scale attacks, were intended to wear down the enemy and confuse him as to the exact point of the main attack. In the period July to December 1916, while the British 4th Army fought on the Somme, the other three armies made a total 310 raids: the 1st Army made 166 raids; the 2nd made 104; and the 3rd made 40.[28] The number of raids reached its highest point during this time. Every British division in France save two was used in the main battle, and as each division left the Somme, it continued the process of attrition with trench war and raids upon other army sectors.

After the Somme, the number of raids decreased somewhat. Between 9 April and December 1917, 270 raids were carried out;[29] and in the period 8 December 1917 to March 1918, 125 raids were made by the B.E.F.[30] In summary, then, 106 raids occurred in the six months before the Somme in 1916; 310 raids were made during the Somme battles, that is, between July and November 1916; about 270 raids were carried out in 1917, from April to December preceding, during and after the battles of Arras and Passchendaele. The scale of this relatively seldom studied other face of attrition suggests that raiding played a not insignificant role in the general policy of ceaseless attrition, which, Haig claimed,[31] weakened the enemy to the point of collapse in 1918. Next we shall see that raiding not only contributed to the wearing-out process but also prevented the disintegration of war into peace.

The first part of this chapter concerned military and political circumstances relating to the introduction of a raiding policy, and the second refers to the interrelations of raiding, the offensive spirit and live and let live. Haig's raiding strategy aroused intense controversy, and, according to one authority, 'So long as men who took part in the war are alive, the subject of raids is like to crop up whenever two or three are met together'.[32] The debate centred around two connected issues. Firstly, some held that raids built up the offensive spirit, while others believed that raids weakened the spirit of aggression. An alternative view will be argued here, namely that a raid increased the incidence of aggression in the trenches but this increase was caused more by the destruction of live and let live than the stimulation of the offensive spirit. Secondly, critics of raiding argued that generally the raiders had greater casualties than the raided, and since the British raided more frequently than the Germans, it followed the British suffered more than their opponents; thus raids were condemned as an ineffective means of attrition.[33] It will be suggested here, firstly, that this view has not been proved, and, secondly, that some critics of raiding could take neither a synoptic nor a detached view of the situation and problems faced by Haig, because of their partial experience of the war, as well as their understandably intense involvement in it.

But who are these critics? And what are their criticisms in detail? Two types of comment exist: firstly, the judgements of infantry called upon to make raids; much of this is unreflective and unconcerned with the strategic or tactical roles of raiding, being more of a gut reaction either to raids just done or to prospects of raids about to happen. Secondly, the considered judgement of military historians and others, often with personal experience of trench war, regarding both the aims of raiding and its success, or otherwise, in respect of these aims. As to the former, it seems the non-élite infantry's attitude was generally critical, and raids were viewed at best as an 'overrated pursuit',[34] or, at worst, as 'a foul, mean, bloody, murderous orgy'.[35] Most infantry would probably agree with Blunden:

> I do not know what opinion prevailed among other battalions, but I can say that our greatest distress at this period was due to that short and dry word 'raid'. Adducing one reason or another, the lowering of the enemy's spirits, the raising of our own, the identification of some supposedly new troops opposite, the damaging of the German trenches, the Great Unknown behind us were growing infatuated with this word.[36]

On the other hand, aggressively inclined persons were most probably attracted to raiding, and others were motivated either by rewards such as medals, promotion and leave, or by needs to prove their skill and bravery both to themselves and others. For instance, one divisional historian, a trench fighter himself, wrote:

'Underlying the keenness of the officers and men who carried out these raids . . . was a restlessness, not only a vague desire for action, but a definite wish to be given the opportunity of proving above all to themselves that they were as anxious as ever to meet the Bosche face to face, and confident of the result of the encounter'.[37]

Nor did the élite infantry give unqualified support to raiding. An élite battalion liked to manage its own raids; but high command sometimes imposed a raid of its own design upon a unit, and, if high casualties resulted, high command's compliments for a job well done did not assuage a battalion's sense of loss or its animosity against the generals.[38] Moreover the aims of high command could arouse bitter comment, especially when a raid was ordered to stimulate the offensive spirit. To a battalion with fighting prowess, such an order seemed a libel against its honour, and the reaction of the C.O. of the élite 1st Gloucesters cannot have been untypical: 'raids for the sake of raiding were the worst part of the war. Nobody minded going over to get a necessary identification, but the other kind "to maintain the fighting spirit of the troops" was loathed by everyone . . . A unit that needed such an encouragement should have been disbanded, or at least its commander should have been replaced'.[39] This is understandable enough, yet less than fair, perhaps, to units of less renown; but to disband such units was not practical from high command's point of view, although battalion commanders were sometimes sent home for a lack of fighting spirit. However, other regular officers, who served with fighting battalions, had similar misgivings about raiding. For instance, Jack referred to a raid as a 'disagreeable prospect',[40] while Hitchcock declared that raids 'became unpopular with regimental officers and the rank and file, for there grew up a feeling that . . . [raids] . . . owed their origin to rivalry between organisations other than battalions'.[41]

The considered judgements of historians are mostly against raiding. As regards these, one can distinguish between an unqualified and qualified disapproval. Liddell Hart, trench fighter and eminent military theorist, rejected both raiding and active trench war, which, he argued, forced the Germans to strengthen trench defences, thus causing higher British casualties in large battles.[42] However, one object of active trench war was to destroy defences, and it is arguable that if active trench war were absent, the Germans would have had more time for, and less interference during, their defensive work, whereupon casualties would be higher and not lower in battles. But a qualified disapproval of raiding is more frequently found than total condemnation (though Liddell Hart is joined by Lord Moran, whose opinion is examined below), and an example of the former is given by Cyril Falls, the military historian, who held that 'Raids were frequently useful, and sometimes imperatively necessary; but the British raided too often'.[43] Possibly this reflects the majority opinion. Falls identified three functions of raiding around which dispute centred. Firstly, he referred to the tactical role of raids; secondly, he distinguished raiding designed to keep the 'enemy on the stretch', which presumably meant raiding to wear down the enemy morally and materially (what is here identified as the strategic role of raids in attrition). Unlike some critics, Falls argued that these two functions were justifiable; but he unequivocally condemned the third type of raid, namely, raiding aimed to stimulate or prime the aggressive spirit. More generally, critics objected either that raiding decreased rather than increased the fighting spirit, or raiders suffered disproportionate casualties, often among the best officers and men, or both.

As regards raids and attrition, whether raiding was generally successful or not can be answered only by comparing the material and moral damage inflicted on the Germans, with that suffered by the British. Morale is difficult to measure, but casualty figures exist. However, those who argue against raids on grounds of an unfavourable net balance of casualties do not demonstrate that British casualties exceeded those of the German.[44] It is not claimed here that raiding was a profitable means of attrition, but merely denied that the contrary has been proved, and whether raids were effective in this sense is an open question. Assuming, however, that fewer casualties were suffered than inflicted during a successful raid, some evidence in the official history suggests the balance favoured the British for some of the war at least.[45]

The objection to raiding as a means of priming or sustaining the offensive spirit was quite simply that, in general, raids did not achieve this. One authority asserted that the preparation and execution of a raid 'took heavy toll of even the biggest thruster';[46] Moran would have agreed and likened the 'nervous energy' and 'will power' of trench fighters to a fixed capital, which was used up, or added to, according to circumstances. The conditions of trench war—'the daily drain of the trenches'—depleted this capital continuously: 'in the trenches a man's willpower was his capital and he was always spending, so that wise and thrifty company officers watched the expenditure of every penny lest their men went bankrupt. When their capital was done, they were finished'. Moran believed that an overlong exposure to trench war exhausted nervous energy, and, in his view, to initiate a policy of raiding was 'to dissipate like a spendthrift not only the lives but the moral heritage of the youth of England'. Moran did not doubt that raiding eroded the fighting spirit and he vigorously and bitterly condemned Haig's policy: 'That doctrine grew out of the fanatical sens of duty of a Scotch covenanter unversed in the workings of the human mind. The Army was to be blooded in a hundred raids, a hundred limited offensives, as the only way to preserve, or was it create, the offensive spirit'.[47]

Raiding, then, was a mistaken policy, stemming from Haig's misunderstanding of human minds during war. Such criticism needs careful consideration since Lord Moran was a notable medical man as well as a battalion medical officer with nearly three years experience of trench war. On the other hand, to believe that Moran's experience gave a generality to his judgement, which otherwise might appear partial, could be misleading; for his experience was, in fact, singular. Firstly, he served with an élite battalion, and these were a small proportion of the total. Secondly, this was an élite battalion in an indifferent division. The problem of divisions with élite and non-élite formations was that high command might order élite battalions to carry out not only their own part in battle and trench war but also that of lesser units, which either had defaulted or could not be trusted. This placed a great and disproportionate strain upon élite units. For instance, Moran recorded that a unit with a poor reputation in his division retreated in disorder during the Somme,[48] and this incident and its consequences were described in more detail by another author, who served with a good battalion in the same division: a battalion left the battlefield in disarray, whereupon three other battalions of the same division were ordered to retake the abandoned position; this was accomplished but at the cost of many casualties.[49] A similar position could occur in respect of raiding, where élite units sometimes carried out their own share of raids as well as that of less reliable units. At the same time, raiding to stimulate the offensive spirit was more frequent in poor than other divisions, and, further, élite units defined such raids as unnecessary and a slur on their honour, as we have seen. Thus Moran's battalion was in a difficult and peculiar

position, and suffered the consequences of the failure of others. This
should be borne in mind when considering his evaluation of raiding.
One can agree with Moran that raiding neither created nor
sustained aggression in élite units, without accepting that the effects
were similar in all battalions, or denying that raiding increased
aggression in non-élite units, which is our argument below.

Lord Moran's experience of trench war, though personal and
direct, was nevertheless particular; on the other hand Douglas
Haig's knowledge of the war, though based on reports, was more
general and representative, and Haig, not Moran, knew best the
problems of trench war. He understood that where live and let live
prevailed, trench war involved neither a surfeit nor a sufficiency of
aggression but a lack of it, and, further, that zealous, prolonged
fighting did not always entail the attenuation of aggression, as
argued by Moran and others. Haig's problem as commander-in-
chief was not the high morale of a few élite units, but the fighting
spirit of the greater number of non-élite battalions; for the latter
carried out the major part of active trench war (although élite units
set examples and standards), which was integral to his wider
strategy of ceaseless attrition. Possibly, the British commander
would have agreed that raids were not necessary to stimulate
aggression in élite units, but it would have been impractical and
unwise to institute different raiding policies for different units.

We have accepted, then, that raiding was a mistaken policy for
some formations but questioned the view that raids generally decreased aggression. However, no positive connection between raiding
and the fighting spirit has yet been here suggested or demonstrated.
Whether raids incited the offensive spirit depends on what one
means by the latter. The concept was used ambiguously. The
aggressive or fighting spirit can be taken to mean an inborn, *sui
generis* impulse to attack, existing to some extent in all men, but
needing constant or periodic priming in others. Given this meaning,
one can argue both that raiding increased aggression and that it did
not. For instance, some probably believed that raids primed an
innate aggressive disposition and that this was then either self-
sustaining, in which case soldiers became thrusters, fire-eaters or
natural killers, or that the inborn motives needed periodic building
up, in which case a recurrent priming policy such as raiding must
be established. In both cases raiding stimulated aggression which
subsequently diffused into other areas of trench fighting.
Alternatively, it is equally plausible to argue with Falls and Moran

that the aggressive spirit could be primed and sometimes increased, but limits existed beyond which it was diminished rather than augmented by incitement, and raiding which passed these limits was therefore counter-productive.

However, it is unwise to increase the number of explanatory concepts without need, and, further, there seems little reason to use an explanation which refers to a non-observable, unverifiable entity, while simpler explanations seem adequate. For instance, it is more economic and less misleading to connect one observed set of aggressive behaviours to other observed aggressive behaviours or alternative social facts, and to construe both as created and sustained by learned social rules, which certainly exist, rather than to mysterious, unlearned impulses which might or might not exist. This has been the type of explanation employed in this study.

One might object that the slaughter of the First World War was evidence for an aggressive instinct in man of the type we have just sought to deny. But it should be clear by now that if such an instinct, impulse or motive existed, in either conscious or unconscious form, trench war would have been far nastier, brutish and more violent than it actually was. Therefore aggressive acts will be interpreted as parts of an ongoing reciprocal exchange and quite unrelated to a hypothetical aggressive instinct or any such construct.

Thus, if by an aggressive spirit is meant an innate impulse of some kind, the question of whether this was incited by raids can be settled only by those who believe such entities exist. On the other hand, if aggressive spirit means observable acts of aggression between antagonists, the short answer is: yes, raiding augmented aggression in non-élite battalions. Raids increased the number of situations where antagonists aggressed each other, and decreased the number of situations where violence was ritualised. More exactly, raiding primed and sustained the exchange of aggression because, firstly, it destroyed live and let live, thereby creating identifiable motives for aggression, and, secondly, it could not be ritualised.

Of course, a raid itself was a sequence of violent acts and advanced aggression in this narrow sense alone; but the present argument is that raids enhanced aggression not only directly, during a raid itself, but also indirectly, during the aftermath and as a consequence of a raid. In a vague way, some persons were aware of this connection. For instance, a medical officer of the 23rd division observed of one raid that high command had sanctioned for his unit that: 'it would help to check the growing tendency to fraternise, a

manifestation of goodwill and war weariness which had appeared in
that part of the line, and which alarmed and horrified the powers
which directed battles from the base'.[50] Elsewhere he commented
more generally upon raiding:

> How those raids came to be abominated by those who had to
> make them . . . No doubt the staff knew best and these raids did
> keep up the fighting spirit of the troops . . . But all the same the
> thought often did occur to me, what would have happened if that
> fighting spirit had not been continually whipped up. The French,
> until egged on by us, did not go in for raids. Their comfortable
> policy between battles was to live and let live, and the French are
> no mean warriors. I still wonder what would have happened if
> the friendly meetings between German and English soldiers in
> No-Man's-Land, where they exchanged cigars for cigarettes and
> chattered together, had not been nipped in the bud.[51]

This medical officer did not say whether raiding stopped inertia and
ritualisation as well as fraternisation, nor did he exactly explain how
raiding disrupted the peace; instead he wrote vaguely of a fighting
spirit, which, once primed by raiding, ended live and let live.

A not dissimilar view of the relation of raids and aggression was
held by a brigadier of the 36th division, who originated many raids
and thus had opportunity to observe and compare their effects upon
a number of battalions. He affirmed that 'no doubt a successful raid
had a good effect in a unit, but not always upon the raiding party.
The meticulous preparation made the "waiting for the dentist
period" hard and trying . . . Many units had to deplore the loss of
the very cream of their officers, N.C.Os and men in raids. And the
cold-blooded courage demanded of all took heavy toll of even the
biggest thruster'.[52] Like Lord Moran, this officer seems to have
thought of the fighting spirit as a fixed, quantifiable thing, which
diminished with overuse among members of a raiding party, but,
further, and unlike Moran, he thought that this loss was offset by an
increase in fighting spirit among members of a unit who were not
raiders.

The idea that raids added to the aggressive spirit not of raiders
but of non-raiders is interesting but not altogether clear. The
reasoning was, perhaps, that a successful raid added to regimental
pride among non-raiders, and this pride was expressed after the raid
by aggressing the enemy with greater frequency and zeal than

before. But did this effect occur in élite or non-élite units, or both? Not in élite battalions; for either élite units were zealously aggressing the enemy before a raid, in which case a 'good effect' was unnecessary and would not have been visible anyway, or, if one accepts Moran's view, raiding had bad, not good effects, on élite units, especially when intended to incite the offensive spirit. But how, then, did non-élite battalions benefit from a raid? It is unlikely that the raiders' example persuaded the non-raiders to aggress the enemy more than before because, as we have seen, the prevailing impulse was to restrain rather than to imitate fire-eaters. If, however, the 'good effect' referred neither to élite nor non-élite units, then at least two other types of unit remain: élite battalions which had suffered a temporary eclipse and were seeking to regain reputation by a raid, or ordinary battalions striving for élite status. In each case, it seems plausible that successful raids exhausted the raiders, yet at the same time either reinforced, attenuated or stimulated nascent, regimental pride, thereby eroding informal controls against aggression, which consequently augmented violence. Yet such battalions were at any one time a small proportion of the total, and the brigadier who held that raiding had a 'good effect' on non-raiders, neither asserted nor implied that the effect occurred only in special cases. Therefore, one assumes that the connection held for average units in variable divisions, such as the 36th division (which was the brigadier's division) where some battalions for some of the time kept truces with the enemy.

But if one accepts that raiding had a 'good effect' on non-raiders and, further, assumed that the effect held for battalions in variable and non-élite divisions, the question still remains: how was this effect produced? By what means were raiders constrained to attack the enemy more zealously after a raid than before? In the sources, some clues are found in trench fighters' comments, often expressed in figurative language, as to the way raiding disrupted the continuity of trench war. For example, raids are said by one author to disturb 'the even tenor' of trench war.[53] But no 'even tenor' existed in active trench war; on the contrary, it comprised frequent, often irregular and thus unpredictable exchanges of violence and escalated counter-violence. Probably the author had in mind here the routinised aggression of quiet fronts. Describing the same phenomenon, an officer of the 38th division observed that trench warfare like all routine, 'was subject to cataclysmic upheaval from time to time, when orders came to the infantry to carry out a raid'.[54]

Both authors were referring to systems of ritualised violence and intimated that raiding disturbed these regular and predictable exchanges so radically that their re-establishment was problematic. The analysis of trench warfare in this book has shown that ritualised violence was not only a means whereby the mandatory discharge of lethal missiles was rendered harmless but, quite as significantly, was also a means of indirect communication among antagonists. Ritualised missiles and activities conveyed to the initiated the message that each side was content to restrict aggression and intended, in both present and near futures, neither injury nor harm to the other for so long as he conformed with the rules of live and let live. The constant flow of ritualised violence allowed each antagonist to know the other's current mood as well as to predict, with some confidence, his future behaviour. Moreover, as this communication persisted, the degree of mutual confidence increased. Without doubt, one consequence of this process was the growth among trench fighters of feelings of security and peace of mind, which compared favourably with the unrelenting anxiety and apprehension of active front lines.

A raid, however, abruptly shattered both peace and communication as well as the security these engendered. While in progress the raid was a massive break in communication, but, further, and this is the crucial point, neither communication among enemies nor mutual trust was automatically re-established during the aftermath of a raid. On the contrary, an uncertain and apprehensive interval emerged where neither side knew what to expect from the other: the side which had raided expected retaliation, but could not predict when, where and how; the side which had been raided was also nervous, wondering whether the attack was an isolated event or the first of a series, which marked the arrival in the trenches opposite of an élite unit bent on further aggression.

Raids thus destroyed the mutual conveyance of benevolent meanings, substituting suspicion for trust, and anxiety for assurance, thereby creating a situation where soldiers shot first and asked questions afterwards; consequently, the informal control over aggression within battalions was removed. In the 35th division an officer described the result of such a 'cataclysmic upheaval' thus: 'Generally a raid had the same effect as stirring the muddy bed of a stream, where the water remains discoloured long after the discolouration. Ever expectant of another visitation, the subsequent period found both sides harassing one another'.[55] As regards the same effect of raids, another soldier in the 56th division commented, 'Raids were becoming more frequent on either side, with the object of keeping the enemy in a constant state of nerves'.[56] To sum up, before a raid mutual trust, confirmed by ritualised violence, prevailed among antagonists; after a raid, a background expectancy of mutual caution was general, where each act of the enemy, whatever its real meaning or intent, was defined and reacted to as a potential and lethal attack. Such a situation inhibited the re-emergence of peace; for where mutual distrust had replaced trust, the cycle of aggression and escalated counter-aggression was likely to recommence at any time.

The reason for the brigadier's belief that successful raiding had a good effect on non-raiders but enervated the raiders themselves should now be more clear. On the one hand, a raid might lessen morale among the raiders because it involved great strain. On the other hand, a raid might seem to heighten morale, that is have a good effect, among non-raiders, for it encouraged mutual harassment among trench fighters on both sides of the line, who did not take part in the raid, and who would otherwise have kept the peace. The presence of fighting in place of inertia following on from a raid was no doubt judged by the brigadier, and more generally high command, as a good effect. Raiding increased aggression, however, not because it improved morale or invigorated the offensive spirit, but because it destroyed understandings to restrict violence among non-raiders. Moreover, the effect of a raid was most probably independent of its success or failure. Both efficient and abortive raids destroyed peace, communication and restraints against aggression, thereby facilitating mutual violence. Either way adversaries were left in a 'state of nerves', as the formal rules of war replaced the informal rules of peace.

Incidentally and *à propos* our analysis of raids, one criticism of Haig's raiding policy might usefully be looked at again. As we saw, raiding was condemned, not only for its negative effect on the aggressive spirit, but also for its unprofitability as a means of attrition. In detail, some part of the second criticism went as follows. Casualties incurred in raiding and in active trench war were of two kinds: the former comprised a high proportion of skilled and experienced trench fighters, while the latter included, to a greater degree, trench fighters of more average abilities. The policy of raiding therefore meant a disproportionate and systematic loss of seasoned soldiers. However, if the present analysis is correct, the loss of skilled raiders must be balanced against the gain in fighting skills among non-raiders. Before raids were established, soldiers could more often choose whether to fight or not, and some chose not. Therefore fighting skills, which would have developed in active trench war, remained undeveloped during live and let live. But raiding removed this choice for, in the aftermath of a raid, trench fighters had no alternative but to evolve and practise fighting abilities in order to stay alive.

On the subject of the B.E.F.'s fighting skills in 1916, some authorities have justified the Somme battles of July to November on the grounds that the survivors, who had been amateurs at the battle's beginning, had by its end become the hardened veterans who later smashed the German army.[57] Whether this view is correct is not an issue here; but it misleads inasmuch as the B. E. F.'s fighting ability before the Somme was underestimated. It is suggested here that without the fighting techniques developed during six months raiding and, more importantly, the aftermath of raiding, in the wearing-down time before the Somme, the B. E. F. would have been less prepared for the protracted struggles of that battle. Small-scale attrition was a sensible and steadying preparation for large-scale attrition, and, to some extent, the British were veterans when the Somme commenced.

It has been argued that raids generally destroyed live and let live in the case of non-élite units. But the role of raids was different regarding élite units, on whose sectors the rules of kill or be killed normally prevailed. Here, the pattern of trench war was constant aggression and counter-aggression, which often escalated to a point where one side raided the other. Thus a raid might be the final and most violent in a sequence of reciprocal aggressions. Moreover, some evidence suggests that after such a raid a period of tranquillity intervened until the cycle of mutual violence restarted. For example, a soldier of the 2/Royal Welch observed after a night-time raid: 'It was a glorious summer morning the next day and anyone who had visited this part of the front would have thought it was the most peaceful spot in France. No shells were coming over, no reports of rifles . . . It was generally like this after a show'.[58] In conclusion, then, with non-élite units raids destroyed peace and primed aggression, whereas with élite units, a series of violent exchanges culminated in a raid, which brought about a lull until fighting recommenced.

In earlier chapters, however, we showed that trench fighters rendered weapons and tactics consistent with live and let live. Was raiding similarly adapted to peace? The short answer is no: raids and truces could not be made mutually consistent since exchange and ritualisation were impossible when raids occurred or just before they occurred. The nature of raiding excluded any form of peace exchange with the enemy. Exchange among antagonists occurred where each chose peace when war was possible, and received peace in return. Exchange persisted as the benefits accruing to each party were roughly equal. Equal exchange could not occur with raiding. Raiders, ordered to kill and capture the enemy, would have required a body or prisoner in return for the choice not to raid. But to those who were raided, the cost of exchange with the raiders, namely of giving corpses and/or prisoners in return for immunity, and of actually being raided was the same: either way some would lose life and/or liberty. No advantage accrued to the recipients of a raid, and thus no basis for exchange existed with raiding.

One trench fighter wrote a short tale where special circumstances, not without humour, created the basis for exchange in connection with a raid. The story starts with British and Germans living in peace, when the British high command wants a corpse or prisoner for identification and orders a raid. The British soldiers are dismayed and one visits the German taking a pet German dog, which had strayed into British trenches. He attempts to persuade a German to volunteer as a prisoner, offering money and dog in exchange. The Germans naturally refuse; but they appreciate the common predicament, and propose that if the British call off the raid, they could have the newly dead body of a German soldier, providing he would be given a decent burial. The exchange was concluded; the raid officially occurred; high command got the body; and all parties were satisfied.[59] All this is fiction, however, and I have found no evidence in sources that such an exchange, or one similar, ever occurred.

Thus no basis existed in normal circumstances for a conspiracy among antagonists to ritualise a raid. Moreover, no opportunity existed for a conspiracy among raiders themselves to do so. High command might accept a scrap of German wire or cooked report as proof of a fighting patrol but not as proof of a raid. Accordingly, a raiding party had two choices, firstly, to refuse to leave their trenches, which was a serious crime; or secondly, to raid the enemy, and thereby destroy the peace. As to the latter choice, the raid would be either a success or a failure, but each way high command had proof the raid had occurred: if it were successful, a prisoner would be taken; if the raid were a failure, the raiders' casualties would be proof of an attempt. It is difficult to conceive that raiders, acting alone without the enemy's help as in the above fiction, could ever successfully conspire not to raid where a raid was ordered. The raiding party was a large body of men organised into a complex division of labour, such as field gunners, trench-mortar crews and infantry groups. While a tacit conspiracy among a few trench fighters to ritualise a patrol was feasible, a conspiracy among many and diverse groups of men to ritualise a raid would clearly have been as complex as the raiding plan itself and thus detected without difficulty. There is an account of a ritualised raid in a French war book, but whether this is fact or fiction is not clear. In this case, the French soldiers did not obtain dead bodies from the Germans but instead gave their own casualties from normal trench war to high command as proof that a raid, although a failure, had been attempted.[60] The raiders protected the conspiracy from suspicious, fire-eating compatriots by sending them elsewhere when the raid was supposed to take place.

To continue with the subject of the incompatibility of raiding and peace, raids obstructed live and let live because they recruited bellicose persons and thus made available and mobilised for official aims a pool of aggression, which was otherwise unofficially controlled. We have seen that small, informal cliques maintained peace by punishing aggressive deviants, who would have attacked the enemy. But raiding released these from group control; for raids were carried out in many cases by volunteers, who were most probably either of an aggressive temper or more willing than others to use violence as a means to an end, such as promotion, leave, decorations and so forth.

Raiding was therefore inconsistent with live and let live for several reasons: it replaced a background expectancy of trust with one of mistrust, making problematic the communication of peace motives; raids could not be ritualised; the nature of raids precluded any basis for exchange among adversaries; and raiding mobilised aggression otherwise controlled by informal cliques. Another trench war tactic essentially inconsistent with live and let live was mining, that is, the practice of burrowing under and blowing up enemy trenches. Moreover, mining and raiding obstructed live and let live for a similar reason, namely, each hindered the communication of peace needs among adversaries. Mining adversaries, burrowing from different levels and points towards each others' trenches could communicate neither by inertia nor by word of mouth, and mining, like raiding, could not be ritualised. Inertia as a means of communication was out of the question, for it was entirely ambiguous. The sudden stop of audible enemy burrowings could mean one of several things: that the enemy had given up; that he had changed direction; or that he had finished, laid explosives, and was about to blow one's trenches sky high. Thus a miner could not certainly know the meaning of his enemy's inertia; but the infantry was not always aware of this barrier to communication, and one officer, displeased when mining started on his sector, commented generally of miners:

> There is a class of Englishmen to whom even the present methods of trench warfare are not satisfying . . . Unhappily there is a class of Germans of the same morbid disposition, but the two lots have not yet come to any understanding to 'live and let live' as amongst themselves . . . They prefer to burrow in an ominous silence and get at their antagonists below, with a thousand tons pressure of blasting powder.[61]

The tension below ground generated tension on the surface; for mine explosions were unpredictable, occurring any time of the night or day, and, further, explosions were sometimes accompanied by small attacks. No wonder trench fighters found 'the continued uncertainty as to whether one's trench was undermined proved a strain on the nerves',[62] and that 'The dread of being suddenly blown into the air kept men on edge'.[63] In the 38th division, an officer declared 'Mining puts an end to all repose',[64] and, in the 39th division, Blunden observed 'one could never feel at ease'[65] where mining was going on, and further, 'a mining sector . . . never wholly lost the sense of hovering horror'.[66] A similar ethos of apprehension and uncertainty obtained on mining and raiding sectors, producing similar effects in each case. Any movement or sound of the enemy, which would cause no alarm on quiet fronts, was at once perceived as an incipient attack and reacted to accordingly. Thus mining, like raiding sectors facilitated the aggression and counter-aggression of active trench war, and, indeed, most parts of the line where mining proceeded were very active, whether held by élite or other troops.

In the first phase of trench war, in 1915, miners were controlled by local infantry commanders,[67] who sometimes tried, it seems, to prevent mining in order to preserve the peace.[68] In the second phase—in and after 1916—control of mining, like that of raiding, was centralised, and an Inspectorate of Mines was established at British G.H.Q.[69] Douglas Haig encouraged mining[70] and viewed both it, and raiding, as integral to trench war. Thus, during 1916, the infantry lost control of mining, which, like other trench war operations, was at that time coordinated into a comprehensive, centrally directed and conceived plan of active trench warfare.

Until now the argument has been that raids and mining primed aggression in trench war. To prime means to bring into activity by a preliminary act; but the process whereby raiding primed aggression was more complex than has hitherto been described. Raids not only ended truces, creating backgound assumptions of uncertainty, thus indirectly promoting aggression, but they also generated self-sustaining and direct motives for aggression, of at least two kinds. Firstly, raids triggered the technical rule of retaliation, that is, the formal military precept that counter-aggression, preferably escalated, must always follow aggression. Secondly, raids often elicited the moral rule of negative reciprocity, namely, an eye for an eye, a tooth for a tooth. The former defined retaliation as rational, expedient and technically correct behaviour and belonged to the formal, bureaucratic structure of relationships of men at war. The latter defined retaliation as retributive justice, that is, behaviour correct and proper in an ethical sense, and operated at the level of informal relationships.

As to the technical norm of retaliation, should the Germans raid the British (or conversely), high command invariably ordered a counter-raid. Raids 'naturally provoked retaliation',[71] affirmed the official history; and, moving into a sector well suited to raiding, Blunden averred that the future, 'promised two hateful excitements—the order to raid the enemy thereabouts, the receipt of a raiding party from him'.[72] But while retaliation was mandatory, it did not necessarily follow either that the raiders of the first instance were the counter-raided of the second, or that those raided in the first instance were the counter-raiders of the second. Some battalions expiated the sins of others. For instance, the Germans raided an unprepared battalion of the 24th division, capturing 50 prisoners so swiftly and silently that the British knew nothing of the raid until the Germans announced it over their wireless. To add insult to injury, the raiders hoisted opposite the British line a notice reading, 'Say What About Those 50 Rations'.[73] Understandably, a battalion other than the one raided was ordered to counter-raid. A raid, then, not only created a time when each antagonist, apprehensive of the other's intentions, tended to make pre-emptive attacks, but also set going the technical norm of retaliation in the form of official orders to counter-raid.

Secondly, a raid frequently evoked the rules of revenge, ethical precepts recognised as right and proper by trench fighters themselves. Sentiments of revenge were called forth by several circumstances. For instance, if an élite battalion were successfully raided, retaliation was obligatory, not only for technical, but also for moral reasons, since only a reprisal raid restored regimental honour. The élite 2/Royal Welch carried out a good example of a revenge raid. The battalion was holding the line at Givenchy, a notoriously active mining sector, when the Germans fired a mine, causing 93 casualties and blasting a crater 40 yards in diameter, and simultaneously raided the Royal Welch, who instantly reorganised to beat off the attack. According to the battalion history, 'the disaster . . . aroused a general wish for a return blow',[74] and, on receiving high command sanction, the battalion at once planned and practised the reprisal raid. 'Never has a raiding party gone over the top with such a thirst for blood and revenge',[75] wrote a divisional gunner, and a Royal Welch officer remarked, 'our fellows fought like demons'.[76] The raid was successful. Much damage was done and 43 German prisoners were taken; but, more importantly, the battalion was avenged.

Most probably, revenge was a frequent and important motive in much raiding and counter-raiding, and the need for vengeance appeared particularly intense and powerful following the death of a comrade. For example, Bucher, an experienced German N.C.O., graphically described the reactions and sentiments of the German survivors of a French raid. Immediately after the attack, Bucher had forcibly to restrain another N.C.O. from foolhardy revenge: 'I laid Gaaten out with my pistol butt because he was about to climb out of the trenches and seek vengeance for the three heaps of shattered flesh which had been men under his command'.[77] Several of Bucher's comrades were dead as well as an officer, highly esteemed by his men: 'How tiny the 5th company had become. Kolbe was dead too. There was now a double score for us to settle with the enemy . . . Our day of reckoning would come without a doubt'.[78] Later, a senior officer spoke of a revenge raid, and the author commented: 'We, the 5th company, refreshed and brought up to strength, were to speak the last word. A terrible and pitiless word it was to be'.[79] Meanwhile the sector was becoming more active: 'The enemy seemed to be aware that we meant to get even with them—they were always on the alert . . . the day or the night of our revenge was to come nonetheless. Our front line casualties had become heavier'.[80] The mood of the raiders just before the act of reprisal is portrayed: 'The men who, steel helmeted, bristling with weapons and loaded with hand grenades, crowded around the ladders, were to be the avengers of the old 5th company. Men dead and buried were in a few minutes to cost us still more dead—an eye for an eye and a tooth for a tooth'.[81] The author revealed his own avenging impulse: ' "If I'm not hit getting across, I'll settle the account for Vonau" I said fiercely. Riedel and Gaaten assured me that they too had scores to pay off'.[82] The reprisal did not fail, and the raiders inflicted many casualties; consequently, the front line became even more active, and Bucher remarked, 'For two days life in our sector was no laughing matter. Then we were relieved and we hurried to the rear with no thought but to escape from that murderous zone'.[83] The uncertain aftermath of a raid with its heavy casualties, the order to counter-raid, and the strong revenge needs of the counter-raiders are well illustrated here. Likewise shown is the manner whereby a raid not only primed but also sustained aggression; for the highly motivated Germans inflicted many casualties among the French and thereby generated still further revenge motives for subsequent raids and active trench war.

.

In conclusion, the argument regarding two major topics of this chapter, namely, the interplay of raids, live and let live and aggression, and the effect of raids upon the infantry, is summarised. Concerning non-élite units, raiding not only primed aggression, by dissolving truces and thus causing distrust conducive to aggression, but also primed and maintained aggression by creating formal constraints towards counter-raiding and informal constraints to revenge. As to the effect on non-élite infantry of raiding, the present conclusion is consistent with the views of both the forementioned authority that raiding had a 'good effect', on non-raiders, and the commander of a non-élite division that raiding was 'The type of warfare best calculated to improve the offensive spirit of the men'.[84] Raiding therefore had a latent function, to prevent peace breaking out. Some higher commanders seemed aware of this function in a general sense but did not clearly grasp the details of the mechanism involved, and speculated instead on the effect of raids on a loosely conceived offensive spirit. Finally, this latent function was independent of the success or failure of a raid. Raids involved no priming function on sectors held by élite battalions, where active trench war was generally progressing. In some cases, however, raiding intensified aggression by creating revenge motives for dead comrades and regimental honour as well as counter-raids. As to the effect of raids on élite units, the conclusion here is that raiding to stimulate the offensive spirit generally had a bad effect, but was not always harmful where vengeance was involved.

9

One major concern of this study has been to gain some general understanding of why men fight, and, more particularly, to account for the way men performed in combat in the First World War. Why were some trench fighters more zealous, aggressive and disciplined in their combat roles than others? How were these men able to endure the harshness and horrors of combat? What exactly was this ability to endure? What were its correlates, and from what did it derive?

There are four major types of explanation for the way men perform in combat roles.[1] The first holds that identification with the traditions and symbols of military organisations motivates soldiers. It is my impression that identification with regimental tradition was a powerful force for efficient role performance among élite battalions, where leaders, and led, had discipline, skills and a sense of duty. However, élite battalions were relatively few, and the influence of regimental tradition on non-élite units was more problematic. Again, identification with divisional symbols and traditions seems to have been important in the case of élite units, such as the 29th, 7th and Guards divisions. 'It was a matter of pride to belong to one of the recognised top notch divisions',[2] wrote Graves. On the other hand, it seems that divisional *esprit de corps* was entirely lacking in some non-élite units, for instance, some trench fighters, interviewed during the course of this research, could not remember the divisions in which they served.

The second explanation is that men act bravely in combat in order to fulfil an aggressively masculine code of behaviour. It could be argued that in non-élite units this code had little effect since trench fighters rejected their bellicose peers. Yet one could counter that, even on quiet fronts, trench war could be nasty enough for men to feel that their behaviour conformed to male precepts. I think, however, that the code of being a man had much the same force in both élite and non-élite units; but the courage required to realise this code, while it did not differ in kind, certainly differed in degree between élite and non-élite units. Bravery was relative: what was heroic in one battalion was routine in the next.

A third explanation adduces the abstract values and symbols of the wider and especially civilian society, such as the nation state, the flag, political ideologies and a way of life. The influence of these factors is not clear. Sources show that trench fighters from élite units referred less to patriotic symbols than to regimental or divisional ones; but this might mean that the former, while not without influence, were less powerful than the latter. Nor was identification with symbols of the larger society entirely lacking in non-élite units. For instance, a private soldier of an indifferent division observed candidly: 'there wasn't one in a hundred of us who, if he could have crawled home with a shred of honour, wouldn't have taken the opportunity'. Yet he qualified this at once: 'On the other hand we knew that the war had to be fought out and that somebody had to do the fighting. But had we been asked the plain question: "Will you go on, or will you let Germany win?" I don't think there was more than one in a hundred of us who would have thrown in his hand'.[3] The present tendency of some is to devalue nationalistic sentiments in general. Yet I believe that some commitment to country and cause existed among most trench fighters, and further, that on both active and quiet fronts this made the war more tolerable than it would otherwise have been. Moreover, this factor could explain the different reactions of French and Austro-Hungarian trench fighters to extreme disenchantment with the war. With but little commitment to the Empire, the latter tended to surrender to the enemy in relatively large numbers; whereas French soldiers, typically more patriotic, did not give themselves up as prisoners during the 1917 mutinies. Instead they refused to attack the enemy unless first attacked by him, or, put another way, French soldiers publicly declared their support for live and let live, which privately had existed for a long time.[4] The conclusion is, then, that identification with the wider society, although insufficient itself for exemplary behaviour,[5] did influence combat behaviour in indirect but positive ways.

A fourth type of explanation, pursued for the most part in this study, emphasises informal social relationships among combatants. These are often termed primary groups, in contra-distinction to secondary groups, formed by the formal military division of labour. Primary groups have an independent significance in military organisation, which has been systematically explored in researches dating from the Second World War. The findings of some of these and of the present study will be compared later. The attainment of the aims of large military bureaucracies is either supported, or obstructed, by primary groups within them. Such goals include, of course, the zealous, aggressive performance of combat roles. In a study of the Second World War, social scientists found that the German soldier's battle efficiency derived from membership of a primary group which 'met his basic needs, offered him affection and esteem from both officers and comrades, supplied him with a sense of power, and adequately regulated his relations with authority'.[6] Further, the authors argued that secondary symbols, that is, the symbols of wider national, political and military organisations, were most inspiring when directly associated, often in the person of an officer, with the gratification of basic needs. What is meant by this is well illustrated by the author of a First World War classic. After a hard time in the trenches where it is reduced from one hundred and fifty to eighty men, an infantry company returns to base, where the cook has prepared rations for the full complement. The survivors argue that double rations should be served to them; but the cook asserts in a legalistic way that he lacks authority for this. However, a company officer, who chances upon the situation, orders the distribution of all rations, not hesitating to cut through the red tape in order to satisfy the needs of his men.[7] From the perspective of social exchange, it seems that German commanders gave to their men a paternalistic concern for their emotional and material welfare, perhaps beyond the call of official duty, and received in return conscientious combat performance. Other studies, however, indicated that the influence of primary groups was not always consistent with the values and interests of the larger military bureaucracy.

One reason, then, why men do or do not fight, concerns the informal social relations which emerge among soldiers on the battlefield, and the present research has explored and confirmed this theme in respect of the First World War. Nevertheless, there is a difference here: whereas other works relate combat performance to informal groups of compatriots, this research relates performance not only to compatriots, but also to informal networks of antagonists. Thus unofficial negotiation among adversaries determined what happened on the battlefields of the First World War.

Until now the present study has for the most part attempted to show that men in non-élite units sometimes did not fight very vigorously. At other times, however, they fought well enough. Why was this? What had it to do, if anything, with primary groups? Doubtless many factors affected non-élite soldiers' propensity for fighting. Some factors had a partial effect, influencing particular men and groups at particular times and places; but others were more pervasive, constraining most trench fighters, élite as well as non-élite, at most times and places. It seems to me that revenge was ubiquitous in trench warfare, and certainly it was connected not only with raiding, but also with most other forms of fighting. One cannot read widely among the personal documents of trench fighters and remain unaware of the role of vengeance in trench war. Many sources recount incidents of revenge, while in some nemesis is almost a theme. In this concluding chapter, I shall suggest an interpretation of trench warfare as comprising two basic and interrelated processes, each involving exchanges, albeit of contrary kinds. Further, I shall argue that the reasons why men sometimes fought, yet at other times did not, had much to do with each of these two processes, as well as their interplay.

We have been dealing with one of these processes throughout this book. It is, of course, the mutually contingent exchange of gratifications, or positive exchange, where trench fighters exchanged peace. This has been revealed as a theme or dynamic of trench warfare. But this theme alternated with another. Each theme concerned exchange, but whereas the first referred to the give and take of benefits, the second had to do with the give and take of losses.[8] I will call the latter the mutually contingent exchange of deprivations, or negative exchange of trench warfare, and it took the form of reciprocal exchanges of aggression, such as exchanges of weapon fire causing death, injury or discomfort among trench fighters. As we have seen, all fire exchanges concerned the formal, technical rules of retaliation; but some negative exchange was in addition constrained by an ethic of retributive justice. Moreover, this ethic of vengeance was a corollary of cooperative exchanges within small primary groups of compatriot soldiers. It is here that the two themes of trench war were causally related. To grasp this interplay of positive and negative exchange, it is useful to describe again the cooperative exchange of small combat groups.

It will be remembered that such exchange produced intense sentiments of solidarity, since it was both synchronic and successive, that is, at each point in time as well as at successive points in time.

Each member guarded not only his own welfare but also the welfare of all others, and received in exchange the same service from everyone else. Further, on quiet as well as active sectors, such simultaneous and successive exchange maximised the survival chances of both individual and group. On active fronts, each trench fighter was a warning system for every other during incessant fire exchanges, and a transitory lapse of concentration by one trench fighter could bring disaster not only to himself, but also to his comrades. On quiet fronts, the lives of all depended on each man's constant choice of peace; for should one choose war, retaliation might kill or injure all others. Thus at all times during combat the life of each member of the primary group was in the hands of every other. Consequently, the frequency of cooperative exchange was extremely high and generated strong feelings of fellowship, and these latter entailed intense needs for revenge when fellow trench fighters were killed. Here fellowship and vengeance were inextricably linked. War produced comradeship, which produced vengeance, which in turn, produced war. Vengeance appeared on quiet as well as active fronts, for casualties also occurred on the former, though in fewer numbers and more by chance than design. In this, perhaps, lies a blend of pathos and irony which rendered unique the trench war of 1914–18. Initially, the war set apart men who later became bonded by its working; yet who, despite this bond, were then compelled to mutual killing.

In summary, it is suggested that the creation of vengeance, which primed and sustained aggression, was inherent in trench war; for cooperative exchange, which was a group response to war on both quiet and active fronts, generated comradeship, while the death of a comrade produced needs for revenge. At this point the two themes of war were causally related in a circular way.

Many personal documents of trench fighters illustrate the thematic nature of vengeance, and amply show that the technical act of retaliation was simultaneously a moral act of revenge. A moral matrix surrounded, suffused and supported the exchange of aggression in trench war. For instance, when a soldier of his section was killed by a sniper, Junger commented: 'His comrades lay in wait a long while behind the parapet to take vengeance. They sobbed with rage. It is remarkable how little they grasp the war as an objective thing. They seem to regard the Englishman who fired the fatal shot as a personal enemy. I can understand it'.[9] Presumably the phrase, 'war as an objective thing', means war as a set of rational and specialised techniques for the exchange of aggression with an impersonal enemy (unlike a feud and vendetta where enemies are personal), which are bureaucratically established, administered and controlled. To what extent soldiers understood the war in such an objective way is an interesting question; but, as Junger shows, their actions were constrained not only by rational objective factors, but also by non-rational subjective sentiments of revenge, which while not part of a bureaucratic blueprint for trench warfare were nevertheless a central dynamic of the conflict. The search for retributive justice according to the trench fighters' code was endemic not only to sniping and raiding, but throughout trench war operations. For example, a 'hate' was a frequent, recurrent and violent event of the war, defined by one trench fighter as: 'a short intensive shoot by all the infantry weapons that could be got into action: rifle and machine gun, fixed rifle, rifle grenade, and trench mortar. It was usually directed on some object, or a place where movement was seen. Often it was in revenge for some local incident'.[10] Vivid accounts of such hates, planned as vengeance for the death of comrades, occur in the sources, and they frequently convey the intensity of feelings aroused.

For instance, on the death of two friends, an officer of the 7th division, 'swore hard at the devils that had done this', and immediately planned with two trench-mortar officers a hate, which duly occurred: 'I was elated. "This for Thompson and Robertson" I said, as our footballs [mortar shells] went on methodically . . . and then our guns began . . . grim exaltation filled me. We were getting our own back . . . my blood was up . . . the Boche was sending heavies over . . . I would go on until he stopped. My will would be master. Again our shells screamed over'. The hate continued until the instigator commented to a colleague, "I think we've avenged Tommy"'.[11]

In the 12th division strong sentiments of revenge were generated by a German *ruse de guerre* which killed many British. A machine-gunner recorded that about three hundred Prussians, 'came across No-Man's-Land feigning surrender . . . their hands held high, but with pockets full of egg bombs. Just before reaching our wire they flung themselves to the ground and hurled a rain of bombs into B Company's trench, causing many casualties . . . the rest of the battalion was sullen and furious . . . many vowed dark revenge . . . Most Vickers gunners swore a private vendetta'.[12] Occasionally, one side manipulated live and let live in order to inflict loss upon the other. For example, an infantry officer described an incident where a British band sited in the front line played music to entice musically inclined Germans into exposed positions:

> at six minutes to midnight, [the band] opened with 'Die Wacht am Rhein'. It continued with 'God Save the King' and 'Rule Britannia', each tune being played for two minutes. Then, as the last note sounded, every bomber in the battalion, having been previously posted on the fire-step, and the grenade-firing rifles, trench-mortars, and bomb-throwing machine, all having registered during the day, let fly simultaneously into the German trench; and, as this happened, the enemy, who had very readily swallowed the bait, were clapping their hands and loudly shouting 'encore'.[13]

No doubt some Germans swore private vendettas on that occasion also.

The sources contain many more illustrations of revenge. Our object here, however, is not to estimate exactly the role of retribution in the maintenance of violence, but, firstly, to point out in a preliminary and general way the origin and endemic nature of vengeance in trench war, and, secondly, to suggest that revenge needs were at all times powerful and potential counters to live and let live. Further it was argued that revenge was a comprehensive constraint towards aggression, for it influenced all kinds and categories of trench fighter. Whereas other constraints, if comprehensive, were relatively weak, for instance, rewards for aggression; or if strong were local in effect, for instance, *esprit de corps* in élite battalions. One final important point should be underlined: revenge created revenge. A vengeance-inspired hate was a response to a comrade's death, but at the same time it killed the opponent's comrade, which, in turn, produced still further vengeance needs.

During the First World War trench war occurred not only on the western front but also on several others: in Italy, where the Italians and British (the latter from 1917 only) fought Austro-Hungarians and Germans; in Salonika, where British and French fought the Bulgarians from 1915 until the war's end; in Gallipoli, where Anzac, British and French confronted the Turk during 1915; on the eastern front, where the Russian armies clashed with the Austro-Hungarian. Did live and let live develop on all these fronts, or was the western front unique? The answer is not wholly clear; but evidence from sources suggests that tacit truces emerged on all these fronts except Gallipoli.

In 1917, five British divisions were sent to Italy and took over part of the Italian front line, where one officer of the 48th division observed, 'it was obvious that the war on this front had been conducted by the Italians and the Austrians on the live and let live principle'.[14] According to this officer, the British at once established active trench warfare; but some British units maintained truces taken over from the Italians. For example, in the 41st division, an officer said of the Austrians, that 'their policy was live and let live', and affirmed that 'Life was so peaceful here that it was possible to walk around the front line in broad daylight quite safely'.[15] On the other hand, the Austrians and Italians were aggressive enough on some fronts, and another officer of the 41st division noted that 'Austrian artillery and sniping were extremely quick and accurate' when his unit relieved the Italians.[16]

War likewise alternated with peace in Salonika. There is no mention of quiet fronts in the 60th division's history,[17] and active trench war with raiding is recorded by a battalion in that division.[18] Yet on the 28th division's front:

the Bulgars not only favoured a policy of 'live and let live' but had the qualities of sportsmen. A game of football, for instance, could be played in full view of the enemy without fear of molestation – unless it was watched by a very big crowd; nor was hunting ever interfered with. A drill parade, however, was more than they could put up with: once one was observed, shells were sure to follow.[19]

An artilleryman also recalled that the British played 'football within range of the Bulgarian guns', and further, that:

The Bulgars took no notice when our infantry hung their washing on the barbed wire . . . on the other hand, whenever one of our batteries dropped some shells that were too close for the Bulgars' comfort, they would promptly respond with a salvo . . . which would fall uncomfortably close to the British battery, just to let us know that they had no intention of putting up with that sort of thing. Here, as on the Struma, the Bulgars had demonstrated their willingness to pursue a live and let live policy; but if we preferred to be unpleasant then they could be unpleasant too.[20]

Live and let live also appeared on the eastern front: 'For some time now not a shot has been fired on either side although everybody is calmly walking about on top, and even taking an afternoon kip up there', wrote a German infantryman. 'We keep an eye on one another but we think it would be foolish to disturb one another by shooting. When the Russian sentry goes on duty, he thinks it necessary to inform his *vis à vis* of the fact. "Morning ayoosht" he calls'.[21] A German gunner described similar scenes among Hungarian and Russian troops, 'At the moment not a shot is being fired—the two sides are even bartering goods and newspapers'.[22]

No evidence exists, however, that tacit truces took place in Gallipoli, and some evidence suggests that they did not. I have found in the sources only one mention of a truce, and this was described by John Monash, an Australian brigade commander at the time. The purpose of the truce was to bury the dead, and its entirely formal and legal mode of arrangement was, perhaps, indirect evidence that informal truces happened rarely in Gallipoli. Monash was told in the trenches that the enemy wanted an armistice to bury their dead and he described the subsequent events thus:

> I asked for a staff officer to come forward, and a . . . Turkish officer . . . came up and spoke very good French. I told him I had no power to treat, that this would have to be arranged, if at all, between the Army Corps Commanders and with proper Articles of Armistice; that his commander had better send an accredited *parlementaire* half-way to discuss the matter. This was at 4.30, and I gave them 10 minutes to get all their men into their trenches or we should fire upon them. That same night General Birdwood sent out to General Liman von Sanders practically repeating the terms of my offer, and sure enough next day a meeting took place and drew up an agreement for an armistice from 8 a.m. to 5 p.m. on 24 May.[23]

One suspects that the matter would have been arranged more quickly and less formally on the western front; but the trench fighters of Gallipoli lacked knowledge of the principle and workings of live and let live, and thus had none other than a legal formula for truces. Elsewhere Monash described trench war on Gallipoli which seemed to conform closely to the officially approved pattern:

We have been amusing ourselves by trying to discover the longest period of absolute quiet. We have been fighting now continuously for 22 days, all day and all night, and most of us think that the longest period during which there was absolutely no sound of gun or rifle fire throughout the whole of that time was 10 seconds. One man says he was able on one occasion to count fourteen but nobody believes him.[24]

Further, an infantry officer of the 63rd division with experience of both Gallipoli and the western front contrasted 'the trenches of the peninsula', with 'the normal or "peace time" sectors of France'. He wrote, 'For, in truth, it was all very different. Above all, from dawn to dawn it was genuine infantry warfare . . . in those hill-trenches of Gallipoli the Turk and Gentile fought each other all day with rifle and bomb, and in the evening crept out and stabbed each other in the dark. There was no release from the strain of watching, and listening and taking thought'.[25] All this, and the absence of any account of truces in other sources, suggests that active trench war was typical of Gallipoli, and that live and let live did not develop for some reason. However, conclusions based on these sources are provisional; for the sources, unlike those concerning the western front, were not systematically sampled, and, further, they are relatively scarce.

It seems then, that in the First World War live and let live occurred not only on the western front, but also on several other battlefields. What of other wars, however? Have truces emerged in different conflicts and at different times? Or is it the case that live and let live was peculiar to the First World War? Does other research corroborate the findings of the present study, or do no comparable data exist? Sociological research into men, morale and war is sparse, and much work on morale by non-sociologists seems more concerned with high morale and its causes, and low morale and its cure, than social patterns of low morale, war weariness and combat fatigue, the exact analysis of which was a prime aim here. Nonetheless, social scientists have made some studies and their data and findings are not inconsistent with those of this study, and additionally lend some support to the present research.

A seminal study into the battle behaviour of United States soldiers in the Second World War is that of S. L. A. Marshall, *Men Against Fire*,[26] which one eminent authority described as 'perhaps the only truly successful attempt to analyse the nature of combat in the Second World War'.[27] Marshall's data are compatible with this study. His interpretation, however, differs from our interpretation of the data in this research. Some comment will now be made both on the facts found by Marshall and his explanation of them.

The range of Marshall's research was remarkable. He interviewed in the Pacific and European war theatres about 400 infantry companies, that is, approximately 70,000 men. Interviews took place soon after combat when the men in full assembly spoke publicly as witnesses in the presence of their commanders. The research aim was to find the infantry fire ratio, that is, the proportion of actual fire achieved in combat measured against the total possible volume of fire. The latter concerns factors such weapon technology, physiology and geography, whereas the former relates to more intangible factors like morale. One of Marshall's major findings was that in an infantry company of average efficiency only 20 per cent of soldiers used a weapon against the enemy during battle. In élite units, the proportion of weapon users increased but did not exceed 25 per cent. With rare exceptions, the ratio of active to non-active soldiers did not vary throughout the 400 companies interviewed. The ratio remained constant despite variations in, firstly, tactical situations such as attack and defence; secondly, concerning geography and climate such as between the Pacific and Europe; and thirdly, types of battleground. The fire ratio was the same both for battle-experienced and freshly trained troops. Most soldiers ignored the enemy even when his person presented a clear target. The size of the discrepancy between the actual and expected fire ratio surprised both the author of the research and the commanders of the units interviewed.

Marshall partly explained his data as follows. Most persons have a fear or horror of committing homicide, and, during combat, this fear of killing sometimes exceeds that of being killed. Moreover, its intensity causes passing paralysis, which renders soldiers incapable of killing the enemy. The fear of homicide is a learned moral constraint, deeply embedded in the core of the personality. Killing, or the thought of it, is thus traumatic, since persons simultaneously violate themselves as they violate others. As a result the fear of self-violation causes a fear of aggression, which often makes men unable to act against the enemy.[28] In addition, Marshall supports his argument with, firstly, psychiatric evidence from the Second World War, which shows that the fear of killing was the most common cause of battle fatigue among soldiers,[29] and, secondly, his own experience as an infantry officer in the First World War, recalling the 'great sense of relief' one felt upon a quiet sector when not forced to kill. According to the author, a 'remark frequently made when the enemy grew careless and offered himself as a target' upon a quiet front was, ' "Let 'em go; we'll get 'em some other time".'[30]

One can agree with Marshall that most persons do not find homicide gratifying, but it does not follow, therefore, that a fear of killing leads to battle paralysis on a large scale. In this connection, a distinction between impersonal and hand-to-hand combat encounters is useful. As to the former, little evidence exists to suggest that the tension between humane impulses and orders to kill caused paralysis. After analysing thirty-three autobiographies by soldiers of the First and Second World Wars, one researcher found that most soldiers kill without feeling or shock after their first exposure to violence, and, further, most think of killing as natural or instinctive.[31] This conclusion is borne out by the behaviour both of Robert Graves, who affirmed that he shot Germans whenever they were visible,[32] and another, who alternated command of a company with bouts of sniping and who commented, 'it is a novel and pleasant sensation to see the fellow you hit fall'.[33] While each reaction shows a certain *sang froid*, real or assumed, neither suggests paralysis or reluctance to kill. Further, I have found little evidence in the personal documents used in this research that soldiers experienced either a fear of aggression or temporary paralysis. Many expressions of revulsion against war exist in the sources; but these did not make men inert, although they were probably a factor in perfunctory weapon use.

On the other hand, some sources show that violent hand-to-hand fighting caused responses not dissimilar to those described by Marshall. For instance, raids involved vicious hand-to-hand combat, which caused an officer to comment: 'one sees the raid as a foul, mean, bloody, murderous orgy which no human being who retains a grain of moral sense can take part in without the atrophy of every human instinct', and the same officer affirmed that without hatred, 'such as I seem psychologically incapable of feeling towards an unknown enemy . . . I . . . don't see how it's [the raid] to be done'.[34] This attitude seems somewhat similar to Marshall's idea of battle paralysis. At the same time, other combatants saw hand-to-hand fighting as a situation where one either killed or was killed, and their response was instant and lethal action against the enemy, not an inertia borne of paralysis. Moreover, impersonal encounters were typical, and hand-to-hand combat infrequent, in both world wars; and if the fear of killing merely concerned hand-to-hand combat, then it could not have been the reason why men frequently and typically did not fire weapons in those wars.

The psychiatric evidence supporting Marshall's argument is not convincing; for it shows only that the small proportion of soldiers hospitalised with battle fatigue had a fear of killing. One cannot infer from this atypical sample that the majority of soldiers, who were neither hospitalised, nor suffered battle fatigue, also experienced a horror of killing. Another criticism is that the argument is inconsistent in parts. On the one hand, Marshall argued that an involuntary paralysis of the will caused fire restraint; yet according to this own testimony, conscious decision prevented fire against the enemy, ' "Let 'em go, we'll get 'em some other time".' Further, one might infer from the term 'we' that the decision was a group and not an individual thing, that is, a social rather than psychological event, whereas Marshall's interpretation of fire restraint is, for the most part, psychologistic. It is possible that if Marshall were more concerned to interpret his trench experience in terms of social exchange and less concerned with speculative psychology, he would have guessed that the low fire ratios of the Second World War were linked with live and let live. It is likely that the fire restraint on the Le Tour front cited by Marshall expressed a tacit understanding among adversaries. The German disregard for personal safety derived from expectancies, tested by experience, that the enemy fired neither instantly nor zealously on quiet fronts. Similarly, American restraint derived from assumptions, verified by events, that Germans also exercised restraint on quiet fronts; and, further, that past German restraint should be reciprocated by present American restraint. It is more likely that antagonists were conforming to live and let live than that they were rendered inert by thoughts of killing each other.

The suggestion here is not that tacit truces of a First World War kind entirely explain low fire ratios in the Second World War; for the two wars differed in many respects. But facts clearly show that low fire ratios were common to both wars, and the possibility that part of the low fire ratios of the Second World War concerned live and let live systems of a First World War kind cannot be ruled out. It is at least plausible to contend, firstly, that seasoned soldiers were aware that aggression during combat involved risks of retaliation, while the enemy sometimes reciprocated non-aggression; and, secondly, that some American soldiers acted on these assumptions in the Second World War and thereby determined to a degree the low fire ratios revealed in Marshall's research. This view, of course, does not wholly deny Marshall's explanation. What is rejected is the relative importance given by him to the fear of killing.

Marshall's interpretation can be criticised on the grounds that it lacks rigour. Two kinds of explanation underlie his work, and neither of these is explicitly developed. Consequently, a strict course cannot be followed when doubts occur during analysis. Instead, one type of interpretation is substituted *ad hoc* for another, where the explanatory force of the first, if more clearly defined, would have been greater than the second. This is not an argument for reductionism. Both kinds of explanation used by Marshall are valid. The point is that unless different modes of, and concepts used in, explanation are clarified sufficiently, material best analysed by one kind of concept is sometimes less well analysed by another. For example, the fact that 80 per cent of infantry failed to fire was thought of by Marshall as a problem of psychology,[35] and explained, as one critic noted, in terms of personality character-istics.[36] At the same time, the fact that 20 per cent fired zealously is explained in a sociological way, that is, in terms of group influence on the individual. Marshall showed that the aggressive 20 per cent were not a random sample of soldiers whose composition varied from battle to battle; on the contrary, the same men in the same groups were aggressive in successive battles.[37] These soldiers acted less as autonomous individuals than as individuals tied into cohesive groups which constrained all members to aggression. The author recognised the force of group constraint—the sociological as distinct from the psychological factor—arguing that passive soldiers should be sent to gun crews where 'the group will keep them going. Men working in groups or in teams do not have the same tendency to default of fire as do single riflemen'.[38] He found that the active groups were mostly composed of weapon specialists, such as machine-gun and bazooka crews. Now one would think that Marshall, having connected group constraint to high fire ratios, would develop this kind of explanation and guess that group constraint could also relate to low fire ratios. For why should group influence operate in one direction only? Indeed, as we have seen, research into the effects of small, informal groups in large formal bureaucracies shows that the former sometimes work against the latter's goals, and this was known when Marshall wrote. Such a lack of rigour derives from imprecise theoretical perspectives and does not add to the merit of this seminal work.

In the matter of high fire ratios, Marshall's material, and the interpretation he gives to it, is consistent with the present research. Both studies find that weapon specialists are relatively aggressive and explain this in terms of sociological factors, that is, group constraints (the present work also accounts for the aggression of élite battalions in terms of social variables). As to low fire ratios, some agreement, but also some disagreement, exists between the two works. On the one hand, both this study and Marshall's agree in that low ratios were endemic in the First and Second World Wars respectively. On the other hand, each research offers a different type of explanation for low fire ratios. Marshall's interpretation relies heavily on psychology, whereas this research more rigorously explains both low and high fire ratios in terms of social factors, which is that group influence is seen as decisive whether trench fighters were active or passive.

However, this lack of concern with group influence and low fire ratios is not found in the work of another American social scientist, Roger Little, who researched into the combat behaviour of U.S. soldiers in the Korean war of the 1950s.[39] Moreover, this author's findings, which show that group influence restricted aggression, support those of the present study and further, his analysis of social relationships within small combat groups is not dissimilar to that offered here. Marshall and Little used contrasting methods of data collection. The former held mass interviews with many men in many different circumstances, whereas the latter's method was intensive rather than extensive. During four months in Korea, Little observed in depth a single infantry company, both in its combat and its reserve roles: the combat role involved garrison duty in the battle zone, and patrolling the forward area near the enemy. The author chose one platoon of the company so that he got to know each member as an individual. Each of the platoon's 30 members was interviewed,[40] firstly, alone on at least two occasions, and, secondly, in a group with his fellow soldiers.

Little's problem was the interplay between the values and

informal relations of soldiers on the one hand, and the ideals and aims of the formal military bureaucracy on the other. According to him, the highly solidary 'buddy' relationship among soldiers was an element of informal infantry social organisation, and this derived from awareness of mutual risks involved in combat. The buddy relation was a set of shared norms which regulated the behaviour of soldiers, that is, buddies, both in and out of combat, in a manner which minimised the hazards of combat, but which was inconsistent with military values. Buddy relationships comprised two parts, each of which involved specific forms of exchange, corresponding to specific areas of welfare. One element was generalised exchange among buddies whereby each platoon member had constant regard during combat for the physical survival and welfare of every other, on condition that concern was reciprocated by all others. Thus each soldier was protected against death,injury and other misfortune not only by his own ears, but also by those of his buddies. As in trench warfare, exchange increased survival chances and decreased anxiety during combat, since all buddies knew that each could depend upon the other not to 'bug out', that is desert during battle, leaving others in a weakened state to continue the fight. Of the importance of mutual dependence during battle, one soldier asserted, 'You've got to make every man in the squad your buddy to get things done. You've got to get down and work with them and get them to feel that they can depend on you to stick by them'.[41] Away from battle, the same principle of generalised exchange applied to other interests, for instance, the practice of sharing with all buddies the contents of a package from home. Further, soldiers clearly saw that sharing both reinforced and was consistent with the other exchange of the battlefield: 'If a guy didn't share', one buddy affirmed, 'maybe some day he'd be in a tough spot and the buddy would remember it and think about when you didn't make an offer. You don't always have a chance to do a favour in combat, but if you share everything, you can be pretty sure that your buddy will remember it if you need help.'[42]

However, 'buddy' was a general term which described not only persons with whom one shared combat dangers but also more restricted exchange between two men. Whereas generalised exchange among all buddies concerned physical welfare, restricted exchange between two buddies concerned needs for emotional welfare and close intimate contact. Battle stress provoked unusual emotional reactions among men, and, as Little observed, 'a buddy had to "understand" in a deeply personal sense. Buddies became therapists to each other . . . One man said of another whom he had chosen as buddy, "Our minds seem to run together" '.[43] All buddies were thus tied together in a general way by collective concern for each other's lives, while, simultaneously, pairs of buddies were bonded by a more restricted intimate exchange which involved mutual emotional support against actual and expected stress.

How did the informal buddy system relate to the goals and ideals of the formal military organisation? Aggression initiative and technical competence in combat were highly esteemed in the official system of values; on the other hand, each of these had low esteem in the unofficial value system of buddies. Moreover, the power of the solidary platoon group ensured that the battle behaviour of buddies did not conform to the official ethos. For instance, men neither boasted of individual combat skills nor compared combat proficiency, and all war talk was customarily discouraged: 'In the bunker the men don't talk much about combat. When they do the old men like Camp and Chap call them "war daddy" and they shut up',[44] affirmed one soldier to the author. Moreover, it was believed that the men who boasted of, and sought recognition for combat skills were those most likely to forget in combat that they had buddies, and that buddies should depend upon each other. But opposition to official values was crystallised in the platoon's ironic use of the term 'hero', to stigmatise soldiers whose behaviour conformed to military ideals but deviated from buddy values. Thus 'hero' was a derogatory value applied to a man who not only boasted of his courage and aggression but also actively sought intensive combat, and, further, whose aggression involved others in unnecessary risks in combat. One soldier voiced the group definition of the deviant hero as follows:

A guy who is just trying to show that he's not scared and sometimes trying to show up the other men. He's not braver. You shouldn't stick your neck out unless you have to. If someone gives me an order, we'll do it but we aren't going to take unnecessary chances. If a guy gets a medal for doing his job its O.K. But if he's taken a chance and exposed his men, he's no hero because he's made it more risky for everyone.[45]

But platoon disapproval was more than merely verbal, for heroes were excluded from the socio-emotional life of the soldier group.

Having violated buddy values, heroes were both deviants and outsiders and were not allowed to join in the exchange of benefits of either the restricted or generalised kind. According to Little, the hero tended to withdraw into a world of his own as the buddy system blocked opportunities for him to live up to his ideals. In this way, the structure of informal values and relationships within the platoon controlled the aggression of its members by stigmatisation and rejection, while it simultaneously deterred other potential heroes among members of the platoon. The similarities between labelling in the small combat groups of both the Korean war and the First World War are marked.

At the same time, the informal system controlled officer attitudes by assimilation. Little observed that the longer units opposed the enemy in the line, the stronger buddy values became. Moreover, platoon officers interacted more frequently and intensely with their platoons when in the line. Therefore officers participated in buddy systems when these were most strong and pervasive, and consequently, they sometimes took over the sentiments of the men they commanded. As time passed, aggression and initiative attenuated to a point where high command was no longer sure that orders involving risk would be carried out by units, which were then withdrawn from combat into reserve for retraining, and officially described as of 'low morale'.

During the Vietnam conflict of the 1960s, another American sociologist, Charles Moskos, observed both U.S. infantry and airborne units. Concerning the tendency of soldiers to restrict the aggressive activity of each other, the findings of this author were similar to those of Little and this study of trench war. In Vietnam, as in Korea, soldiers applied the stigma of hero to any of their number who either 'recklessly jeopardises the unit's welfare', or 'who endangers the safety of others'. Further, the author found that 'Men try to avoid going out on patrols with individuals who are overly anxious to make contact with the enemy'.[46] According to Moskos patrolling was a major part of infantry activity, and the usual patrol missions were to search out the enemy, who was then attacked either from the ground or by air and artillery. A survey made by the U.S. Defence Department in 1970 found that the infantry had replaced the official patrol policy of 'search and destroy' the enemy, with their own unofficial policy of 'search and evade' him,[47] which is a striking parallel to patrolling in the First World War.

This brief survey of related research shows that the type of phenomena found in the First World War existed also in other wars. In particular, there is evidence that low fire ratios are not uncommon, and that constraints within small combat groups determine some part of these. There is less support for the view that informal negotiation between adversaries determines what happens in battle, which is, of course, a theme of this study. On the other hand, the authors of the research reviewed above neither considered nor pursued this possibility in a systematic way. Neverthless, it seems to me that the idea that battle outcomes might be related to such informal negotiation might usefully be employed in exploring wars, both past and present. According to this perspective, it makes sense to ask certain questions concerning the present conflict in Ireland. For instance, do tacit understandings exist between the para-military forces and units of the British army? If they do, are all units involved equally? Or are some more implicated than others? If a unit which customarily operates such understandings is suddenly confronted by an enemy unit which does not, what then happens? What is the relationship between these understandings and wider political goals, immediate and future tactical considerations, and also the morale of the fighters? The men involved in this struggle are brave; but would the limit of their endurance be passed, if such understandings were destroyed? Should tacit agreements therefore be tolerated or, perhaps, reinforced? Maybe there is a case for some, but not other, units to negotiate informally with the enemy. With reason some observers seem to regard parts of Ireland as a battlefield, and any ideas which might further understanding of this tragic and perplexing state are worth considering.

The eminent German sociologist, Max Weber, who was a commissioned officer in a reserve corps of the German army in the First World War, argued that warfare generated discipline and that discipline, in turn, produced bureaucracy.[48] The bureaucratisation of society or, as this is often called, the disenchantment of the world, was a major theme in Weber's work. His attitude towards bureaucracy was ambivalent. He saw bureaucracy on the one hand as the most efficient means of administration and as guarding certain freedoms of man; yet on the other, as a system of domination which transformed the quality of human life by generating impersonality in social relationships, and diminishing the importance of individual action in human affairs generally. Weber averred that where bureaucracy prevailed, 'each man becomes a little cog in the machine, and, aware of this, his one preoccupation is whether he can become a bigger cog'.[49] Further, he believed that the global trend in modern times towards bureaucracy was irreversible, partly because no effective countervailing force existed. Pessimistically, he declared, 'what can we oppose to this machinery in order to keep a portion of mankind free from this parcelling out of the soul, from this supreme mastery of the bureaucratic way of life?'.[50] The bureaucratisation of life has been and is a theme not only of sociology but also of philosophy, literature and other disciplines. New light upon this theme was shed by sociological studies of the nineteen forties and fifties, which showed that a bureaucratic society need not destroy the intimate, personal relationships of primary groups, such as the family, play group, neighbourhood and so forth. Further, some studies also showed that primary groups developed even within large, apparently impersonal bureaucracies themselves, and that such groups protected persons, acting as power centres for collective opposition to bureaucratic domination. Thus men did not always become powerless, compliant cogs in impersonal bureaucratic systems, as Weber feared. Now, it seems to me that if Weber were to have looked more closely at the origins of discipline, and thus bureaucracy, in warfare, he might have found signs of collective resistance to the bureaucratic impulse in the earliest disciplined armies. Perhaps the primordial bureaucratic tendency in military formations, which later pervaded society, simultaneously produced its own counter-force. If so, then Weber's predictions about the social and human consequences of the spread of bureaucracy in modern times would have been different and more optimistic. Certainly, modern research has shown that counter-currents to bureaucracy occur in twentieth-century armies, but whether these happened in historical times, I do not know. In this connection, it is interesting to read of conversations in Kilvert's diary between the diarist and an old soldier, who fought in Spain during the Napoleonic wars:

Went to see the old soldier and talk to him about the war . . . Morgan said there was often a good and friendly feeling between English and French soldiers when they were in the field. He had often been on piquet duty less than 50 yards from the French sentries. He would call out, 'Bon Soir'. The Frenchman would sing out in return 'Will you boire?' Then they would lay down their arms, meet in the middle space and drink together. Morgan liked drinking with the French sentries because they mostly had something hot. He believes and believed then that if they had been caught fraternising he would have been shot or hung.[51]

To return to the First World War, and in particular the French Army mutinies of 1917, both military historians and laymen have been puzzled by the fact that the Germans remained unaware of the upheavals reverberating throughout the French army. Commonsense indicates that where enemies are but yards apart, as in trench war, and one side refuses to fight, the other will surely know. The mutinies were neither isolated nor ephemeral, but widespread and persistent, involving units from more than half the total number of divisions in the French army, in 151 recorded incidents, during the months of May, June, July, August and September.[52] How was it possible, then, that the Germans did not know of the French mutinies? Small wonder that the British official historian commented, 'extraordinary as it may seem, the Germans never had any suspicion of the French troubles'.[53] Another historian thought it astonishing that the French command so effectively suppressed knowledge of the mutinies, that the Germans heard little about them.[54] What was not quite coherent to historians, however, might be more clear to the reader. To a degree, the French mutiny was nothing more than a dramatic demonstration of support for a policy of live and let live. As far as the Germans in the trenches knew, nothing had changed: tacit truces proceeded during the mutiny, according to patterns established long before. The exchange of peace just went smoothly on. Perhaps the term mutiny, meaning tumultuous revolt, was too strong for much that actually happened, especially where French soldiers publicly preached for the first time, what had been privately practised for a long time. For the most part, Frenchmen did not down weapons, walk out and refuse to negotiate with the nation. As one authority put it, the mutinies were not a refusal of war as such, but only a certain way of waging it.[55] 'You have nothing to fear', declared some *poilus* to their divisional commander, 'we are prepared to man the trenches, we will do our duty and the Boche will not get through'.[56] No soldier who practised live and let live would disagree with this. The Frenchmen simply refused to attack the enemy unless first attacked by him, which was a tenet of tacit truces. No conspiracy masterminded the mutiny, although some tried, no doubt, to gain control once it had emerged. The mutiny was a popular and collective act, ostensibly spontaneous, but in fact rooted in the traditions of the trenches.

But why did mutiny on this scale occur only in the French and not the British army? After all, they shared many common circumstances. This is a complex question and no complete answer is intended here. Many reasons have been given for the mutiny, and probably some truth exists in most. One circumstance, however, has not been considered, except in a loose and vague way as war weariness, and this circumstance concerned truces and raids, and, further, it differed between the French and British armies. Many British trench fighters believed that live and let live was more persistent on British than French sectors. Moreover, the official history affirms that the British 'generally found a kind of unofficial suspension of arms or truce prevailing',[57] upon taking over a French sector. Live and let live was thus possibly more developed and frequent with the French than the British. Certainly, however, French raiding tactics were less developed, and raids less frequent, than in the British army. In fact, the French lacked a systematic raiding policy and did not raid much until after the mutinies. Now, if, as appears in the French case, truces were allowed to evolve and pervade trench war, all the while producing fellowship among enemies, and if raids were not systematically disrupting this process, then the unfettered growth of truces could well contribute to a comprehensive collapse of trench war, and an informal and general declaration of peace.

This is not to deny the influence of other, more usually mentioned, causes relating to the mutiny, but merely to suggest that the unrestricted exchange of peace was a contributory factor. It also helps to explain why no widespread mutinies occurred in the British army, where Douglas Haig's raiding policy had hampered the growth of peace. It seems that a similar thought occurred to an officer of the 23rd division, who speculated about the effect of raids upon the war: 'I still wonder what would have happened if the friendly meetings between German and English in No-Man's-Land, where they exchanged cigars for cigarettes and chattered together, had not been nipped in the bud'.[58] According to him, live and let live was 'nipped in the bud' by raids, which 'continuously whipped up' the fighting spirit, and, further, he conjectured that without the continuous stimulation of aggression by such means as raids, the war might not have lasted for so long.

In conclusion, I have been conscious at all times when writing this work that I, as a non-combatant, have been trying to interpret a world which, at best, I can only experience vicariously. There are those who have experienced combat, and those who have not: the worlds of the soldier and of the civilian are hugely different. In some small way, I have tried to bridge these worlds, so that civilians might better understand. In his very interesting work 'The Face of Battle'.[59] John Keegan argues for a new emphasis in the writing of military history, which focuses upon the direct experiences of soldiers in battle. I have tried to do this. One problem here, however, is to present battle experiences in a way which is not merely anecdotal and/or humanitarian but also relevant to wider theoretical perspectives. The perspective here is that of sociology and social psychology, in which war is seen as an ongoing and interrelated system of social action ordered by the principle of social exchange, and it is explicit and well defined. Further, it has been rigorously pursued in analysis, while other perspectives have been firmly eschewed. In particular, I have avoided an ethological perspective, which seeks clues to human behaviour in that of animals, in explaining any part of the present material. For instance, there is no more than a passing resemblance between Lorenz's concept of ritualised aggression in animal societies[60] and the present concept of ritualised aggression; for the former refers to innate, genetically patterned and transmitted social behaviour, while the latter refers to learned and culturally ordered, as well as transmitted patterned behaviour. However, I have sought to interpret only some part of the aggression in this war and a more comprehensive theory would no doubt consider perspectives neglected here. Finally, to return to the world of the trench fighter, an issue raised earlier in this paragraph, the reader might consider the following comment on trench war made to the author by a sergeant of the 47th division. This was a brave and astute man, who had known the many moods of trench war during his three years service on the western front; yet his comment, made during the formative years of this research, was puzzling to me at that time. He observed that naturally trench war was not a pleasant experience, yet continued, somewhat disparagingly, that nevertheless it was not nearly as bad as some would have one believe. I now realise, perhaps, the full meaning of his remark, and I hope to have conveyed something of this to the reader.

Notes

1. Although trench systems varied considerably between sectors, according to local circumstance, the trench system described above is that laid down in an official British manual of 1916. See *Notes for Infantry Officers on Trench Warfare*, (General Staff, War Office, March 1916). This manual set the pattern for most British trenches for much of the war. Two points should be made, however. Firstly, 1915 was mostly a time of experiment in trench war, and the official trench design was then evolving; consequently, trench systems were both less complex and less standardised than after 1915. Secondly, in December 1917, the British G.H.Q. ordered changes to the trench system in anticipation of a major German attack in Spring 1918. Adapted from a captured German manual, this reorganisation emphasised defence in depth and consisted of three separate trench systems: the forward, battle and reserve zones. The forward zone was the old system of front, support and rear trenches, but the element of intersupporting strongpoints was strengthened at the expense of continuous trench lines. By January 1918, the forward zones of defence in depth had been constructed on many British sectors, but shortage of labour had impeded work upon the battle and rear zones.

2. Ll. Wyn Griffiths, *Up to Mametz* (London: Faber, 1931) p. 130 (38th division).

3. C. Carrington, *Soldier from the Wars Returning* (London: Hutchinson, 1965) p. 101 (48th division).

4. R. Graves, *Goodbye to all That* (London: Cassell, 1961) pp. 214–15 (33rd division).

5. See J. Baynes, *Morale* (London: Cassell, 1967) for a study of an infantry battalion as a community.

6. M. Middlebrook, *The First Day on the Somme* (London: Allen Lane, 1971) Chapter 1.

7. H. Gordon, *The Unreturning Army* (London: Dent, 1967) p. 99 (25th division).

8. C. Falls, *War Books* (London: Peter Davies, 1930) Preface p. 8.

9. Some of these totals include cavalry and Commonwealth divisions, for instance, the November 1918 figure included 10 Commonwealth and 3 cavalry divisions.

10. This figure excludes cavalry and Commonwealth divisions.

11. The only division from which I could find no material was the 57th division.

12. Some historians have remarked that the official war diaries make less than satisfactory sources for conventional unit histories. Thus Professor Atkinson commented that: 'To be quite candid, these have proved of very unequal and somewhat uncertain value . . . battalion diaries have varied so much in

fullness and value . . . what applies to battalion diaries applies also to them'.
'Them' refers to division and brigade official diaries. See C. T. Atkinson, *The Devonshire Regiment 1914–1918* (Exeter: Eland Bros, 1926) Preface p. 9.

13. At this time, 58 divisions were in the B. E. F. so that 19 divisions were in reserve.
14. F. Richards, *Old Soldiers Never Die* (London: Faber & Faber, 1933) p. 170.
15. Ibid., p. 92.
16. Richards, ibid., p. 217; p. 157.
17. A. Thomas, *A Life Apart* (Gollancz, 1968) p. 58 (12th division).
18. Anon (Ed.), *The War the Infantry Knew* (London: P. S. King, 1938) p. 177 (2/Royal Welch Fusiliers, 33rd division).
19. H. Sulzbach, *With the German Guns* (London: Leo Cooper, 1973), p. 30.
20. Carrington, op. cit., pp. 101–2 (1/5th Royal Warwickshire Regiment, 48th (T.F.) division).
21. Ibid., p. 107.
22. C. Messenger, *Trench Fighting, 1914–1918* (London: Pan/Ballantine, 1973), Intro. by J. Keegan. The theme of powerlessness is common enough, for instance, another military historian wrote: 'The story of men at war is usually of people caught in events over which they have very little personal control. In gathering material together for this story I have been struck by this factor to an increasing extent. From generals to private soldiers there is a theme of powerlessness infiltrating their activities; nearly always they were controlled by external forces which were well nigh irresistible, and which often forced them into courses quite different from those they would rather have followed'. K. Macksey, *The Shadow of Vimy Ridge* (London: William Kimber, 1965) p. 9.
23. Frank Hawkings, *From Ypres to Cambrai* (London: Morley, 1973). Introduced and edited by Arthur Taylor.
24. A seminal theoretical statement of this is found in P. Selznick, 'An Approach to a Theory of Bureaucracy', *American Sociological Review*, 8:1 (1943).
25. J. Brophy and E. Partridge, *The Long Trail* (London: Andre Deutsch, 1965) pp. 107, 195.
26. Griffiths, op. cit., pp. 71–3 (38th division).
27. M. Gilbert (ed.), *Winston S. Churchill*, vol. 3 (London: Heinemann, 1972) p. 1372.
28. C.R.M.F. Crutwell, *The War Service of the 1/4th Berkshire Regiment (T.F.)*, (Oxford: Basil Blackwell, 1922) p. 46.
29. J. Edmonds, *History of the Great War, Military Operations, France and Belgium, 1915* (Macmillan, 1928) p. 83. I shall refer to the official history from now on as O.H. followed by year and volume—two volumes were published for each year of the war. Thus this reference would appear as: O.H.15.2. p. 83.
30. Middlebrook, op. cit., p. 35.
31. H. M. Davson, *The History of the 35th Division* (London: Sifton Praed & Co., 1926) Appendix 2. The two battalions were the 20/Lancashire Fusiliers (38 casualties) and the 15/Sherwood Foresters (96 casualties). The 19/Northumberland Fusiliers had fewer casualties (32) than the 20/Lancashire Fusiliers but this was a pioneer battalion with different movements in and out of the line than a fighting battalion. It should be noted that the above statistics show the battalion monthly casualty rate, and not the battalion's casualty rate per 30 days in the line. The two are different since a battalion was out of the line for some part of each month. Most battalions spent about 40 per cent of

their time in the trenches. Therefore, to calculate the above battalions' casualty rates per 30 days in the line, one can take 40 per cent of the 150 days (5 months), which is 60 days, divide the total number of casualties by 60, which gives a daily casualty rate, and multiply by 30, which gives a montly rate. For instance, the casualty rate per 30 days in the line of the 20/Lancashire Fusiliers was 38 divided by 60 = 0.63 (daily rate), multiply by 30 = 18.9 (monthly rate). Secondly, the 15/Sherwood Foresters: 96 divided by 60 = 1.6 × 30 = 48 casualties per 30 days in line. The two statistics are different but both illustrate the central point that casualties varied considerably between battalions in routine trench warfare. In many histories, it is not clear whether casualty statistics refer to casualties per month or casualties per 30 days in the line. In general, the calculation of casualties in trench warfare could be improved; for instance, one author calculates that the rate was 7000 per day, which is consistent with his thesis that trench war was a catastrophic experience but hardly tallies with the facts. P. Fussel, *The Great War and Modern Memory* (London: Oxford University Press, 1975).

32. R. B. Ross, *The Fifty First in France*, (London: Hodder and Stoughton, 1918) p. 128 (51st Division, 7th battalion Gordon Highlanders, August 1915, nr. Bécourt, 3rd Army).

33. J. Brophy and E. Partridge, op. cit., p. 194.

34. D. Jerrold, *The Lie About the War* (London: Faber & Faber, 1930). It seems to me that Jerrold, like the authors he criticised, overstated his case. The assertion that most trench fighters were bored for most of the time is as inaccurate as the contrary that most were fighting for most of the time. One must distinguish between sectors. Thus there was neither boredom on active sectors nor continual struggle on quiet sectors.

35. The works of Ian Hay, a new army infantry officer in the 9th division, and Patrick MacGill, a private soldier of the 47th division, are good examples of these informal dispatches.

36. C. Falls, op. cit., pp. 182–3. Professor Falls was a trench fighter and is a distinguished academic.

37. E. Blunden, *Undertones of War* (London: Cobden-Sanderson, 1930) See Preface to the second edition. Blunden served for over two years on the western front and he was involved in the big events, for instance, the Somme and Passchendaele, as well as the small.

38. Ibid., p. 167.

39. Ibid., p. 167.

40. Ian Hay, *The First Hundred Thousand* (London: Wm. Blackwood, 1916) p. 224. This book consists of articles first appearing in the journal *Blackwood* during 1915. See also the same author's *Carrying On – After the First Hundred Thousand* (London: Blackwood, 1917) p. 58. Ian Hay was the pen name of an infantry officer of the 9th division, 10th battalion Argyll & Sutherland Highlanders.

41. See, for instance, A. H. Maude (ed.), *The 47th (London) Division 1914–1919* (London: Amalgamated Press, 1922) p. 51; Owen Rutter (ed.), *The History of the Seventh (Service) Battalion The Royal Sussex Regiment 1914–1919* (The Times Publishing Co., 1934) p. 182 (12th division); D. Young, *Rommel* (London: Collins, 1950) p. 39 (14th division).

42. S. Sassoon, *Sherston's Progress* (London: Folio Society, 1974) p. 174 (74th division).

43. Ross, op. cit., p. 210 (51st division).

44. *The War History of the Sixth Battalion The South Staffordshire Regiment* (London: Heinneman, 1924) p. 125 (46th division).

45. D. V. Kelly, *39 Months* (London: Ernst Benn, 1930) p. 122 (37th division).

46. V. F. Eberle, *My Sapper Venture* (London: Pitmans, 1973) p. 9 (48th division).

47. P. MacGill, *The Great Push* (London: Herbert Jenkins, 1916) p. 87 (47th division).

48. L. M. Newton, *The Story of the Twelfth* (Tasmania: J. Walch & Sons, 1925) p. 173 (1st Australian division).

49. R. G. V. M. Bland, *The Sixth Welsh (T.F.) in France, 1914–1918* (Cardiff: 1920) p. 81 (1st division).

50. Lord Wavell, himself a trench fighter, used the phrase 'kill or be killed' to describe the official trench war policy. See R. H. Kiernan, *Wavell* (London: George Harrap, 1945) p. 173.

51. F. Hitchcock, *Stand To* (London: Hurst & Blackett, 1937) p. 125 (24th division, 2/The Leinster Regiment, November 1915, St. Eloi, 2nd Army).

52. R. O. Russel, *The History of the 11th (Lewisham) Battalion The Queen's Own Royal West Kent Regiment* (London: Lewisham Newspaper Coy., 1934) p. 36 (41st division 11/R.W.K. Regt. May 1916, Ploegstreet, 2nd Army).

53. Like live and let live, quiet or cushy fronts had synonyms which included: 'peacetime sectors' and 'rest cure sectors'.

54. C. V. Molony, *'Invicta' With the 1st The Queen's Own Royal West Regiment in the Great War* (London: Nisbet & Co., 1923) pp. 125, 162.

55. R. Graves, *Goodbye To All That* (London: Cassell, 1961) p. 105.

56. It seems to me assertions like 'the infantryman's was the truly common experience of the war', B. Bergonzi, *Heroes' Twilight* (London: Constable, 1965) p. 190, are misleading, as they oversimplify the complexity and diversity of war experience. There was not one common infantry experience but many.

57. *The War The Infantry Knew*, op. cit., p. 145.

58. Richards, op. cit., p. 154. Richards referred to the 20/Royal Fusiliers, which was in the same brigade as the 2/Royal Welch Fusiliers of which Richards was a member. For an account of the war seen through the eyes of a member of the 20/R. Fusiliers see J. L. Hodson, *Grey Dawn, Red Night* (London: Gollancz, 1929). The comparison refers only to the trench fighting skills of the 20/R. Fusiliers and the 2/R. Welch. There is no implication that the former were less brave than the latter. This is another issue, and one on which the reader must form his own opinion.

59. Wilfred Owen's experience of the trenches was short but nasty—an active front in winter. It seems likely he did not know firsthand of the undertones of war. But perhaps his poems are, for that reason, a more striking evocation of a particular war experience.

60. G. H. Greenwell, *An Infant in Arms* (London: Allen Lane, 1972) p. 251 (48th division). In the preface of his book, Greenwell wrote: 'The horrors of the Great War and the miseries of those who were called upon to take part in it have been described by innumerable writers. For my own part I have to confess that I look back on the years 1914–1918 as among the happiest I have ever spent.'

CHAPTER 2

1. *The War the Infantry Knew*, op. cit., p. 92 (2/Royal Welch Fusiliers, November 1914, nr. Fleurbaix).
2. Hawkings, op. cit., p. 23 (5th division, 1/Queen Victoria Rifles, 1 December 1914, nr. Messines).
3. *The Memoirs of Captain Liddell Hart*, Vol. 1 (London, 1965) p. 21. Liddell Hart served with the 5th, 14th and 21st divisions.
4. *9th Royal Scots (T.F.) B Company Active Service* (Edinburgh: Turnbull & Spears, 1916) p. 44 (27th division, Glencorse Wood, Ypres Salient, 1st Army).
5. Hay, op. cit., pp. 224–5 (9th division, 10/Argyll & Sutherland Highlanders, Summer 1915, nr. Festubert, 2nd Army).
6. Hawkings, op. cit., p. 35.
7. R. Binding, *A Fatalist at War* (London: Allen & Unwin, 1929) p. 35 (nr. Ypres, 8 December 1914). Informal truces were not confined to British and Germans, for the events described by Binding, who was an officer of divisional cavalry, occurred between the Germans and French.
8. For instance, one infantry officer asserted 'There was no truce on the front of my battalion'. J. Terraine (ed.), *General Jack's Diary 1914–1918* (Eyre & Spottiswoode, 1964) p. 94 (1/Cameronians, nr. Houplines). But there are signs that this unit did exchange some form of Christmas greeting with the enemy—see p. 88 of the same diary.
9. Captain Sir E. H. W. Hulse, *Letters* (privately printed: 1916) p. 54 (7th division, 2/Scots Guards, nr. Laventie, November 1914).
10. Ibid., pp. 54–5.
11. Ibid., pp. 56–65 (1st Army).
12. J. E. Edmonds, *A Short History of World War 1* (London: Oxford University Press, 1951) p. 134.
13. A. F. Barnes, *The Story of the 2/5th Battalion Gloucestershire Regiment* (Gloucester: The Crypt House Press, 1930) p. 37 (61st division, 2/5th Gloucester Regt. May 1916, nr. Rouge Croix, 1st Army).
14. P. Gosse, *Memoirs of a Camp Follower* (London: Longmans, 1934) p. 1 (23rd division, 69th Field Ambulance, September 1915, nr. Bois Grenier, 2nd Army).
15. Graves, op. cit., p. 85 (1st division, 2/Welch Regiment, May 1915, Cambrin, 1st Army).
16. P. MacGill, *The Red Horizon* (London: Herbert Jenkins, 1916) p. 84 (47th division, 18/London Regiment, March 1915, nr. Festubert, 1st Army).
17. S. Gillon, *The Story of the 29th Division* (London: Nelson & Sons,) p. 77 (29th division, May 1916, nr. Englebelmer, 4th Army). The 29th relieved the 31st division.
18. R. C. Sherriff and V. Bartlett, *Journey's End* (London: Corgi Books, 1968) pp. 129–30 (24th division, 9/East Surrey Regiment). This is a work of autobiographical fiction and whether the above incident actually occurred is not known; yet it could easily have happened and is probably typical of many actual incidents. As far as I can determine the line which Sherriff described above was Vimy Ridge—although the main event of the book occurs elsewhere. The 24th division was in the line near Vimy when Sherriff first joined his unit—October 1916—and remained in Vimy, Souchez, Loos until

April 1917; this was the main part of Sherriff's trench war experience. Generally the sector was not overactive. In the history of a battalion in the same division as Sherriff's unit, it is interesting to read of a sector where 'The enemy post was within easy bombing distance of our own, and consequently neither side cared about stirring up strife, as it was apt to become unpleasant for the instigator'. *The History of the Eighth Battalion The Queen's Own Royal West Kent Regiment 1914–1918* (London: Hazell, Watson & Viney, 1921) p. 72 (24th division, March 1916, nr. Loos, 1st Army). Possibly Sherriff's battalion occupied the same part of the line at about the same time.

19. *Notes for Infantry Officers on Trench Warfare*, op. cit., p. 34.
20. Kelly, op. cit., pp. 17–18 (37th division, 110th Brigade, Summer 1915, Berles, 3rd Army).
21. A. Smith, *Four Years on the Western Front* (London: Odhams, 1922) p. 277 (56th division, 1/5th London Regiment, September 1917, nr. Baupaume, 3rd Army).
22. P. G. Bales, *The History of the 1/4th Battalion Duke of Wellington's (West Riding) Regiment* (London: 1920) p. 13 (49th division (T.F.) 1/4th Duke of Wellington's Regt., Spring/Summer 1915, Fleurbaix, 1st Army).
23. On 26 December the British divisions in the line were: 1st, 2nd, 3rd, 4th, 5th, 6th, 7th, 8th, and the Meerut (Indian) division. Accounts of some of these truces occur in the following sources: Anon. (Douglas Bell), *A Soldier's Diary of the Great War* (London: Faber & Gwyer, 1929) pp. 77–87 (5/Rifle Brigade, 4th division); B. Bairnsfeather, *Bullets and Billets* (London: Grant Richards, 1916) (1/Royal Warwickshire Regiment, 4th division); F. Loraine Petre, *The History of the Norfolk Regiment*, Vol. 2 (Norwich: Jarrold & Son) p. 13 (1st Norfolk Regiment, 5th division); J. K. Henriques, *The War History of the 1st Battalion Queen's Westminster Rifles* (London: 1923) pp. 34–5 (6th division); J. H. Boraston & C. E. D. Bax, *The Eighth Division in the War* (London: Medici Society, 1926) p. 13 (8th division).
24. *The War the Infantry Knew*, op. cit., pp. 99–103 (2/Royal Welch Fusiliers attached to the 6th division). For an account of the same truce which differs somewhat see Richards, op. cit., pp. 65–70.
25. Loraine Petre, op. cit., p. 13.
26. *The Fifth Battalion The Cameronians* (Glasgow: Jackson & Co., 1936) p. 28.
27. R. Blake, *The Private Papers of Douglas Haig* (London: Eyre & Spottiswoode, 1952) pp. 121–6.
28. W. Ewart, *Scots Guard* (London: Rich & Cowan, 1934) p. 80. For two eyewitness accounts of the 1915 Christmas truce see Ewart, ibid., pp. 76–9; Griffiths, op. cit., pp. 33–5.
29. J. H. Morgan, *Leaves from a Field Note Book* (London: Macmillan, 1916) pp. 270–1. The author was attached to G.H.Q. of the B.E.F. as Home Office Commissioner, and while not a participant, he was an eyewitness of trench warfare, for his duties involved daily visits to the H.Q.s of almost every corps, division and brigade, and took him on one or two occasions into the trenches.
30. W. E. Gray, *The 2nd City of London Regiment (Royal Fusiliers) in The Great War* (London: 1929) p. 33 (6th division, 1/2nd London Regiment, April 1915, nr. Armentières, 2nd Army).
31. C. H. Dudley-Ward, *Regimental Records of the Royal Welch Fusiliers*, Vol. 3 (London: Forster, Groom and Company, 1928) p. 420 (38th division, 2/Royal

Welch Fusiliers, May 1918, nr. Aveluy, 3rd Army). Neither incident nor order is recorded in the history of the 38th division; but there is a mention in the history of the 2/Royal Welch, where the 'ringleader in the exchange of news, views and cigarettes' is reported as falling from favour. However, the history also commented that 'Front and rear have never looked on such incidents from the same angle'. The 'rear' is, of course, high command. See *The War The Infantry Knew*, op. cit., p. 479.

32. Richards, op. cit., p. 155 (33rd division, 2/Royal Welch Fusiliers).

33. E. Junger, *The Storm of Steel* (London: Chatto & Windus, 1929) p. 43.

34. Boraston and Bax, op. cit., p. 56 (1st Army). The history recorded that despite these 'friendly overtures' divisional troops, 'were in no way tempted to abandon the customary aggressiveness . . . or to alter their usual practice of making things consistently as uncomfortable as possible for the other side'.

35. D. Sutherland, *War Diary of the Fifth Seaforth Highlanders* (London: John Lane, 1920) p. 27 (51st division, 5/Seaforth Highlanders, July 1915, Laventie, 1st Army). Both Greenwell and Hay wrote of similar occasions where as part of a live and let live arrangement the Saxons shouted of their impending relief by Prussians, and asked the British to stir it up for the latter; see Greenwell, op. cit., p. 21 (48th division, 4/Oxfordshire and Buckinghamshire Light Infantry, June 1915, Ploegsteert Wood, 2nd Army); I. Hay, *Carrying on After the First Hundred Thousand* (London: Wm. Blackwood, 1917) p. 59 (9th division, 10/Argyll & Sutherland Highlanders, Ploegsteert Wood, Spring 1916, 2nd Army).

36. A. Scott and P. M. Brumwell (eds.), *History of the 12th (Eastern) Division in the Great War* (London: Nisbet & Co., 1923) p. 7 (12th division, 7/East Surrey Regiment, June 1915, nr. Armentières, 2nd Army).

37. T. M. Banks and R. A. Chell, *With the 10th Essex in France* (London: 1921) p. 57 (18th division, 10/Essex Regt. November 1915, La Boiselle, 3rd Army).

38. Scott and Brumwell, op. cit., p. 9 (12th division, 8/Royal Fusiliers, August 1915, nr. Houplines, 2nd Army).

39. J. D. Hills, *The Fifth Leicestershire 1914–1918* (Loughborough: The Echo Press, 1919) p. 46 (46th division, The 5/Leicestershire Regiment, July 1915, Comines Canal sector, Ypres, 2nd Army).

40. Robert Graves, op. cit., p. 121 (2nd division, 2/Royal Welch Fusiliers, August 1915, 1st Army).

41. A. W. Pagan, *An Account of the 1st Gloucestershire Regiment During the War 1914–1918* (Aldershot: Gale & Polden, 1951) p. 83 (1st division, 1/Gloucester Regt. May 1916, Les Brébis, 1st Army).

42. Ewart, op. cit., p. 154 (Guards division, 2/Scot Guards, January 1918, nr. Vimy Ridge, 1st Army).

43. A. L. Raimes, *The Fifth Battalion The Durham Light Infantry 1914–1918* (London: 1931) pp. 79–80 (50th division, 5/Durham Light Infantry, January 1917, nr. Mametz, 4th Army). The same truce was witnessed by a gunner officer who wrote, 'I was being led to our trenches by a sub. [infantry officer] . . . through mud until I saw a row of faces gazing at us about fifty yards away, and I suddenly discovered they were Bosche. I naturally took cover in a trench, . . . and then discovered that in this particular section there was a recognised truce, as the trenches on both sides were so bad that they had stopped fighting until they were improved'. C. H. Ommaney, *The War History*

of the 1st Northumbrian Brigade R.F.A. (T.F.) (Newcastle: 1927) p. 131.

44. Boraston and Bax, op. cit., pp. 13–14 (8th division, January/February 1915, nr. Neuve-Chapelle, 1st Army).

45. Hitchcock, op. cit., pp. 118–26 (24th division, 2/Leinster Regiment, November 1915, St. Eloi, 2nd Army).

46. Gilbert, op. cit., p. 1347 (French 70th division, Vimy Ridge, December 1915).

47. Ibid., p. 1346. The officer was Captain Spiers, the British liaison officer with the French 10th Army.

48. See Ian Hay, *After the First Hundred Thousand*, op. cit., chapters 1, 2 and 3.

49. Gilbert, op. cit., p. 1376.

50. R. Feilding, *War Letters to a Wife* (London: The Medici Society, 1929) pp. 154–5 (16th division, 6/Connaught Rangers, February 1917, nr. Kemmel, 2nd Army). Despite the severity of high command reaction, *ad hoc* truces to collect wounded still occurred; for instance, a battalion of the 66th division recorded that twenty minutes after it had raided the Germans: 'a German climbed on to the top of his parapet and commenced to beckon to men in our line . . . the German said if we would provide stretchers they would fetch our wounded and dead. Stretchers were obtained and the work commenced . . . One of the Germans was quite familiar with Manchester and said he wondered what was on at the "Palace" that week . . . the enemy's parapet was lined with men.' C. H. Potter and A. S. C. Fothergill, *The History of the 2/6th Lancashire Fusiliers* (Rochdale: 1927) pp. 52–3 (66th division, 2/6th Lanc. Fusil., March 1917, Festubert, 1st Army).

51. Blunden, op. cit., pp. 80–1 (39th division, 11/Royal Sussex Regiment, July/August 1916, Givenchy, 1st Army).

52. A. E. Ashcroft, *History of the 7th South Staffordshire Regiment* (London: Boyle, Son & Warchurst, 1919) p. 141 (11th division, 7/South Staffs. Regiment, October 1916, nr. Lens, 1st Army).

53. *History of the Prince of Wales Own Civil Service Rifles* (London: Wyman & Sons, 1921) pp. 90–1 (47th division, 1/15th London Regiment, April 1916, Vimy Ridge, 1st Army). The form of words used varied in the sources. For instance, one author wrote: 'The Arras front was really most charmingly quiet', A. S. Turberville, *A Short History of the 20th Battalion King's Royal Rifle Corps* (Hull: Goddard, Walker & Brown, 1923) p. 48 (3rd division, 20 K.R.R.C. January/February 1917, nr. Arras, 3rd Army).

54. *War Memoirs of David Lloyd George*, vol, 1 (London: Odhams Press, 1938) pp. 124–6, p. 123.

55. *The War History of the Sixth Battalion The South Staffordshire Regiment*, op. cit, p. 37 (46th division, 6/South Staffs. April 1915, Wulvergnem, 2nd Army).

56. *The Letters of Charles Sorley* (Cambridge: The University Press, 1919) p. 283 (12th division).

57. Ibid., p. 283.

58. Ibid., p. 277.

59. Ibid., p. 283.

60. F. W. Bewsher, *The History of the 51st (Highland) Division* (London: Blackwood and Son, 1921) p. 29 (51st division, Summer 1915, nr. Festubert, 1st Army).

61. *Field Service Regulations Part 1. Operations, 1909* (reprinted 1914) (London: General Staff, War Office) Chapter 1.

62. *Field Service Regulations German Army, 1908* (General Staff, War Office) p. 9.

63. Field Service Regulations, British, op. cit., Chapter 8.
64. O.H.15.1. pp. 33–4. The memo was addressed to the commanders of the First and Second armies, and the British and Indian Cavalry Corps.
65. For the same reason the official history is misleading in referring to the 'G.H.Q. memorandum ordering raids' (see O.H.15.1. p. 33); for raiding, which by 1916 had become a specialised and complex trench war tactic, was in February 1915 hardly distinguished from other small operations.
66. *Notes for Infantry Officers on Trench Warfare*, op. cit., Chapter 1, Section 4. The title of this work is somewhat modest, for it consists of five chapters entitled: Special Characteristics of Trench Warfare; Siting and Construction of Trenches; Occupation and Relief of Trenches and General Trench Routine; Organisation of a Trench Line and Action in Case of Attack; Notes on the Attack in Trench Warfare. This manual gives a fuller account of trench war from the infantry point of view than other official works that I have read; yet it is neglected by many historians and commentators.
67. R. M. Watt, *Dare Call it Treason* (London: Chatto and Windus, 1964) p. 79. The passage is from the U.S. Army's translation of the 1917 edition of the *Manual for Commanders of Infantry Platoons (Manual de Chef de Section D'Infanterie)* p. 355. The British literature — both official and personal documents — is misleading with respect to official French policy for trench war. There is much evidence in personal documents that British trench fighters believed that live and let live was the French policy. This view is also found in the British official history which asserts that when the British relieved the French 10th Army in March 1916: 'a state approximating to a suspension of arms existed . . . the enemy . . . seemed used to a policy of "live and let live"' (O.H.16.1. p. 209), and elsewhere that: 'when the British took over from their allies they generally found a kind of unofficial suspension of arms or truce prevailing . . . with a view to cultivating an "aggressive spirit" G.H.Q. did not allow this state of affairs to continue . . . as far as the British were concerned the western front was never quiet' (O.H.16.1. p. 156). This needs qualification. Some British units restarted the war on relieving the French, but others took over the French truce. While it is true that both British and French units practised live and let live, whether the French did so more frequently I do not know (my impression is that probably they did). But what must be corrected is any idea that official French directives ordered a policy of live and let live.
68. O.H.15.1. p. 213.
69. Binding, op. cit., p. 182.
70. Ibid., p. 95.
71. On the other hand specific orders are inflexible, and in a group of high morale might inhibit initiative which otherwise, that is, with general directives, would be used.
72. *The War the Infantry Knew*, op. cit., p. 103.
73. Molony, op. cit., pp. 124–5.
74. *Extracts from the Diary of Brig.-Gen. Hon. Robert White* (Richmond: F. W. Dimbleby & Sons, no date) pp. 30–3.

CHAPTER 3

1. Blunden, op. cit., p. 74.
2. B. H. Liddell Hart, *History of the First World War* (London: Cassell, 1970), p. 266.
3. Some members of high command had thought of attrition before this time, for instance, Charteris, who was on Haig's staff, wrote in his diary before the battle of Neuve-Chapelle in 1915: 'I am gradually being forced into the opinion that we shall not win the war by great victories on land or sea, but by wearing Germany out.' Brigadier General J. Charteris, *At G.H.Q.* (London: Cassell & Co. Ltd.) pp. 74–5.
4. *The War the Infantry Knew*, op. cit., pp. 176–7.
5. Junger, op. cit., p. 109.
6. Richards, op. cit., p. 78 (19th Brigade, 2/Royal Welch Fusiliers, February 1915).
7. *The Fifth Scottish Rifles 1914–1919*, op. cit., p. 38.
8. Hay, *The First Hundred Thousand*, op. cit., pp. 190–1 (9th division, 10/Argyll and Sutherland Highlanders).
9. H. Hesketh-Pritchard, *Sniping in France* (London: Hutchinson) p. 17. The author commanded the 1st Army sniping school in 1916.
10. In 1916 control was further centralised, passing from battalion to brigade, and snipers then received orders from the brigade sniping and intelligence officer, who was a member of high command staff.
11. Both number and siting of posts varied among battalions; but the organisation here outlined was not untypical and corresponds to that described by the battalion sniping officer of the 1/Royal Welch Fusiliers during February and March of 1916. See B. Adams, *Nothing of Importance* (London: Methuen) Chapter 8. Both Adams and Siegfried Sassoon served at the same time in the 1/Royal Welch, and Adams is referred to by Sassoon as 'Bill Eaves'. See S. Sassoon, *Memoirs of an Infantry Officer* (London: The Folio Society, 1974) p. 36.
12. *Notes for Infantry Officers on Trench Warfare*, op. cit., p. 41. 'It may be assumed that a company in the trenches will number about 160 . . . Of these there will be by day about 16–20 men engaged in sniping and observation and another 16–20 ready to relieve them.'
13. The German organisation was somewhat different, but according to one authority each company had six telescopic-sighted rifles for sniping. See Hesketh-Pritchard, op. cit., pp. 30–1.
14. R. H. Mottram, J. Easton and E. Partridge, *Three Personal Records of the War* (London: The Scholartis Press, 1929) p. 327 (2nd Australian division, 7th Brigade, nr. Armentières, Summer 1916).
15. A. R. Fellowes, *The 1st Battalion The Faugh-A-Ballaghs in the Great War* (London: Gale and Polden, 1925) p. 48 (4th division, 1st Royal Irish Fusiliers, July 1915, Ypres Salient, 2nd Army).
16. Ibid., p. 23 (December 1914, nr. the River Douve, 3rd corps).
17. D. Jones, *In Parenthesis* (London: Faber and Faber, 1963) p. 196 (38th division).
18. A. W. Pagan, op. cit., p. 21 (1st division, 1/Gloucester Regiment, May 1915, nr. La Bassée, 1st Army).

19. O.H.15.1. p. 7.
20. Newton, op. cit., pp. 193–4 (1st Australian division, 12th battalion, June 1916).
21. O.H.15.1. p. 11.
22. G. Coppard, *With a Machine Gun to Cambrai* (London: H.M.S.O., 1969) p. 66.
23. O.H.16.1. p. 64.
24. Each division had 48 Vickers guns, but where two battalions were in the line and two out, weapon density was 6000 yards/24 guns = 1 gun per 250 yards.
25. There is some confusion about this allotment. In one part the official history asserts one battalion in six selected divisions had Lewis guns on 14 July 1915, and, further, that this was the first issue in the B.E.F. (O.H.15.2. p. 89). But elsewhere the history states four Lewis guns had been issued to some battalions during June 1915 (O.H.16.1. p. 64). The reorganisation seems to have been accompanied by much variation among divisions; for instance, in the 9th division, some battalions had two and others four Lewis guns in September 1915, and this was before the division's Vickers were brigaded.
26. O.H.16.1. p. 65.
27. O.H.15.2. p. 89 fn.
28. When calculating the density for the 36-gun allotment, one must remember that in 1918 the number of battalions in a brigade was reduced from four to three, and therefore the number of Lewis guns in a 1918 division was 324. The above density assumes six battalions in the line and three in reserve.
29. Terraine, *General Jack's Diary 1914–18*, op. cit., p. 170 (8th division, 2/West Yorkshire Regiment, September 1916, nr. Hulluch, 1st Army).
30. A trench-mortar is a short-barrelled gun which fires a bomb along a high trajectory across a relatively short distance.
31. A. H. Hussey and D. S. Inman, *The Fifth Division in the Great War* (London: Nesbitt and Co., 1921) p. 102.
32. Although control of mortars was made uniform at this date, weapons were still variously manned; for instance, in the 9th division, crews were made up of heavy gunners and infantry pioneers. See J. Ewing, *The History of the Ninth (Scottish) Division* (London: John Murray, 1921) p. 81.
33. Molony, op. cit., p. 104.
34. O.H.15.1. pp. 8–9. The figures for the second and third quarters are 225 and 121 respectively. These totals do not include mortars made in army workshops in France.
35. O.H.16.1. p. 61. These were organised into 61 batteries of 4 guns each.
36. That is 6.5 mortars per division or one for each battalion in the line. I have no figures for French and German armies during this period. It is possible the French and British were not dissimilar, but German mortar technology was more advanced.
37. A. Forbes, *A History of the Army Ordnance Services*, vol. 3 (London: The Medici Society, 1929) p. 40.
38. O.H.15.1. p. 9. Shell output in the first quarter of 1916 was 1,000,000 and in the second quarter over 2,000,000.
39. In June 1917, toffee apples were superseded by another medium mortar with a longer range—1000 yards—and a quicker fire rate. Other and earlier mortars were known as toffee apples, but these were never standardised.
40. J. Shakespeare, *Historical Records of the 18th Battalion Northumberland Fusiliers*

238 *Notes to Chapter 3*

(Newcastle: 1920) pp. 38–9. This was a pioneer battalion which in 1916 built emplacements for the heavy mortars of the 34th division 25 feet below ground.

41. B. Latham, *A Territorial Soldier's War* (Aldershot: Gale and Polden, 1967) p. 49 (47th division).

42. G. F. Wear, '17–21', in C. Purdom (ed.), *Everyman At War* (London: J. M. Dent, 1930) p. 106 (49th division).

43. Lord Moran, *The Anatomy of Courage* (London: Constable, 1945) p. 81 (1/Royal Fusiliers, 24th division).

44. Graves, op. cit., p. 126 (2nd division).

45. Ommanney, op. cit., p. 82.

46. G. K. Rose, *The Story of The 2/4th Oxfordshire and Buckinghamshire Light Infantry* (Oxford: B. Blackwell, 1920) p. 12.

47. O.H.16.1. p. 61

48. The reader should bear in mind this density assumes three brigades in the line on a 6000-yard front. Density varied with conditions. Many divisional fronts were less than 6000 yards; but some divisions had two brigades in trenches and one in reserve, in which case one of three brigade light mortar batteries was also in reserve; but all medium and heavy mortars remained, as these were under divisional not brigade control. Moreover, some brigades had six Stokes in a battery (the official history gives the figure of four). See Latham, op. cit., p. 49.

49. Some divisions received pigs in 1916, and some in 1917. The 34th division got two heavy mortars in June 1916. See J. Shakespeare, op. cit., pp. 38–9.

50. Many targets were found by snipers and observers who recorded their location on a log given to the intelligence officer, who then sent likely items to brigade; the latter forwarded targets to medium and heavy mortars.

51. O.H.16.1., see end paper.

52. O.H.16.1. p. 59.

53. O.H.15.1. p. 55.

54. O.H.17.1. p. 11.

55. O.H.17.1. p. 11.

56. O.H.15.1. p. 55.

57. O.H.15.1. p. 7.

58. O.H.15.2. pp. 193–4.

59. In September 1915 the 15th division had a brigade bombing squad of 181 specialists (O.H.15.2. p. 194). For a short time the 51st division (T.F.) was organised in this way. For an account by a brigade bombing officer see Ross, op. cit., Chapters 3–4.

60. See G. Goold Walker (ed.) *The Honourable Artillery Company In the Great War 1914–1918* (London: Seeley, Service, 1930) p. 61 (61st division, 1/H.A.C. September 1916); Newton, op.cit., pp. 193–4 (1st Australian division, June 1916).

61. E. Parker, *Into Battle 1916–1918* (London: Longmans, 1964) p. 34 (14th division, 10/Durham Light Infantry, October 1915).

62. O.H.15.1. p. 95.

63. Bombing schools were instituted at army and corps level (O.H.15.1. p. 12), probably some divisional and brigade schools existed.

64. For instance, the War Office manual: 40/W.O./3352, *The Training and Employment of Bombers*.

65. Coppard, op. cit., p. 70 (12th division, March 1916, Hohenzollern, 1st Army).
66. G. Seton-Hutchinson, *Warrior* (London: Hutchinson) p. 98 (33rd division, 2/ Argyll & Sutherland Highlanders).
67. *The War The Infantry Knew*, op. cit., p. 120 (6th division).
68. Terraine (ed.) p. 98 (6th division, 19th brigade, January 1915, nr. Armentières, 2nd Army).
69. J. Reith, *Wearing Spurs* (London: Hutchinson, 1966) pp. 177–8, 185–6 (6th division).
70. Graves, op. cit., p. 114 (2nd division, 2/Royal Welch, July 1915, nr. Laventie, 1st Army).
71. Ibid., p. 114. Patrolling was thus defined in the 1/Welsh Regiment (1st division May/June 1915, Cambrin, 2nd Army) in which Graves served before joining the 2/Royal Welch; he also served with the 1/Royal Welch where aggressive patrolling was also a point of honour.
72. Ibid., p. 114.
73. *The War The Infantry Knew*, op. cit., p. 84 (October 1914, nr. Fromelles).
74. Ibid., p. 88 (October 1914, nr. Fromelles).
75. Richards, op. cit., p. 39. Richards served with the 2/Royal Welch from 1914–18 as a private but very 'old' soldier, and asserted this practice held throughout the war; but another source states that patrolling and trench raids, which had been made with volunteers before the Somme, were made after with men detailed for the task. See Dudley-Ward op. cit., p. 305.
76. *The War The Infantry Knew*, op. cit., p. 100 (nr. Houplines).
77. Ibid., p. 122 (nr. Armentières, March 1915).
78. Ibid., p. 134 (nr. Armentières, March 1915).
79. Ibid., pp. 127–8 (La Vesée, March 1915). In the patrol formation, two men led, another followed and was guarded from behind by a fourth.
80. Ibid., pp. 122–3 (nr. Armentières, March 1915).
81. Army formations ran scouting schools. See O.H.15.1. p. 12.
82. See *Notes For Infantry Officers in Trench Warfare*, op. cit., p. 8. 'Minor local enterprises . . . during the tour of duty in the trenches furnish the best means of maintaining the efficiency of the troops.'
83. Ibid., p. 9. There were other means, for instance, aerial reconnaissance.
84. Ibid., p. 9.
85. *O.H.18. Appendices*, Appendix 6, p. 22. 'G.H.Q. Memorandum on Defensive Measures. The enemy's fighting power must be impaired by . . . active patrolling, constant raids.'
86. O.H.15.1. p. 32 fn.
87. See Hulse, op. cit., p. 37 (7th division, 2/Scots Guards, November 1914); Dudley-Ward, op. cit., p. 161 (7th division, 1/Royal Welch Fusiliers, 1914).
88. The 6th and 7/Canadian battalions, 2nd Canadian infantry brigade.
89. O.H.16.1. p. 156 fn.
90. For the official account of the raid see *O.H.16. Appendices*, Appendix 6.
91. *The War The Infantry Knew*, p. 116.
92. *O.H.16. Appendices*, op. cit., pp. 42, 48.
93. Ibid., p. 43.
94. Ibid., p. 43.
95. Parker, op. cit., p. 80 (29th division, 2/Royal Fusiliers, June 1917, Ypres, 2nd Army).

96. Mark Seven, A *Subaltern On The Somme* (London: J. M. Dent, 1927) p. 217 (17th division).
97. A river which needed bridging ran between the lines, and covering groups were placed by the bridges to stop the enemy destroying this means of withdrawal.

CHAPTER 4

1. H. Macmillan, *Winds of Change 1914–1919* (London: Macmillan, 1966), p. 65 (Guards division, 4/Grenadier Guards).
2. R. Blake (ed.), *The Private Papers of Douglas Haig* (London: Eyre and Spottiswood, 1952), p. 79.
3. On impersonal control systems see P. Blau and W. Scott, *Formal Organisation* (San Francisco: Chandler Publishing Company, 1962), pp. 176–83.
4. For an account of regimental *esprit de corps* and fighting ability see Baynes, op. cit. The author, an infantry officer, shows very well how a battalion develops and maintains solidarity, and how this is positively related to combat performance. However, Baynes leaves implicit an important point, namely, that regimental loyalty is a bond cutting right across the hierarchy of formal military rank, thus containing conflict which otherwise might occur between levels of bureaucratic hierarchy and lessen efficiency. The importance of cross-cutting ties in conflict management has, of course, been realised in the behavioural sciences for many years.
5. Solidarity refers to the shared disposition among members of a group to act in concert for certain purposes. Units with high solidarity expressed in aggressive battle behaviour were said by high command to have high morale. On the other hand, solidarity might determine informal limits on aggression, in which case high command defined units as of low morale. It is important to realise that some battalions officially defined as having low morale were highly solidary units. A third possibility is where members of a unit are bound together merely by official ties of function and rank; such a unit had cohesion but no solidarity, and its fighting ability would be relatively low.
6. Gillon, op. cit., pp. ix-xii.
7. G. Belton Cobb, *Stand to Arms* (London: Wells Gardner, Darton & Co., 1916) p. 74. This book contains much minutiae of trench life and war in 1915; unfortunately dates, place and unit names are absent. The author served with the London Irish Rifles and most probably with the 47th division; the period described is March 1915–October 1915.
8. *Notes for Infantry Officers on Trench Warfare*, op. cit., pp. 48–9.
9. Ibid., p. 39.
10. Ibid., pp. 48–9.
11. R. L. Bullard, *Personalities and Reminiscences of the War* (New York: Doubleday, Page and Company, 1925), p. 95. Bullard took command of the U.S. 1st division in December 1917.
12. For an analysis of assembly lines as impersonal, non-human control systems, see Blau and Scott, op. cit., pp. 176–8.
13. Haig's reasons for this are examined in Chapter 7.
14. This is not to deny that a complex technology can serve as a deterrent and

maintain peace.
15. Hay, *The First Hundred Thousand*, op. cit., p. 253.
16. Adams, op. cit., p. 132.
17. S. L. A. Marshall, *Men Against Fire* (New York: Wm. Morrow, 1968) p. 57.
18. G. F. Wear, '17–21', in Purdom, op. cit., p. 102 (49th division).
19. Parker, op. cit., p. 34.
20. Ibid., p. 73.
21. J. A. Blake, 'The Organisation as Instrument of Violence: The Military Case', *Sociological Quarterly*, vol. II, no. 3, (1970) pp. 331–50.
22. Coppard, op. cit., p. 59.
23. All social systems have mechanisms of control which maintain established patterns of behaviour by negatively sanctioning deviance; the control mechanisms which sustained live and let live are examined in Chapter 7.
24. This is not to say battalions were no longer concerned with the activities of these weapon groups after this reorganisation. On the contrary, they were equally if not more concerned, but control of the specialists was more difficult than before. This problem will be examined in Chapter 7.
25. Blunden, op. cit., p. 19 (39th division, 11/Royal Sussex Regiment, Spring 1916, nr. Festubert, 1st Army).
26. *Notes for Infantry Officers on Trench Warfare*, op. cit., pp. 44–5.
27. The C.R.A. was the officer commanding divisional artillery—a member of high command.
28. A. B. Scott *et al.*, *Artillery and Trench Mortar Memories* (London: Unwin Bros., 1932), p. 25 (32nd division, August 1916, nr. Cambrin, 1st Army).
29. Hussey and Inman, op. cit., p. 79.
30. Reith, op. cit., p. 189 (6th and 27th division, 5/Scottish Rifles).
31. Charteris, op. cit., p. 66.
32. *The War the Infantry Knew*, op. cit., p. 125.
33. Ewing, op. cit., p. 15.
34. Duff Cooper, *Haig*, vol. 1 (London: Faber and Faber, 1935), p. 251.
35. J. Terraine, *Douglas Haig* (London: Hutchinson, 1963), p. 133.
36. Graves, op. cit., pp. 112–13, 134.
37. For instances of Williams' humour see, *The War The Infantry Knew*, op. cit., pp. 131–2, 135–6.
38. Richards, op. cit., p. 31.
39. Thomas, op. cit., pp. 56–7 (6/Royal West Kents, 12th division).
40. Graves, op. cit., p. 138.
41. Richards, op. cit., p. 50.
42. J. H. Boraston (ed.) *Sir Douglas Haig's Dispatches* (London: J. M. Dent, 1920), pp. 3–4.
43. E. Wyrall, *The History of the 62nd (West Riding) Division*, vol. 1 (London: Bodley Head, 1924), pp. 60–1.
44. Feilding, op. cit., pp. 248–9 (16th division, 6/Connaught Rangers, January 1918, nr. Ronssoy, 5th Army).
45. B. Peacock, *Tinker's Mufti* (London: Seeley Service & Co., 1974) pp. 57–8 (34th division, 22/Northumberland Fusiliers, September 1917, nr. Hargicourt, 5th Army).
46. C. Headlam, *History of the Guards Division in the Great War*, vol. 1 (London: Murray, 1924), pp. 106–7, fn.

47. Hesketh-Pritchard, op. cit., p. 193. The author was a sniping officer in XI corps for a time.
48. Headlam, op. cit., pp. 108–9.
49. *Notes for Infantry Officers on Trench Warfare*, op. cit., p. 8.
50. Headlam, op. cit., p. 107.
51. J. R. Colville, *Man of Valour* (London: Collins, 1972) p. 42 (Guards division, 1/ Grenadier Guards, Summer 1918, nr. Blairville, 3rd Army).
52. C. Carstairs, *A Generation Missing* (London: Heinemann, 1930), p. 66 (Guards division, 3/Grenadier Guards, Autumn 1916). W. Ewart, who served with the 2/Scots Guards, mentions several sectors where his battalion exchanged peace: see Ewart, op. cit., pp. 16, 22, 26, 77, 153–4.
53. Headlam, op. cit., p. 107.
54. Gilbert, op. cit., p. 1372.
55. Ewing, op. cit., p. 77 (January/May 1916, Ploegsteert, 2nd Army).
56. J. O. Coop, *The Story of the 55th Division* (Liverpool: *Daily Post*, 1919), Spring/ Summer, 1916.
57. Russel, op. cit., p. 40 (41st division, June 1916, Ploegsteert, 2nd Army).
58. *The War Diary of the Master of Belhaven* (London: John Murray, 1924), p. 126 (24th division, December 1915, nr. Ypres, 2nd Army).
59. Carrington, op. cit., p. 103 (48th division, 5/Warwickshire Regiment).
60. Goold-Walker, op. cit., p. 300 (7th division, 2/H.A.C., December 1916, nr. Mailly-Mallet, 5th Army).
61. Seton-Hutchinson, op. cit., p. 148.
62. For instance, a 56th divisional memo stated, 'the vital importance of imbuing all ranks with the offensive spirit will be insisted on, this will be the personal concern of brigade and other commanders'. Henriques, op. cit., pp. 76–7.
63. W. R. Elliot, *The Second Twentieth, being the History of the 2/20th London Regiment* (Aldershot: Gale and Polden, 1920), p. 23 (60th division (T.F.), 2/20 London Regt., July 1916, Neuville St. Vast, 3rd Army). General Studd commanded the 180th brigade.
64. F. P. Crozier, *A Brass Hat in No-man's-land* (London: Jonathan Cape, 1930), pp. 133, 144–5.
65. Ibid., pp. 145–7, 157. I have seen no other instances of this practice among higher commanders.
66. C. C. R. Murphy, *The History of the Suffolk Regiment* (London: Hutchinson), p. 137 (3rd division, 2/Suffolk Regt., January 1916).
67. *Notes for Infantry Officers on Trench Warfare*, op. cit., p. 46.
68. Bales, op. cit., p. 34.
69. *The War The Infantry Knew*, op. cit., p. 224, fn.
70. *The Fifth Scottish Rifles*, op. cit., p. 85.
71. Ashcroft, op. cit., p. 57.
72. Feilding, op. cit., p. 140 (December 1916).
73. A. Vagts, *A History of Militarism* (New York: Meridian Books, 1959), p. 234.
74. *General Jack's Diary*, op. cit., p. 98 (6th division, 1/Cameronians, January 1915, nr. Bois Grenier, 2nd Army).
75. Ibid., p. 170 (8th division, 2/West Yorkshire Regt., September 1916, nr. Hulluch, 1st Army).
76. Ibid., pp. 87–90. Such brigadiers were far fewer from 1916.
77. Blunden, op. cit., p. 36 (39th division, 11/Royal Sussex, May/June 1916,

Cuinchy, 1st Army).

78. Jack, op. cit., p. 167 (8th division, 2/West Yorkshire Regt., September 1916, nr. Vermelles, 1st Army).
79. Dudley Ward, op. cit., p. 163.
80. *The War the Infantry Knew*, op. cit., p. 192.
81. Hussey, op. cit., p. 142.
82. A. Hilliard Atteridge, *History of the 17th (Northern) Division* (Glasgow: R. Maclehose, 1926) p. 69.
83. W. D. Croft, *Three Years with the 9th (Scottish) Division* (London: John Murray, 1919) p. 232.

CHAPTER 5

1. *The War History of the Sixth Battalion The South Staffordshire Regiment*, op. cit., p. 48 (46th division, 6/South Staffs. Regt., April–June 1915, Wulverghem, 2nd Army).
2. C. Haworth, *March to Armistice* (London: William Kimber, 1968) p. 45 (14th division, 14/Argyll & Sutherland Highlanders, Summer 1918, nr. Ypres, 2nd Army).
3. Blunden, op. cit., p. 121.
4. Griffiths, op. cit., p. 33 (38th division, December 1915, Neuve-Chapelle, 1st Army).
5. Ibid., p. 35.
6. Jack, op. cit., p. 170 (8th division, 2/West Yorks. Regt., September 1916, nr. Hulluch, 1st Army).
7. F. P. Gibbon, *The 42nd East Lancashire Division 1914–1918* (London: 1920) p. 94 (Ypres, June 1917).
8. Sorley, op. cit., p. 283 (12th division, 7/Suffolk Regt., Summer 1915, Ploegsteert, 1st Army).
9. J. Aston and L. M. Duggan, *The History of the 12th (Bermondsey) Battalion East Surrey Regiment* (London: The Union Press, 1936) p. 89 (41st division, 12/East Surrey Regt., March 1917, St. Eloi, 2nd Army).
10. S. Sassoon, *Memoirs of a Fox Hunting Man* (London: The Folio Society, 1973) p. 287 (7th division, 1/Royal Welch Fusiliers, Spring 1916, nr. Fricourt, 4th Army).
11. *The War The Infantry Knew*, op. cit., p. 120 (6th division, 2/Royal Welch Fusiliers, Spring 1915, nr. Armentières, 1st Army).
12. H. Read, *Annals of Innocence and Experience* (London: Faber & Faber, 1946) pp. 142–3 (21st division, 10/Green Howards, nr. St. Quentin, 5th Army).
13. E. A. Atkins, 'Tommy Atkins, P.B.I.', in M. Moynihan (ed.), *People At War 1914–1918* (Newton Abbot: David & Charles, 1973) pp. 90–1.
14. Hay, op. cit., pp. 224–5 (9th division, 10/Argyll & Sutherland Highlanders, June/July 1915, nr. Festubert, 1st Army).
15. MacGill, *The Great Push*, op. cit., p. 87 (47th division, 18/London Regt., Spring/Summer 1915, nr. Maroc, 1st Army).
16. F. Manning, *Her Privates We* (London: Peter Davies, 1964) p. 260 (3rd division, 7/Kings Shropshire Light Infantry, Summer/Autumn 1916, nr. Colincamps, 5th Army).

17. W. V. Tilsey, *Other Ranks* (London: Cobden-Sanderson, 1931) pp. 169–71 (55th division, 164th brigade, Spring 1917, Lille Gates, Ypres, 2nd Army).
18. Ibid., pp. 193–4, same time and place.
19. Seven, op. cit., pp. 106–8 (17th division, September 1916, nr. Hebuterne, 5th Army).
20. F. P. Crozier, *A Brass Hat In No Man's Land* (London: Jonathan Cape, 1930) p. 157.
21. F. P. Crozier, *The Men I Killed* (London: Michael Joseph, 1937) p. 71.
22. Tilsey, op. cit., pp. 169–70.
23. Haworth, op. cit., pp. 24–5.
24. Crozier, *The Men I Killed*, op. cit., pp. 71–2.
25. L. Renn, *War* (London: Martin Secker, 1929) pp. 274–5. Renn was Golssenau's pseudonym.
26. Mottram *et al.*, op. cit., p. 328.
27. Griffiths, op. cit., p. 33.
28. *Purnell's History of the First World War*, vol. VI, no. 4 (London). The soldier was Henry Williamson. What appears to be the same event was also described by a soldier of the 5/Rifle Brigade. See D. Bell, *A Soldier's Diary of the Great War* (London: Faber & Gwyer, 1929) p. 81.
29. O. H. Bailey and H. M. Hollier, '*The Kensingtons*' *13th London Regiment* (London: 1935) p. 27 (8th division, 13/London Regt., December 1914, Laventie, 2nd Army).
30. With the exception of hand-grenades, there was no shortage of small arms ammunition in the B.E.F. in the first or second phase of trench war. See O.H.15.1., p. 58.
31. Russel, op. cit., p. 106 (41st division, 11/Royal West Kents, Spring 1917, nr. St. Eloi, 2nd Army).
32. *The War The Infantry Knew*, op. cit., p. 98 (6th division, 2/Royal Welch Fusiliers, December 1914, nr. Armentières, 3rd corps).
33. Hay, *The First Hundred Thousand*, op. cit., 1916, pp. 205–6 (26th Brigade attached to 6th division, 10/Argyll and Sutherland Highlanders, May/June 1915, nr. Armentières, 2nd Army).
34. Griffiths, op. cit., p. 35 (38th division, Spring 1916, nr. Laventie, 1st Army).
35. A. F. Wedd, *German Student's War Letters* (London: Methuen, 1929) p. 182. The incident was described in a letter by a German soldier and took place in August 1915, on the Vosges sector.
36. F. Delamain (ed.), *Going Across* (Newport: R. H. Johns,) p. 65 (19th division, 9/Welsh Regiment, September 1916, nr. Kemmel, 2nd Army).
37. Excepting, of course, where one party has power.
38. G. Dugdale, *Langemarck and Cambrai* (Shrewsbury: Wilding and Son, 1932) pp. 94–6 (20th division, 60th brigade, October 1917, nr. Villers Pluich, 4th Army).
39. C. T. Atkinson, *The Seventh Division 1914–1918* (London: John Murray, 1927) (July 1915, nr. Givenchy).
40. *The War Diary of the Master of Belhaven 1914–1918* (London: John Murray, 1924) pp. 371–2 (24th division, 12/Royal Fusiliers, August 1917, Ypres, 2nd Army).
41. Gordon, pp. 103–4 (25th division, 112th brigade (R.F.A.) November 1917,

nr. Festubert, 1st Army).
42. A. Thomas, op. cit., p. 149 (12th division, 6/Royal West Kents, October 1918, Vimy, 1st Army).
43. J. Goss, *A Border Battalion. The History of the 7/8 (Service) Bttn. King's Own Scottish Borderers* (Edinburgh: 1920) p. 259 (15th division, August 1918, Loos, 1st Army).
44. F. G. Stanley, *The History of the 89th Brigade* (Liverpool: Daily Post Printer, 1919) (30th division, 89th brigade, June 1916, nr. Maricourt, 4th Army).
45. Smith, op. cit., p. 195 (56th division, 1/5th London Regiment, December 1916, Laventie, 2nd Army).
46. G. Chapman, *A Passionate Prodigality* (MacGibbon and Kee: 1965) p. 70 (37th division, 13/Royal Fusiliers, Summer 1916, nr. Bailleaumont, 3rd Army).
47. Reith, op. cit., p. 126 (19th division, September 1915, nr. Béthune, 1st Army). At this time Reith was on detachment from the Royal Engineers of the 7th division.
48. Carrington, op. cit., p. 130. The author used the phrase to describe the Le Sars sector in the winter of 1916.
49. Ashcroft, op. cit., p. 54 (Nr. Wanquentin, July 1916, 3rd Army).
50. Ibid., p. 141 (Cité St. Auguste nr. Lens October 1917, 1st Army).
51. Blunden, op. cit., p. 74 (39th division, 11/Royal Sussex Regt., July 1916, nr. Festubert, 1st Army).
52. Seven, op. cit., p. 91 (17th division, September 1916, Hebuterne, 5th Army).
53. Aston and Duggan, op. cit., pp. 244–5 (41st division, 12/East Surrey Regt., Summer 1918, Kemmel, 2nd Army).
54. H. S. Clapham, *Mud and Khaki* (London: Hutchinson) p. 223 (3rd division, 1/ H.A.C., Ypres, 2nd Army).
55. Taken from a machine-gunner's notebook — Private Ribbans, D.C.M. — which was compiled during training.
56. A. Aitken, *From Gallipoli to the Somme* (London: Oxford University Press, 1963) p. 71 (New Zealand division, Spring 1916, nr. Armentières, 2nd Army).
57. Ewart, op. cit., p. 88 (Guards division, 2/Scots Guards, Summer 1916, Ypres, 2nd Army). For an autobiographical document containing a good account of aggressive machine-gun tactics, see Coppard, op. cit.
58. Bewsher, op. cit., p. 14 (1915, Festubert, 1st Army).
59. C. H. Cooke, *Historical Records of the 19th (Service) Battalion Northumberland Fusiliers* (Newcastle: 1920) p. 23 (35th division, February 1916, nr. Festubert, 1st Army).
60. Russel, op. cit., p. 25 (41st division, August 1916, nr. Ploegsteert, 2nd Army). Numerous instances of musical machine-guns appear in the literature.
61. C. J. Arthur, 'A Boy's Experiences', in Purdom, op. cit. (41st and 12th divisions).
62. Ibid., p. 176.
63. Ibid., p. 179.
64. Clapham, op. cit., pp. 27–30 (3rd division, 1/H.A.C., February 1915, Kemmel, 2nd Army).
65. Feilding, op. cit., p. 220 (16th division, 8/Connaught Rangers, October 1917, nr. Croisilles, 5th Army).
66. *9th Royal Scots. (T. F.): From a Private's Diary* Edinburgh: 1916 (27th division,

9/Royal Scots, April 1915, Glencorse Wood, Ypres, 2nd Army).

67. Feilding, op. cit., p. 217 (16th division, 8/Connaught Rangers, October 1917, 5th Army).
68. E. Junger, op. cit., pp. 30–1.
69. Rutter, op. cit., pp. 30–1 (12th division, 7/Royal Sussex Regt., September 1915, nr. Houplines, 2nd Army).
70. J. Tyndale-Biscoe, *Gunner Subaltern* (London: Leo Cooper, 1971) p. 86 (14th division, March 1916, Blangy, nr. Arras, 3rd Army).
71. Thomas, op. cit., p. 79 (12th division, 6/Royal West Kent Regt., January 1917, Blangy, nr. Arras, 3rd Army).
72. D. Philips, 'At a Sap Head', in Purdom, op. cit., p. 50 (60th division, 23/London Regiment, Autumn/Summer 1916, Ecurie, 1st Army).
73. C. E. Jacomb, *Torment* (London: Andrew Melrose, 1920) pp. 177–8 (2nd division, 23/Royal Fusiliers, September/October 1916, nr. Mailly-Maillet, 5th Army). The Canadian corps was near the 2nd division. It is unlikely the mortar crew were shelling a target in no-man's-land, since there was no retaliation, or that the crew were finding the range of enemy trenches because of the length of time involved. The Canadians were almost certainly ritualising aggression.
74. R. Scott, *A Soldier's Diary* (London: Collins, 1923) pp. 70–1 (41st division, July 1918, Ypres).
75. Rutter, op. cit., p. 213 (12th division, Mailly-Maillet, May 1918).
76. C. Falls, *The History of the 36th (Ulster) Division* (London: McCaw, Stevenson and Orr, 1922) p. 35 (36th division, Spring 1916, Mailly-Maillet, 4th Army).
77. H. F. Barnes, *The Story of the 2/5th Battalion The Gloucestershire Regiment, 1914–1918* (Gloucester: The Crypt House Press, 1930) p. 38 (61st division, 2/5 Gloucester Regt., June 1916, Laventie, 1st Army).
78. Newton, op. cit., p. 173 (1st Australian division, 12/bn. A.I.F., April 1916, nr. Fleurbaix, 2nd Army).
79. Dudley Ward, op. cit., p. 140 (2nd division, 2/Royal Welch Fusiliers, September 1915, Cuinchy, 1st Army).
80. Reith, op. cit., pp. 171–2 (6th division, 5/Scottish Rifles, April 1915, nr. Bois Grenier, 2nd Army).
81. A 'Jack Johnson' was army jargon for a large shell.
82. Feilding, op. cit., p. 5 (1st division, 3/Coldstream Guards, May 1915, Cuinchy, 1st Army).
83. Russel, op. cit., p. 90 (41st division, 11/Royal West Kent Regt., Winter 1916–17, nr. St. Eloi, 2nd Army).
84. Crutwell, op. cit., p. 38 (48th division, 1/4th Royal Berkshire Regt., Summer/Autumn 1915, nr. Hebuterne, 3rd Army).
85. Jacomb, op. cit., pp. 176–7.
86. Hawkings, op. cit., p. 67.
87. E. Koppen, *Higher Command* (London: Faber and Faber, 1931) p. 205.
88. Goold-Walker, op. cit., p. 52.
89. R. Haigh and P. Turner (eds.), *The Long Carry* (London: Pergamon, 1947) p. 21 (47th division, 1/7th London Regt).
90. Raimes, op. cit., p. 47.
91. Hills, op. cit., p. 118.
92. R. Blaker, *Medal Without Bar* (London: Hodder and Stoughton, 1930) p. 150

(11th division, July 1916, nr. Arras, 3rd Army).

93. A. P. Herbert, *The Secret Battle* (London: Chatto and Windus, 1970) pp. 114–16 (63rd division, Summer 1916, Souchez, 1st Army).

94. Ashcroft, op. cit., pp. 55–6 (11th division, 7/South Staffs Regt., July 1916, Achincourt, 3rd Army).

95. Ewing, op. cit., p. 147 (9th division, August/September 1916, nr. Vimy, 3rd Army).

96. Binding, op. cit., p. 92 (January 1916, nr. Ypres, opposite British 2nd Army).

97. O.H. 1918. Appendices, p. 91. The VI corps defence scheme asserted that with respect to artillery, 'the method of fire will be salvoes at irregular intervals'.

98. F. G. Stanley, *The History of the 89th Brigade* (Liverpool: *Daily Post Printers*, 1919) pp. 230–1 (30th division, September 1917, Hollebeke, 2nd Army).

99. Delamain (ed.) op. cit., p. 20 (9/Welsh Regt., 19th division, Spring 1916, nr. Laventie, 1st Army).

100. Gilbert, op. cit., p. 1403 (9th division, 6/Royal Scots Fusiliers, January 1916, nr. Ploegsteert, 2nd Army).

101. Henriques, op. cit., p. 62 (6th division, 1/Queen's Westminster Rifles, September 1915, Ypres, 2nd Army).

102. Ibid., p. 55, same place and date. 'Little Willies' were German shells.

103. Crutwell, op. cit., pp. 10–11 (48th division, May 1915, nr. Ploegsteert, 2nd Army).

104. Kelly, op. cit., p. 36 (21st division, 110 brigade, July 1916, Arras, 3rd Army).

105. Hills, op. cit., p. 96 (48th division, 5/Leicestershire Regt., November 1915, nr. Festubert, 1st Army).

106. D. Clayton-James, *The Years of McArthur*, Vol. I (London: Leo Cooper, 1970) p. 156 (U.S. 42nd division, February 1918, nr. Luneville, French sector).

107. Junger, op. cit., p. 133 (April 1917, Arleux, nr. Douai).

108. Koppen, op. cit., p. 135–7 (September 1915, opposite the 1st British Army).

109. E. Remarque, *All Quiet on the Western Front* (London: Putnam, 1929) p. 62. No reference to time and place.

110. Renn, op. cit., p. 141 (Winter 1915–16, Chailly, opposite French army).

111. G. Bucher, *In the Line 1914–1918* (London: Jonathan Cape, 1932) pp. 136–7 (January/February 1917, Champagne, opposite the French army).

112. Hay, op. cit., *The First Hundred Thousand* p. 191. (10/Argyll & Sutherland Highlanders, May 1915, Armentières, 2nd Army).

113. Haig and Turner (eds) op. cit., p. 88.

CHAPTER 6

1. Sorley, op. cit., p. 283.

2. Hesketh-Pritchard, op. cit., p. 112.

3. Hussey and Inman, op. cit., p. 17 (5th division, Bray/Fricourt sector, August 1915, 3rd Army).

4. G. H. F. Nichols, *The 18th Division in the Great War* (London: Blackwood & Sons, 1922) p. 17 (7/R. West Kent Regiment, August/December 1915, Ovillers, 3rd Army).

5. Gordon, op. cit., p. 101 (25th division, Givenchy, October 1917, 1st Army).

6. Molony, op. cit., p. 123 (1/R. West Kents, 5th division, July 1915, Ribemont, 3rd Army); Nichols, op. cit., p. 17 (18th division, Autumn 1915, Bécourt, 3rd Army); T. S. Williams, 'The Carnoy Cow', in Purdom (ed.) op. cit., pp. 78–81 (30th division, 19/King's Liverpool Regiment, Spring 1916, Carnoy, 3rd Army); Banks and Chell, op. cit., p. 28—on an instructional tour with the 51st division, the 10/Essex found one unit kept a cow in trenches (August 1915, Authuille, 3rd Army); P. L. Wright, *The First Buckinghamshire Battalion 1914–1918* (London: Hazell, Watson & Viney, 1920), p. 17 (48th division, 1/1st Bucks Bn., June 1915, Hebuterne, 3rd Army).

7. Delamain (ed.), op. cit., p. 21 (19th division, 9/Welsh Regiment, April 1916, nr. Béthune, 1st Army).

8. Bales, op. cit., p. 124 (49th division, 1/4th Duke of Wellington's Regiment, March 1917, Femme du Bois).

9. Goss, op. cit., pp. 193–4 (15th division, 7/8th King's Own Scottish Borderers, November 1917, nr. Blangy, 3rd Army).

10. Hodson, op. cit., p. 265 (33rd division, 20/R. Fusiliers, Autumn 1916, nr. Pommiers, 3rd Army).

11. Brophy and Partridge, op. cit., p. 99.

12. Banks and Chell, op. cit., p. 225 (18th division, 10/Essex Regiment, March 1918, Fontaine, 5th Army).

13. Blunden, op. cit., p. 80 (39th division, 11/R. Sussex Regiment, Summer 1916, 1st Army).

14. Ibid., p. 74 (Summer 1916, nr. Festubert, 1st Army).

15. Raimes, op. cit., pp. 34–5 (50th division, 5/Durham Light Infantry, July 1915, nr. Houplines, 2nd Army).

16. R. B. Carver, *A History of the 10th (service) Battalion The East Yorkshire Regiment* (London: A. Brown & Sons, 1937) p. 166 (31st division, 10/East Yorks Regiment, July 1918, Nieppe Forest).

17. W. G. Hall, *The Green Triangle. Being the History of the 2/5th Battalion The Sherwood Foresters in the Great European War* (Letchworth: Garden City Press, 1920) p. 91 (59th division, 2/5th Sherwood Foresters, June 1917, Villers Pluich, 4th Army).

18. J. Glenn Gray, *The Warriors. Reflections on Men in Battle* (New York: Harper Torchbooks, 1965) Chapter 5.

19. H. Read, *The Contrary Experience* (London: Faber and Faber, 1963) p. 231. Read served with the 17th and 21st divisions.

20. Mottram *et al.*, op. cit., p. 33.

21. Ex-Private X, *War Is War* (London: Gollancz, 1930) pp. 72, 193 (63rd division).

22. Moran, op. cit., p. 60. Moran served with the 6th and 24th divisions.

23. Purdom, op. cit., p. 6.

24. L. Houseman, *War Letters of Fallen Englishmen* (London: Gollancz, 1930).

25. W. K. Pfeiler, *War and the German Mind* (New York: A.M.S. Press, 1966) pp. 78, 289.

26. H. Saunders, 'Trenches at Vimy Ridge', in Purdom (ed.), op. cit., p. 59. The author served with the 60th and 56th divisions.

27. G. C. Homans, *The Human Group* (London: Routledge & Kegan Paul, 1965) Chapter 5. The statement must be qualified, for conflict produces malevolence and ill feeling.

28. A. W. Gouldner, 'The Norm of Reciprocity' *American Sociological Review*, vol. 25, April 1970, pp. 161–78.
29. C. E. Montague, *Disenchantment* (London: MacGibbon & Kee, 1968) pp. 108–9.
30. Ibid., p. 108.
31. *The War History of the Sixth Battalion The South Staffordshire Regiment (T. F.)*, op. cit., p. 32 (46th division, March 1915, nr. Armentières, 2nd Army).
32. Chapman, op. cit. (37th division, 13/Royal Fusiliers, Spring 1916, Hannescamps, 3rd Army).
33. Crutwell, op. cit., p. 16 (48th division, 1/4th R. Berks Regiment, May 1915, Ploegstreert, 2nd Army).
34. Nichols, op. cit., p. 17 (18th division, Fricourt-Mametz, Autumn 1915).
35. Davson, op. cit., p. 72.
36. McGill, *The Red Horizon*, op. cit., pp. 234–5 (47th division, 18/London Regiment, Cuinchy, Summer 1915, 1st Army).
37. Maude, op. cit., p. 51 (Carency-Souchez, March/April 1916, 1st Army).
38. Brophy and Partridge, op. cit., p. 23.
39. Adams, op. cit., pp. 31–2 (7th division, 1/R. Welch Fusiliers, Cuinchy, October 1915, 1st Army).
40. Richards, op. cit., p. 103 (6th division, 2/R. Welch Fusiliers, Bois Grenier, Spring 1915, 2nd Army).
41. Middlebrook, op. cit., p. 59.
42. Stanley, op. cit., p. 180 (30th division, 19/King's Liverpool Regiment, December 1916, nr. Humbercamps, 3rd Army).
43. Houseman, op. cit., p. 38 (6th division, 2/Leinster Regiment, nr. Ypres, January 1915, 2nd Army).
44. Jack, op. cit., p. 94 (19th Brigade, 1/Cameronians, Bois Grenier, January 1915).
45. Ibid., pp. 121, 137, 139, 143, 156, 170, 184, 187, 190 (two comments), 192 (two comments), 198.
46. N. Lytton, *The Press and the General Staff* (London: Collins, 1920) p. 15 (39th division, 11/R. Sussex Regiment).
47. Hitchcock, op. cit., p. 100.
48. Jack, op. cit., p. 172.
49. Ibid., p. 170.
50. Feilding, op. cit., pp. 131, 225; see also Jack, op. cit., p. 190.
51. *The War The Infantry Knew*, op. cit., p. 298 (33rd division, 2/R. Welch Fusiliers).
52. Blunden, op. cit., p. 59 (39th division, 11/R. Sussex Regiment).
53. S. Westman, *A Surgeon with the Kaiser's Army* (London: William Kimber, 1968) p. 63.
54. Jones, op. cit. (38th division).
55. Griffiths, op. cit.
56. Anon., *A Soldier's Diary*, op. cit., p. 97 (6th division).
57. Brophy and Partridge, op. cit., p. 137.
58. Westman, op. cit., p. 43.
59. Pfeiler, op. cit., pp. 293–300.
60. C. Barnett, *The Swordbearers* (London: Eyre & Spottiswoode, 1963) pp. 211–12.

61. Brigadier General Count Gleichen, *The Doings of the Fifteenth Infantry Brigade* (London: Blackwood, 1917) p. 273 (5th division, nr. Messines, 2nd Army).
62. C. H. Dudley Ward, *The 56th Division* (London: John Murray, 1921) p. 141.
63. Haig and Turner (eds), op. cit., p. 52 (47th division).
64. Greenwell, op. cit., p. 66 (48th division, 1/4th Ox. & Bucks Light Infantry, November 1915, Hebuterne, 3rd Army).
65. Rutter, op. cit., p. 29 (12th division, 7/R. Sussex Regiment, August 1915, nr. Armentières, 1st Army).
66. C. Douie, *The Weary Road* (London: Murray, 1929) p. 20 (1/Dorsetshire Regiment).
67. Graves, op. cit., p. 201.
68. Montague, op. cit., p. 110.
69. Hussey and Inman, op. cit., pp. 85–6.
70. Adams, op. cit., pp. 137–8 (7th division, 1/R. Welch Fusiliers, February/March 1916, nr. Morlancourt, 4th Army).
71. Belhaven, op. cit., p. 162 (24th division, March 1916, Ypres, 2nd Army).
72. Gibbon, op. cit., pp. 119–20 (42nd division, December 1917, La Bassée, 1st Army).
73. Ibid., pp. 115–20.
74. Ommanney, op. cit., p. 77 (50th division, May 1916, Kemmel, 2nd Army).
75. Greenwell, op. cit., pp. 16–17 (48th division, 1/4th Ox. & Bucks light Infantry, May 1915, Ploegstreert, 2nd Army).
76. Bland, op. cit., pp. 81–3 (1st division, 6/Welsh Regiment, Winter 1915–16, Loos, 1st Army).
77. Blaker, op. cit., pp. 150–2 (11th division, July 1916, Agny, nr. Arras, 3rd Army).
78. Blunden, op. cit., pp. 70–1 (39th division, 11/R. Sussex Regiment, Richebourg, May/June 1916, 1st Army).

CHAPTER 7

1. This form of exchange is defined by Ekeh as Group Focused Net Generalised Exchange where 'Individuals . . . successively give to the group as a unit and then gain back as part of the group from each of the unit members'. P. Ekeh, *Social Exchange Theory* (London: Heinemann, 1974) pp. 53–4. This type of exchange operates among group members over a period of time, for example, in a 5-man friendship group when each member invites all others together as a unit to dinner parties at intervals such as a month. But the present concept refers to exchange which occurs among all combinations of group members both simultaneously, that is, at a given moment in time, and successively, that is, at each consecutive moment in time without cease. Such exchange is not confined to war but commonly occurs in groups whose members are exposed to danger, for instance, miners, mariners and the like. Such intensive exchange is associated with solidarity.
2. See, for instance, E. Shils and M. Janowitz, 'Cohesion and Disintegration in the Wehtmacht in World War 2', *The Public Opinion Quarterly*, Summer 1948; R. Little, 'Buddy Relations and Combat Performance', in M. Janowitz (ed.),

The New Military (New York: Russell Sage, 1964); C. C. Moskos, *The American Enlisted Man* (New York: Russell Sage, 1970).
3. Brophy and Partridge, op.cit., p. 151.
4. Montague, op. cit., p. 33.
5. Ibid., p. 33.
6. *Infantry Training 1914*, op. cit., p. 145.
7. MacGill, *The Red Horizon*, op. cit., pp. 232-3.
8. Graves, op. cit., p.92.
9. *Scrapbook of the 7th Battalion Somerset Light Infantry* (Aylesbury: Kingsbury Press, 1932) p. 111.
10. D. Young, *Rommel* (London: Collins, 1950) p. 39 (17th division).
11. Graves, op. cit., p. 14 (1st division, 2/Welsh Regiment, Summer 1915, Cambrin, 2nd Army).
12. MacGill, *The Red Horizon*, op. cit., p. 97 (47th division, 18/London Regiment, Summer 1915, nr. Festubert, 1st Army).
13. For instance, facist, racist, revolutionary, reactionary.
14. *The History of the Prince of Wales' Own Civil Service Rifles*, op. cit., p. 152 (47th division, 15/London Regiment).
15. *The Times*, 25 June 1917.
16. Douie, op. cit., p. 141 (32nd division).
17. Hay, *The First Hundred Thousand*, op. cit., p. 252 (9th division).
18. Ibid., p. 243.
19. Griffiths, op. cit., pp. 44-5 (38th division).
20. Koppen, op. cit., pp. 205-7.
21. Hesketh-Prithard, op. cit., p. 14.
22. Brophy and Partridge, op. cit., p. 196.
23. G. Seton-Hutchinson, *The Thirty-Third Division in France and Flanders* (London: Waterlow & Sons, 1921) p. 6.
24. Hussey and Inman, op. cit., p. 79.
25. J. Shakespear, *The Thirty Fourth Division 1915-1919* (London: H.F. & G. Wetherby, 1921) p. 18.
26. Greenwell, op. cit., pp. 197-8 (48th division).
27. Bell, op. cit., p. 154 (1st division).
28. W. Lewis, *Blasting and Bombardiering* (London: Caldaer and Boyars 1967) Chapter xi.
29. Hussey and Inman, op. cit., p. 79. It has been asserted the infantry's hostility towards mortars derived from their technical inferiority in phase 1 and diminished as mortars became more reliable in phase 2. This is partly true but misleading. As mortars improved, infantry were less hostile, but not because the enemy was then aggressed more accurately, but because mortars could then be used effectively as a negative sanction to restore live and let live. This process is explained in respect of artillery later in the chapter.
30. Ewing, op. cit., p. 16.
31. Scott, op. cit., p. 25.
32. J. Stewart and J. Buchan, *The Fifteenth (Scottish) Division* (London: Blackwood, 1926) pp. 57-8.
33. Scott *et al.*, op. cit., pp. 36-7 (32nd division).
34. Hay, *The First Hundred Thousand*, op. cit., pp. 254-6 (9th division).
35. Russel, op. cit., p. 98 (41st division, 11/R. West Kents, Winter 1916-17,

St. Eloi, 2nd Army).
36. Eberle, op. cit., p. 9.
37. Mottram, *et al.*, op. cit., p. 47.
38. Gordon, op. cit., p. 59.
39. Sulsbach, op. cit., p. 64.
40. From a letter in the present author's possession writen by an F.O.O. of the 63rd division. All junior artillery officers did duty in trenches, and many battery commanders had, as junior officers, done tours in the line; non-commissioned gunners, except signallers, did not serve in trenches.
41. Ibid.
42. Aston and Duggan, op. cit., p. 35 (41st division, 12/East Surrey Regiment).
43. Sulsbach. op. cit., p. 78.
44. Ibid., p. 71.
45. Feilding, op. cit., pp. 206–7 (16th division, 6/Connaught Rangers, October 1917, Ervillers, 5th Army).
46. Lewis, op. cit., pp. 200–1 (Canadian Corps Siege Artillery, Winter 1917, Vimy Ridge, 1st Army).
47. Neither divisional nor regimental histories contain sufficient data of the day-to-day life of units in the line; diaries and memoirs frequently do but are often intermittent or concern short periods only. Official war diaries are of less use since the distinction between ritualised and non-ritualised aggression is not drawn, and consequently the data is misleading.
48. The 1/4th Duke of Wellington's Regiment was a pioneer battalion, but pioneering duties took a small proportion of its time—about four months—and the rest of the unit's time was spent either in trench war or battle—except for training and rest intervals.
49. Mottram *et al.*, op. cit., pp. 127–8.
50. Graves, op. cit., pp. 160–2. Graves was an instructor for several weeks in the winter of 1916.
51. For instance the history of an élite battalion—2/R. Welch Fusiliers—states, 'We took over a tacit live and let live arrangement'. *The War the Infantry Knew*, op. cit., p. 285 (33rd division, December 1916, Bouchavesnes, 4th Army).
52. To say the least the samples are small and the conjectures great; but I do not see how the sample size could be substantially increased without great time and expense; secondly, this study is exploratory, that is, the main problem is to identify rather than precisely measure a phenomenon, and to the best of my knowledge no other study has attempted either to conceptualise or measure live and let live.

CHAPTER 8

1. Duff Cooper, *Haig* (London: Faber and Faber, 1935), pp. 300–2.
2. Ibid., p. 301.
3. Blake, op. cit., p. 137. For an earlier reference in Haig's diary to the B.E.F.'s lack of training, see p. 129 (14 February 1916).
4. On 20 January Haig met Joffre who confirmed this was the French view; but, prior to that meeting, he had learned of the French view both from Major

Cavendish of the British mission at Chantilly and Captain Gemeau of the French mission at B.E.F. headquarters.

5. Duff Cooper, op. cit., pp. 298-9.
6. Blake, op. cit., p. 125.
7. The La Bassée–Ypres sector was chosen by Haig and Joffre in February for these preparatory battles, and the Somme was chosen for the decisive battle. In the event, however, the former attacks were not made (raids were substituted) since the Germans seized the strategic initiative at Verdun, and the British concentrated, not on preparatory attacks, but the major battle, that is, the Somme. But the issue here is Haig's strategic thinking at the beginning of 1916, not events as they actually happened.
8. J. H. Boraston, *Sir Douglas Haig's Dispatches* (London: J. N. Dent and Son, 1920) p. 326.
9. Blake, op. cit., p. 96. Diary entry of 14 June 1915. See also diary entry of 14 January 1916, p. 125.
10. Ibid., p. 101. Diary entry of 19 August 1915.
11. Boraston, op. cit., p. 319. According to one of Haig's biographers, the study of this document has been neglected. See Terraine, *Douglas Haig*, op. cit., p. 480.
12. Boraston, op. cit., pp. 3-4.
13. *The War The Infantry Knew*, op. cit., p. 192.
14. *Notes For Infantry Officers on Trench Warfare*, op. cit., pp. 48-9.
15. *Field Service Regulations*, Vol. 2, Operations, 1920, p. 241.
16. Blake, op. cit., p. 80.
17. Ibid., p. 86.
18. Ibid., p. 89.
19. Haig also expressed concern about inactivity and the erosion of the fighting spirit among French troops. For instance, commenting on the fighting ability of the French, Haig wrote in his diary: 'Then came Nivelle's fiasco in the spring of 1917, and for the rest of last year the French armies "rested". And now, when the result of the war depends on their "fighting spirit" many of their divisions won't face the enemy.' (Blake, op. cit., p. 314).
20. *Notes For Infantry Officers On Trench Warfare*, op. cit., p. 8. This was published in March 1916.
21. *Field Service Regulations 1920*, op. cit., p. 234.
22. See Chapter 4.
23. Terraine, *Douglas Haig*, op. cit., pp. 181-2.
24. O.H. 16.1., p. 27, fn.
25. Blake, op. cit., pp. 145-6. The French generals Joffre, Foch and Castelnau and the French President, Prime Minister and Minister of War were present.
26. O.H. 16.1., p. 242.
27. O.H. 16.1., p. 310. The three armies were: the 1st (14 raids); 2nd (17 raids); 3rd (12 raids).
28. O.H. 16.2., p. 543.
29. Boraston, op. cit., p. 135.
30. Ibid., p. 181. The Germans reciprocated with 225 raids during this period.
31. Ibid., pp. 319-27.
32. Falls, op. cit., p. 71.
33. Such criticism would not apply to raiding for tactical purposes, that is, the identification of enemy troops, destruction of defences and so forth, because

the tactical advantage gained from a few such raids might outweigh an unfavourable balance of casualties.
34. The Story of the 2/5th Gloucestershire Regiment, op. cit., p. 51 (61st division).
35. Seven, op. cit., p. 217 (17th division).
36. Blunden, op. cit., p. 177 (39th division). The period referred to was the 1917 winter, and the 'Great Unknown' was, of course, high command.
37. H. R. Sandilands, *The 23rd Division 1914–1919* (London: Blackwood and Sons, 1925) pp. 58–9.
38. Moran (op. cit., pp. 143–50) described a situation where a battalion C.O. was told by a divisional commander that he must not worry about the casualties which had been caused by a raid as the latter was a success from high command's point of view.
39. Pagan, op. cit., p. 140.
40. Jack, op. cit., p. 170 (8th division, 2/West Yorkshire Regiment):
41. Hitchcock, op. cit., p. 229 (24th division, 2/Leinster Regiment).
42. Liddell Hart, *A History of the First World War* (London: Cassell, 1970) p. 308. See also *The Memoirs of Captain Liddell Hart*, Vol. 1, op. cit., p. 13.
43. Falls, op. cit., pp. 71–2.
44. See, for instance, Terraine, *Douglas Haig*, op. cit., p. 192; Falls, op. cit., p. 71; O.H. 16.1., p. 310.
45. Of the 63 raids made by the British between December 1915 and May 1916, 47 were successful; of the 33 raids made by the Germans in the same period, 20 were successful (O.H. 16.1., p. 310).
46. Falls, op. cit., p. 71.
47. Moran, op. cit., pp. 67–71.
48. Moran, op. cit., p. 84.
49. Hitchcock, op. cit., pp. 163–9.
50. Gosse, op. cit., p. 23 (23rd division, 9/Green Howards, Bois Grenier 2nd Army, December 1915).
51. Ibid., pp. 25–6.
52. Falls, op. cit., p. 71.
53. Shakespear, op. cit., p. 80 (34th division).
54. Griffiths, op. cit., pp. 71–2 (38th division).
55. T. Lloyd, *The Blazing Trail of Flanders* (London: Heath Cranton 1933) p. 126 (35th division, 15/Cheshire Regiment).
56. Smith, op. cit., p. 119 (56th division, 5/Rifle Brigade).
57. Cooper, op. cit., pp. 331–69.
58. Richards, op. cit., p. 169 (33rd division, 2/Royal Welch Fusiliers, June 1916, Givenchy, 1st Army).
59. C. E. Montague, *Fiery Particles* (London: Chatto and Windus, 1923) pp. 211–33. This is not a work of autobiographical fiction, as far as I can judge, and it is not considered here as a source.
60. J. Romain, *Verdun* (London: Mayflower Books, 1973) Chapter 19.
61. The War History of the Sixth Battalion The South Staffordshire Regiment, op. cit., pp. 76–7 (46th division, 6/South Staffs, Autumn 1915, nr. Hill 60, 2nd Army).
62. Nichols, op. cit., p. 17.
63. Ewing, *The Royal Scots*, op. cit., p. 111.
64. Griffiths, op. cit., p. 77.

65. Blunden, op. cit., p. 35.
66. Ibid., p. 41.
67. O.H. 16.1., p. 73.
68. A. Barrie, *War Underground 1914–18*, (London: House Publications, 1964) p. 112. 'The local infantry commander made it clear that he wished no protective tunnelling to be carried out . . . Almost certainly, he hoped—as other infantrymen were simultaneously hoping a mile or so further north at Hill 60—that if they stopped the underground war, the Germans would do the same.'
69. O.H. 16.1., pp. 75–6. The German mining organisation was centralised about the same time—see Barrie, op. cit., p. 159.
70. Barrie, op. cit., p. 158.
71. O.H. 16.1., p. 156.
72. Blunden, op. cit., p. 168.
73. Hitchcock, op. cit., pp. 230–1.
74. *The War The Infantry Knew*, op. cit., p. 218.
75. J. Macartney Filgate, *The History of the 33rd Divisional Artillery* (London: Vacher and Sons, 1921), p. 21.
76. *The War The Infantry Knew*, op. cit., p. 220.
77. Bucher, op. cit., p. 147. The French raid and German counter-raid occurred early in 1917 upon the Champagne sector.
78. Ibid., p. 153.
79. Ibid., p. 154.
80. Ibid., p. 155.
81. Ibid., p. 161.
82. Ibid., p. 157.
83. Ibid., p. 167.
84. R. E. Priestly, *Breaking The Hindenburg Line: The Story of The 46th (North Midland) Division* (London: Fisher and Unwin, 1919) p. 20. The commander was Major General Thwaites.

CHAPTER 9

1. Little, op. cit., pp. 204–7.
2. Graves, op. cit., pp. 161–2.
3. Ex-Private X, op. cit., p. 96.
4. Frenchmen mobilised into the army numbered 8,410,000, and 537,000 of these became prisoners or were posted missing; Austro-Hungarians numbered 7,800,000, and 2,200,000 were taken prisoner or were missing. In Britain and the Commonwealth, 8,904,467 men were mobilised, and 191,652 were prisoners or missing. See: V. J. Esposito, *A Concise History of World War I* (London: Pall Mall Press, 1965) p. 372.
5. My own conclusions are similar to those of Charles Moskos, who argued that the combat motivation of the U.S. soldier in Vietnam in the 1960s was influenced by 'an underlying commitment to the worth of the larger social system for which he is fighting. This commitment need not be formally articulated, nor even perhaps consciously recognised. But the soldier must at some level accept, if not the specific purposes of the war, then at least the

broader (moral virtue) of the society of which he is a member'. See: C. C. Moskos, 'Why Men Fight', in D. Popenoe, *Sociology* (New York: Appleton-Century-Crofts, 1971) pp. 119–26. Moskos' paper first appeared in: *Transaction Magazine* (New Jersey: November 1969).

6. Shils and Janowitz, op. cit.
7. Remarque, op. cit., pp. 10–13.
8. This type of exchange is referred to by Homans as the exchange of punishments, and by Ekeh as negative exchange. See G. C. Homans, *Social Behaviour* (London: Routledge, and Kegan Paul, 1961) p. 57; Ekeh, op. cit., p. 150.
9. Junger, op. cit., p. 49. See also Richards, op. cit., p. 78. The author describes his reaction to the death of a friend: 'any man could go sniping if he wished to. I felt very sore after Stevens' death and for a number of days I spent many hours in that sniping post. A man needed plenty of patience when sniping and might wait hours before he could see a man to fire at. I was very fortunate on two days and felt I had amply revenged Stevens.'
10. *The War The Infantry Knew*, op. cit., p. 116.
11. Adams, op. cit., pp. 177–9 (7th division, 1/Royal Welch Fusiliers, Spring 1916, nr. Mametz, 4th Army).
12. Coppard, op. cit., p. 71 (12th division, 37th Machine Gun Company, March 1916, Hohenzollern Redoubt, 1st Army).
13. Feilding, op. cit., p. 30 (1st division, 1/Coldstream Guards, August 1915, Cambrin, 1st Army). Another incident illustrating the manipulation of live and let live occurred on the 23rd division's front: 'The peace which had reigned on the front prior to our arrival was exemplified shortly after we took over. A tin of bully beef having been thrown into No-Man's-Land . . . a German soldier emerged to retrieve what he took to be a peace offering. The simultaneous arrival on the spot of a heavy trench mortar bomb, however, could not be accepted in the same spirit.' Sandilands, op. cit., p. 48 (23rd division, March 1916, nr. Souchez, 1st Army).
14. Eberle, op. cit., p. 156 (48th division, Royal Engineer Field Company, Asiago, Spring 1918).
15. Aston and Duggan, op. cit., p. 196 (41st division, 12/East Surrey Regiment, February 1918, Monte Grapp sector).
16. Russel, op. cit., p. 191 (41st division, 11/The Queen's Own Royal West Kents, December 1917, Monte Grapp sector).
17. F. H. Dalbiac, *History of the 60th Division* (London: Allen and Unwin, 1927).
18. Bailey and Hollier, op. cit., p. 273.
19. H. R. Sandilands, *The Fifth in the Great War* (Dover: Grigg and Sons, 1938) p. 244 (28th division, 2/Northumberland Fusiliers, May 1917, Struma Valley). According to the same source, upon the Struma front in April 1918, the 'Divisional panto staged for the amusement of the troops a song entitled "Boris the Bulgar" and it had made a great hit. On a night in April notices were left on our wire by an enemy patrol, quoting two verses of the song, and requesting that the music be supplied' (p. 249).
20. C. Packer, *Return to Salonika* (London: Cassell, 1964) pp. 91, 104.
21. Wedd, op. cit., p. 266.
22. Sulsbach, op. cit., p. 108 (18th Austrian army corps). The infantry were the 10th Hungarian Infantry Regiment. Sulsbach's battery was attached to the Austrian army.

23. A. J. Smithers, *Sir John Monash* (London: Leo Cooper, 1973) pp. 98–9.
24. Ibid., p. 101.
25. Herbert, op. cit., pp. 42–3.
26. Marshall, op. cit.
27. Quoted from a review by Professor Michael Howard. See the *Sunday Times*, 30 May 1976.
28. Marshall, op. cit., pp. 70–1, 78–9. The author does take account of other fears which make men inert; but the fear of aggression is basic to his analysis. He asserts that 'This is his greatest handicap when he enters combat' (see p. 78).
29. Ibid., p. 78.
30. Ibid., p. 79.
31. Blake, op. cit.
32. Graves, op. cit., p. 116.
33. Hulse, op. cit., p. 82.
34. Seven, op. cit., pp. 217–18.
35. Marshall, op. cit., p. 70, 'the increasing of fire volume must be considered primarily as a psychological matter'.
36. Little, op. cit., p. 206. Little offers an alternative sociological explanation for some part of low fire ratios. He argues that Marshall did not consider problems of ammunition supply in attacks when accounting for low fire ratios. But morale, like morality, is indivisible. In élite units men of high morale will fire, while others of equally high morale will overcome, with great personal risk, problems of supply. For instance, in World War One, some élite units of the B.E.F. fired so rapidly that Germans mistakenly thought that they were attacked by machine-guns, not rifles (see O.H. 14.1. p. 92). Moreover, Marshall showed that fire ratios remained constant both during attack and defence, while Little's explanation refers to low fire ratios of attacking units only. Thus, even if Little's interpretation were true, he would still have to account for the low fire ratios of defending units, where supply problems are less acute.
37. Marshall, op. cit., p. 56–8.
38. Ibid., pp. 75–6.
39. Little, op. cit.
40. The platoon comprised 39 men; but 9 were Korean soldiers and not interviewed.
41. Little, op. cit., p. 202.
42. Ibid., p. 217.
43. Ibid., p. 200.
44. Ibid., p. 201.
45. Ibid., p. 203.
46. Moskos, *The American Enlisted Man*, op. cit., p. 33.
47. *The Times*, 5 January 1971.
48. H. H. Gerth and C. Wright Mills, *From Max Weber* (London: Routledge and Kegan Paul, 1957) Chapter 10. By discipline is meant 'the consistently rationalised, methodically trained and exact execution of the received order, in which all personal criticism is unconditionally suspended and the actor is unswervingly set for carrying out the command' (ibid., p. 253).
49. M. Weber, 'Some Consequences of Bureaucratisation' in L. A. Coser and B. Rosenburg, *Sociological Theory* (New York: Macmillan, 1957) pp. 442–3.

50. Ibid., p. 443.
51. W. Plomer (ed.), *Kilvert's Diary*, Vol. 1 (London: Jonathan Cape, 1969) pp. 212–13.
52. J. C. King, *The First World War* (London: Macmillan, 1972) p. 269.
53. Edmonds, *A Short History of World War I*, op. cit., p. 223.
54. King, op. cit., p. 259.
55. M. Ferro, *The Great War* (London: Routledge & Kegan Paul, 1973) p. 184.
56. King, op. cit., p. 265.
57. O.H.16.1. p. 156.
58. Gosse, op. cit., pp. 25–6.
59. J. Keegan, *The Face of Battle* (London: Jonathan Cape, 1976).
60. K. Lorenz, *On Aggression* (London: Methuen, 1966).

Index

Battalions mentioned in the text may be found under both the names of their Regiments and the general heading 'Battalions'. Divisions are listed in numerical order under the heading 'Divisions'.